Defense Engagement since 1900

Defense Engagement since 1900

GLOBAL LESSONS IN SOFT POWER

Edited by

Greg Kennedy

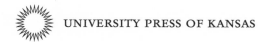 UNIVERSITY PRESS OF KANSAS

Published by the University Press of Kansas (Lawrence, Kansas 66045), which was
organized by the Kansas Board of Regents and is operated and funded by Emporia
State University, Fort Hays State University, Kansas State University, Pittsburg
State University, the University of Kansas, and Wichita State University

Library of Congress Cataloging-in-Publication Data

Names: Kennedy, Greg, editor.
Title: Defense engagement since 1900/ edited by Greg Kennedy.
Description: Lawrence, Kansas : University Press of Kansas, [2020] | Series:
Modern war studies | Includes bibliographic references and index.
Identifiers: LCCN 2019045400
 ISBN 9780700629473 (cloth)
 ISBN 9780700629480 (paperback)
 ISBN 9780700629497 (epub)
Subjects: LCSH: Military attachés—Case studies. | Military intelligence—Case
studies. | Security, International—Case studies. | National security—Case studies.
Classification: LCC UB260 .H57 2020 | DDC 355/.032—dc23
LC record available at https://lccn.loc.gov/2019045400.

British Library Cataloguing-in-Publication Data is available.

Printed in the United States of America

10 9 8 7 6 5 4 3 2 1

The paper used in this publication is recycled and contains 30 percent
postconsumer waste. It is acid free and meets the minimum requirements of
the American National Standard for Permanence of Paper for Printed Library
Materials z39.48-1992.

CONTENTS

Defense Engagement since 1900

Introduction

Greg Kennedy

This collection is what has come to be known as applied military history, or case-study history, a particular form of analysis favored for use with military and political topics that require historical analysis to comment on contemporary defense/security problems.[1] The methodology is relatively simple: a current policy issue of interest to a particular military organization is selected for historical interrogation and comparison. Along with the historical "lessons learned" material, contemporary analysis is provided. This combination creates a synthesis of chronological perspectives, varying national experiences, a wide range of strategic and operational contexts, and a base of "reality" (the historical experience) and practitioner theory (the expectations of current actors) that provides a truly comprehensive and holistic commentary. So rather than this being simply the exploration of the performance of multiple military attachés (although they do feature largely in the cases selected), it is a question of looking at the ability of the state's military to move away from thinking of its role as the applicator of force and toward thinking of itself as an applicator of power.

This historical evaluation, combined with a contemporary context/value-setting condition, is useful not just as an academic exercise or methodology. When done with an appropriate degree of research rigor and analytical clarity and disseminated and embedded into contemporary policy-making dialogues or national-security-supporting mechanisms, it can assist national-security-policy practitioners to better understand the issue in question and appreciate the full matrix for the utilization of military power in a more comprehensive fashion to influence events.[2]

It is influence that is at the core of much that this application of military power aspires to accomplish. That ability to influence, and the associated difficulty of measuring the effectiveness or impact of any assumed influence, is linked to the concept of soft power.[3] Now, as in the past, the purpose of defense engagement is to attempt to tackle the causes of designated security threats and not simply to manage their consequences. It is in the measurement of effectiveness of such applications of soft power that things get difficult. What do you measure, where, for how long, and in what manner, are the questions that pose a challenge for those wishing to champion defense engagement's greater use. In circumstances in which resources are scarce, time is limited, and manpower at a premium, the thought of "wasting" such critical assets on an immeasurable, and therefore unknown, preventative effect permeates much of the debate on the true utility of defense engagement as a bespoke or core task for a nation's military apparatus. It is for this reason that historical evidence is one of the few reliable methods of adjudicating this question of utility and effect.[4] In this collection, the focus is on bringing history to bear on the United Kingdom's and other nations' experiences in defense engagement in different times and places. By providing analysis through the use of historical case studies to test the veracity of some of the beliefs of the worth of defense engagement to a nation's defense and security strategies, it is hoped that this initial foray into the ongoing debates surrounding the need for clarification of the modern concept will provide sound historical truths that will act as catalysts for further dialogue.[5] Such an approach is but a first step in analyzing the Kantian principles related to the problems or impossibilities of causality and effect: if the military contribution to all aspects of strategy cannot be measured or understood, difficulties arise not only in comprehending the true nature of the situation but also in the further selection of appropriate applications of power.[6]

Defense engagement is not a new concept. It is the desire to achieve influence and advantage by engaging with neutral nations, allied nations, and even adversarial nations through military interactions. As such, it is a matter more of imagination than of doctrine or policy: being able to creatively use military power in circumstances that are not usually places where such power would be found or applied. More important, successful defense engagement requires a holistic and comprehensive understanding of just what military power actually is, what its constituent parts are being applied for (what is to be achieved), and against what or whom. Also, there must be some ability to coherently attach those actions performed by the military to the higher elements of a national-security strategy (coordination to diplomacy, finance, economic, politics, intelligence, etc.).[7] Only then can any expectation of greater influence or leverage, or for any deterrence, coercion, compellence, prevention, or assurance be expected. Therefore, defense engagement should be seen by a state's strategic planning organizations as another use of soft power in pursuit of such aims.

The interactions put forward above are not simply kinetic in nature. Instead, the intention is to utilize what Joseph Nye would categorize as "soft power" attributes within the military power sphere.[8] These activities and actions run the gamut from war-gaming, exercising, and common-doctrine creation through to technological exchanges, professional military education interactions on staff courses and training events, and intelligence sharing. The aim of defense engagement is multifold in current Western military thinking: to deter, assure, attract, and prevent. However, such a myriad array of aims may reflect a lack of appreciation of the limitations of what defense engagement can actually achieve in practice.[9] Indeed, gaining some clarification as to what defense engagement can reasonably be expected to achieve for the strategic level, and what it cannot, is a core aim of this collection.

The chapters that follow are focused primarily, but not exclusively, on the British experience of defense engagement throughout the twentieth century. The British Empire and its use of military power is perhaps the most extensive example of the use of military power in a nonkinetic fashion in pursuit of policy goals. However, irrespective of the nations' military used in any individual case study, the main focus of the chapters is to highlight various characteristics of defense engagement regardless of the national context: intelligence, technology exchanges, planning, coordination, influence and strategic narrative creation, the use of indigenous troops, or the use of paramilitary or police forces with regular troops to achieve security objectives. The particular environment in which the engagement activity took place—land, sea, or air—has some bearing on the character of defense engagement but not on its nature, which is again a core feature of analysis at the heart of this collection.[10] However, the operational priorities of each of the environments regarding operational art characteristics does mean that each domain has particular strengths and weaknesses with regard to the range of expectations for success that various defense-engagement activities can have. Perhaps, in the future, a further study that combines all three environments and their historical experiences could be a worthwhile area of investigation for those interested in the topic. As the discussions of grey-zone, subthreshold, and hybrid conflict continue to occupy the minds of strategic thinkers in democratic states, there is no doubt that the ability to comprehend and use effectively military power to its fullest extent will continue to be a topic of interest and importance.

NOTES

1   Peter N. Stearns, "Applied History and Social Science," *Social Science History* 6, no. 2 (Spring 1982): 219–226; George Lawson and John M. Hobson, "What Is History in International Relations?," *Millennium—Journal of International Studies* 37, no. 2 (2008): 415–435.

2   Göran Swistek, "The Nexus between Public Diplomacy and Military Diplomacy in Foreign Affairs and Defense Policy," *Connections* 11, no. 2 (Spring 2012): 79–86;

3   K. A. Muthanna, "Military Diplomacy," *Journal of Defence Studies* 5, no. 1 (January 2011): 1–15.

4   Peter Leahy, "Military Diplomacy," 2016, accessed September 12, 2019, http://ips.cap.anu.edu.au/sdsc/publications/centre-gravity-series.

5   Daniel Baldino and Andrew Carr, "Defence Diplomacy and the Australian Defence Force: Smokescreen or Strategy?," *Australian Journal of International Affairs* 70, no. 2 (2016): 139–158.

6   Immanuel Kant, Marcus Weigelt, and F. Max Müller, *Critique of Pure Reason*, 1st ed. (London: Penguin, 2017).

7   Lech Drab, "Defence Diplomacy: An Important Tool for the Implementation of Foreign Policy and Security of the State," *Security and Defence Quarterly* 20, no. 3 (2018): 57–71.

8   Joseph S. Nye Jr., "Soft Power," *Foreign Policy* 80 (Autumn 1990): 153–171.

9   Kevin Rowlands, *Naval Diplomacy in the 21st Century: A Model for the Post–Cold War Global Order* (New York: Routledge, 2019).

10 Patrick Blannin, *Defence Diplomacy in the Long War Beyond the Aiguillete* (PhD diss., Bond University, 2018).

The Development of the Role of the Military Attaché, 1900–1919

Tim Hadley

At the end of the Napoleonic period, the military attaché was transformed gradually from ad hoc observer to permanent member of an embassy staff with extensive official responsibilities, including, in rare cases, participating in state-to-state negotiations on military security.[1] From the outset, the military attaché's primary responsibility was to establish the size and quality of the armed forces in the country to which they were assigned and to identify their locations. As early as 1810, Austrian general Josef Graf Radetzky was the first to provide detailed reporting guidelines for military officers assigned to diplomatic facilities.[2] Subsequent technical improvements to weapons, ammunition, and equipment demanded adjustments to strategy and tactics. As military arts developed into military sciences, it became essential to know how foreign armies were reacting to these developments. As international treaties and alliances were created, military staffs required information on their allies as well as their enemies. Although there were some military attachés present in this period in European capitals from states outside Europe, including those from Japan and the United States, this chapter will focus on the representation of military attachés in European capitals.[3]

In 1873, the Austrian army produced an "Instruction" for military attachés that included a list of topics on which they were to report routinely. Not long thereafter, the list began to grow, as new topics were added at a growing rate in response to the evolution of technologies and doctrine. It soon became clear that it would be better for staffs to levy general requirements and defer to the military attaché to refine or expand them as he saw fit, relying on his tact and professionalism to determine the best way to satisfy them. The French followed this trend, as did others in time.[4] Although the targets of the reporting increased in number and variety, many military attachés arrived at their posts with limited preparation—if any at all. The British military attachés in the late nineteenth and early twentieth centuries apparently received no training at all, according to Douglas Dawson (who served in Vienna, Bucharest, and Belgrade, 1890–1895; also Paris, Brussels, and Bern, 1895–1901).[5] Sir Edward Gleichen in Berlin (1903–1906) and Washington, DC (1906–1907), summed up his experience for future military attachés by observing that intelligence officers could learn much from the reading of the adventures of Sherlock Holmes, but that they should be careful not to emulate Dr. Watson. By contrast, the British navy provided a comprehensive training program for its naval attachés in 1903.[6]

In the early 1890s at the latest, Austria's 1873 Instruction for military attachés was no longer in effect. Some military attachés arrived at their new posts with the most limited preparation. Eugen Straub passed several weeks in Vienna to prepare for his assignment to the Scandinavian kingdoms (1913–1914) but received little in the way of briefings or training and was forced to leave Vienna earlier than planned. He stopped in Berlin for several days, where he met with his Austrian colleague Karl von Bienerth (1908–1918). Bienerth opened his reporting files to Straub to give him a sense of the topics Vienna was interested in. This was the closest he came to getting any instruction on just what he was supposed to collect.[7] Many other Austrian military attachés recalled a very shallow preparation for their new posts. Josef Graf Stürgkh, assigned to Berlin (1897–1902); Gustav Hubka to Cetinje (1912–1914); Wladimir Giesl von Gieslingen to Constantinople, Sofia, Athens, and Cetinje (1893–1909); Joseph Pomiankowski to Constantinople (1909–1918); and Lelio Graf Spannocchi to St. Petersburg (1907–1911) all recalled having been provided very little in the way of preparation, if any.[8] There are no records suggesting that the German military attachés received any formal training before they assumed their new duties. In 1854, the first Prussian military attaché assigned to Vienna, Prince Kraft zu Hohenlohe-Ingelfingen, was concerned that he had not been provided any training for the job. The war minister assured him that "everything in Austria can be found out by a man who knows how to court women." With this in mind, and with a flair for improvisation, Hohenlohe proved to be very effective.[9] Despite the lack of training programs, the military attaché's responsibilities were generally and widely understood by 1909. The French revised their guidance even further, simply exhorting the military attaché to "do his job, speak little, and observe much."[10]

The Russian military attachés in Germany and Austria had more specific requirements to fill than their colleagues did. In addition to the vague instruction to collect that which seemed to them important, they were directed to acquire sensitive military information. This included official military codes, military laws, military railway estimates, and the latest technology. To this end, they were authorized to negotiate the purchase of foreign military inventions. They were also directed to cultivate a network of secret agents who could report on sensitive topics in their host country.[11] In Vienna, Mitrofan Martchenko (1905–1910) reported on all the new technologies developed and implemented in Austria, including new lower-visibility uniforms, mobile kitchens, and a bread that could be stored six months without spoiling. Martchenko needed no clandestine agent to obtain the secret of the nonspoiling bread. Although an informant offered to sell him the recipe, Martchenko decided to call on the war minister, who simply gave it to him.[12] For fulfilling normal requirements, the direct approach to local authorities was sufficient. Walscourt Waters in Berlin (1900–1903) recorded that despite tension between the two countries during the Boer War, the German General Staff (GGS) was very helpful to the British military attachés. The GGS provided new cartridges, a new form of range-finder, and field glasses—all unsolicited. In return, GGS officers and the kaiser called on Waters from time to time for his views on a variety of matters, including uniforms and volunteer recruitment programs.[13]

The military attachés' presence at maneuvers provided them an opportunity to see the host army performing under simulated battlefield conditions. Nevertheless, the military attachés were not free to roam about the maneuver field unaccompanied. Their viewing positions were prearranged so as to permit them to see only what the host army wanted them to see. The chief of the Austrian military intelligence section, August Urbanski von Ostrymiecz (1909–1914), was the official responsible for shepherding the military attachés at maneuvers. He reported that it was a challenge to restrain the wily Martchenko, who was not above wandering off from the herd on his own.[14] British accounts from Berlin describe the similar situation of military and naval attachés being closely chaperoned to the point that they were able to observe little of serious interest.[15] Gleichen recalls that the largest and most spectacular annual maneuver, the *Kaisermanöver*, was not the place to observe new tactics, techniques, or technologies of the German Army. These trials were held in smaller maneuvers to which the military attachés were not invited.[16] Military attachés who were permitted to accompany their host army to wars were treated as they were in peacetime, being kept as far away from the action at the front as possible. In this case, their minders would claim that their primary interest was the safety of their guests.[17]

It has been suggested that in the late nineteenth and early twentieth centuries military attachés developed a sense of common identity based on their common professions, despite growing nationalism and international competition.[18] To the extent that this is at all discernible, there were characteristics that the military attachés shared that would have encouraged, if not accounted for, a certain camaraderie. Some of these characteristics would have been the shared social background of many of them: wealth and noble birth. Their being military officers in an otherwise exclusively civilian environment would have drawn the military attachés closer to one another naturally.[19] Encouraging this cohesion were activities in which they participated as a group: maneuvers and exercises; tours of military installations; technical trials and demonstrations; military ceremonies. They occasionally went off in smaller groups. In Berlin, Gleichen teamed up with his American colleague William S. Biddle II (1902–1906) for a tour of the Krupp works in Essen and to the Ehrhardt Laboratory in Potsdam. He joined the French military attaché Pierre de Laguiche (1906–1909; St. Petersburg, 1912–1916) on a visit to the stud farms in East Prussia, which supplied the German cavalry.[20] Otto Hein, the American military attaché in Vienna (1889–1893), joined his British, Russian, and French colleagues on a visit to the Austerlitz battlefield. He obtained official permission to visit military installations by himself, including the military academies in Wiener Neustadt and Báblona, Hungary, and horse farms in eastern Hungary.[21] Despite the tensions between Austria and Russia, Martchenko was included in visits to Austrian military facilities: a railway communications office in Korneuburg; gunnery schools and factories in Skoda; a cavalry school in Vienna; and an automobile school in Klosterneuburg. He also made personal tours of Galicia, Transylvania, upper and lower Austria, Croatia, Bohemia, and Hungary.[22]

There was a gray side as well. They must have considered each other as sources of information, at least on the local situation and perhaps on their own armed forces. The American Hein pooled information and impressions on the Austrian army with his colleagues, including the British, French, and Russian military attachés.[23] German military attaché Maximilian Yorck von Wartenburg in St. Petersburg (1885–1894) approached his Austrian colleague Eduard von Klepsch (1882–1899) for help obtaining good sources on the Russian army. Klepsch could only advise that the Russians were extremely secretive and that using agents to get information was dangerous because they tended to talk a lot when drunk.[24] The German military attaché Lüttwitz (1900–1904) helped his Austrian colleague Gottfried Prinz von Hohenlohe-Schillingsfürst (1902–1906) to better understand the Russian army when he first arrived. As a result, Hohenlohe was quickly integrated into Russian society and was able to return the favor by providing Lüttwitz insights into the Russian court and government.[25] Gleichen in Berlin acknowledged seeking help from his Japanese colleague Kikutaro Oi. The Japanese had a network of informants among civilians and Japanese officers in exchange programs.[26] Their French colleague Maurice Pellé (1909–1912) helped the British military attaché Alick Russell (1910–1914) in preparing a report on German military transport. In return, Russell provided Pellé with information from British sources.[27] The British military attaché in St. Petersburg, Guy Wyndham (1907–1909), was able to advise London that his own assessment of the Russian army was more favorable than that of his German and Austrian counterparts.[28] His Austrian colleague, Lelio Spannocchi (1907–1911), recorded that he often met with Wyndham at Wyndham's house and exchanged views on many subjects.[29] The German military plenipotentiary in St. Petersburg, Paul von Hintze (1908–1910, a naval officer), was able to report a unanimity of views among military attachés on the question of Russia's response to the German and Austrian positions during the Bosnian Annexation Crisis.[30]

Faced with difficulties, or under pressure to succeed, some military attachés resorted to stealing or buying the restricted information they sought: if espionage were discovered, diplomatic relations could be severely damaged. Accordingly, most states prohibited their diplomats, civilian and military, from engaging in the practice. There were exceptions and gray areas. Some British military attachés were tasked with undertaking semiclandestine reconnaissance. They used their status as diplomats openly, or only as necessary to provide natural reasons for traveling to areas they were directed to reconnoiter. Dawson did this along the Adriatic coast on a trip from Vienna to report on coastal fortifications.[31] Alfred Knox in St. Petersburg (1911–1914) traveled through Russian Poland by bicycle from Warsaw and over the border into Germany to examine border defenses in both countries. To disguise his intent, he carried historic maps in the event he needed support for his claim to be studying Napoleon's eastern battles.[32]

From 1909 to the outbreak of World War I, the Russian military attachés were directed to cultivate confidential sources to obtain secret information on army plans, military dispositions, and secret technical developments.[33] In Bern, D. I. Romejko-Gurko (1908–1914) was frustrated by the failures of his agents in Germany. He complained that he had not received proper training for his role as a spy master. This likely contributed to his management style, which was aggressive, threatening, and ruthless. The result was a vicious circle of low productivity.[34]

The espionage efforts of Martchenko in Vienna were revealed when a joint police-military investigation identified him as the leader of a ring of confidential paid informants that included some Austrian military officers. Among them was a watchman at the Vienna arsenal who admitted to selling technical information on Austrian artillery in January 1910. Martchenko was withdrawn.[35] A few months later, Spannocchi in St. Petersburg was accused of espionage after he paid for secret documents in St. Petersburg. Spannocchi had undertaken the operation at the express direction of the Austrian military intelligence section, which provided funds for the payment.[36] Martchenko's successor in Vienna, Michail Zankiewitsch, was caught in April 1913. He had been managing several agents, including two brothers, one of whom was a military cadet classmate of a son of the Austrian chief of staff, Franz Conrad von Hötzendorff.[37] The Russian military attachés in Vienna may have been more successful because their approaches to targets were subtle and their management skillful once the relationship was fixed. Since there was little if any training in the discipline, their successes seem to come down to the ability of individual military attachés to adjust to new duties requiring creativity and imagination. The Alfred Redl case in Vienna the same year indicates that the Russians were capable of a high degree of professionalism even if it was not on view in every case.[38] The Russian military attaché accredited to Sweden, Norway, and Denmark, Peter Assanovitsch (1910–1913), managed a network of spies in Sweden that was administered from Copenhagen. The network's primary target was the armed forces of the Scandinavian kingdoms. Assanovitsch also directed some of his agents to enlist subagents, including a servant in the house of the Austrian military attaché. The standards of this particular Russian military attaché were not high: he sent his agents detailed instructions in his own hand, often signing the letters with his full name.[39]

While the German and Austrian prohibitions against military-attaché espionage in both countries remained in effect till the war, it did not forbid them from talking about it. Straub in Sweden developed a good relationship with his German colleague, Major Giese, and the two shared information on the Russians when they had it.[40] Once the war broke out, German and Austrian military attachés in Switzerland cooperated in espionage operations, primarily against Italy. They even had some success in encouraging their official contacts in the Swiss army to support their efforts.[41]

As states and their economies matured, the military attachés occasionally needed to address political topics to provide the relevant background or context for military issues, such as: Where will the government find the money for essential new arms purchases or equipment? How will the populace react to a lengthening of mandatory military service? This led, in many but not all cases, to a more cooperative relationship between the military attachés and their civilian colleagues.

Austrian military attachés were permitted to report on political topics only to the extent that such reporting conveyed insights that would contribute to a fuller, more accurate understanding of the armed forces in the host country. To this end and in some cases, the military attachés developed a healthy relationship with their ambassadors. Giesl and Pomiankowski in Constantinople had excellent working relationships with Ambassador Johann von Pallavicini (1906–1918), who let them read his reports sent to the foreign ministry. In return, they shared their military reports with him before they were sent to Vienna. This worked to mutual advantage, and to the advantage of Vienna generally, in its receiving clear and comprehensive views of the situation in the Ottoman capital.[42] Hubka shared his reporting with Ambassador Giesl in Cetinje, and Giesl gave him access to relevant diplomatic reporting.[43] The Austrian ambassador in St. Petersburg Leopold Graf Berchtold (1906–1911, and subsequently foreign minister, 1912–1915), occasionally shared his reporting with Spannocchi, who passed it on to the chief of staff in Vienna, noting that it had been given to him confidentially. During the Bosnian Annexation Crisis of 1908, Spannocchi mostly addressed the tone of the press and prospective financing for the Russian army. At the end of the year he argued that Vienna should prepare to join Germany in a "final accounting" with Russia for her resistance to Austrian interests in the Balkans. Not surprisingly, the ambassador objected to this last paragraph.[44]

In Germany, overlaps in the reporting from civilian diplomats and their military colleagues was a management issue left to the ambassadors. If differences between two reporters on a given topic could not be reconciled, the ambassador submitted both views to ensure that Berlin understood the differences.[45] By the turn of the century this was becoming rare. The German military attachés were very busy and focused on their hosts' military readiness. Reporting from Russian military attachés at the turn of the century stands in high contrast to that of the generally businesslike and dispassionate reporting from German, French, British, and Austrian military attachés. In Berlin, the Russian military attachés exaggerated German military strength and, without presenting specific evidence, concluded that this indicated preparations for war against Russia. They provided no indication *why* Germany might choose to attack; much less did they offer authoritative reporting to support that conclusion. This raises the question of whether the Russian general staff solicited their views at least in part because they matched their own. This might have encouraged the military attaché, consciously or unconsciously, to provide the views the general staff wanted to hear, and emboldened them to speculate on broad geopolitical questions and offer unsolicited advice tinged with warning. All this may have contributed to the narrowing of the general staff's outlook.[46]

After the Bosnian Crisis of 1908, Russian military attaché Alexander Michelson in Berlin (1909–1911) submitted a report on German preparedness that concluded that Germany was nearly capable of dominating Europe; its next goal might be the Baltic coast. He offered assessments of the growing influence of the German Social Democrats, on the changing attitudes of the Center Party, and the economic effects of bad harvests in 1909. Michelson's successor, Pavel Bazarov (1911–1914), was directed to comment on the United Kingdom's Haldane Mission to Germany in late January to early February 1912. Bazarov wisely turned to his colleague, the naval attaché Captain Berens, for help. In a very short time, Bazarov was submitting long and expansive reflections on geopolitical strategy with references to public opinion—in contrast to military opinion. In November 1912, he warned that the celebrations around the anniversary of the battle of Leipzig would likely inflame German national feeling and arouse a German Army long bored by the lack of activity in the last forty years. In January 1913, Bazarov let his imagination loose, suggesting to the general staff that Russia should reach a "compromise" with Germany in which the lands populated by German Austrians could be ceded to Germany while Russia and the Balkan states attacked Austria simultaneously and brought the dual monarchy down.[47] The accumulation of such reporting coming out of Berlin from the military attaché, and from agents directed from other embassies, may have fed the general staff's appetite for reports of German aggressiveness and hostility. This could have discouraged taking a more critical look at the reporting: once a consensus emerged in the general staff that Russia might be invaded by Germany at any moment, few officers could have been expected to challenge that assumption. Since the damage would be catastrophic if they were wrong, anyone who challenged the assumption might fall under suspicion of pro-German tendencies.

The British rules that governed political reporting were reasonably clear in presentation, but their application was anything but uniform. In most embassies an accommodation was reached to satisfy both military and civilian diplomats, but there were occasions in which military-attaché reporting did not find its way to the foreign office, where it would have been useful. The source of that problem was in London, not the embassies.[48] There is enough of the surviving reporting in this period to indicate the attention the military attachés dedicated to political reporting in Germany, especially as concerned the behavior and statements of its chief political figure after 1890, Kaiser Wilhelm II. The kaiser's behavior was a problem for reporting: he seemed to like having the military attachés around him, but much of his time with them was spent in scolding, dramatic posturing, and general attention-seeking. Nevertheless, given his position, the kaiser's commentary could not be ignored. As a safeguard against any misinterpretation of their accounts in London, military attachés Frederick Trench (1906–1910) and Alexander Russell (1910–1914) always tried to provide a proper context.[49] The relationship between French military attachés and their ambassadors evolved, as did those of most other powers. In addition to collection on routine military matters, the French military attachés provided the war minister with appraisals of the political situation as warranted.[50] The French military attachés in Berlin, like the British ones, reported the kaiser's comments and, like the British, did not spare the reader the kaiser's brutal judgments on their country's policies and the political figures who executed them. To provide a proper perspective on the kaiser, Laguiche forwarded the war minister a lengthy and rather unflattering character sketch.[51]

While the French were certainly pleased with their warming relations with Russia that ended their isolation, it was no easy road. The French military attaché Louis-Etienne Moulin (1891–1908) reported on the difficulties the Russians were having in improving their armed forces and reducing their mobilization times. His long service in Russia, which began with an assignment as deputy military attaché (1881–1891), enabled him to report with authority his unfavorable opinion of the political leadership as well.[52] When it became clear that Russia was to embark on a war against Japan, Moulin described the lumbering pace of the preparations and pointed out the need for Paris to factor in the "Russian coefficient": "for every day that a German or a Frenchman needs to accomplish a task, a Russian needs three." He added that there were three qualities that characterized Russian preparation in all things: slow, lazy, and lacking in foresight. Once again, he wrote, Russia is going off to a war for which it is not prepared.[53]

By the end of the nineteenth century, the military attaché's duties sometimes included engaging in diplomatic activity. The transition from the exclusive role of information collector to active diplomat grew out of the experience of successful ad hoc missions. The use of a military attaché for a diplomatic mission had the advantage of his being able to apply expertise without necessarily signaling an elevated diplomatic intervention or presence. This was the case in the settlement of the short war between Serbia and Bulgaria in November 1885. An international commission of military attachés met the German-born Bulgarian prince Alexander von Battenberg to direct him to cease hostilities and retire from Serbian territory without reparation or compensation. Carl Graf von Wedel in Vienna (1877–1887) represented Germany; in a private meeting, he made it clear to the prince that the commission had come to dictate a settlement, not to negotiate one. Since Alexander was a governor of an Ottoman principality, not a chief of state, the visit of a military attaché commission avoided the impression that the undertaking was a policy matter between states and spared the Turkish government some embarrassment.[54] The governments of both France and Britain would soon recognize the advantages that certain skilled and capable military attachés could bring to the diplomacy of alliance-building, especially in the delicate first stages of the relationship. Wedel was one such; he later became ambassador in Stockholm (1892–1894), Rome (1899–1902), and Vienna (1902–1907).[55]

France and Russia

The Franco-Russian alliance of 1894 is addressed here because of its significance for succeeding developments and represents a seminal event in the evolution of the military attachés. The French government would use the military attachés in negotiations with Russia over their entente and alliance as much to keep contacts discreet as to draw on their expertise and experience. By the early 1880s, France and Russia were each concerned about their situation vis-à-vis Germany. After a long estrangement dating back to Napoleon, Russia began to take an interest in developing closer contacts with France and expressed interest in purchasing artillery. These contacts provided the basis for considering other possibilities.[56] When the time seemed ripe to talk about a closer relationship, the French did not use civilian diplomats; they lowered the profile of their undertaking and brought more expertise to bear by using two specialists ideally suited to the task: the serving military attaché and his predecessor.

When French general Antoine Chanzy was named ambassador to Russia, he selected Major Raoul de Boisdeffre, who had served under him in Algeria, to be his military attaché (1879–1882). Boisdeffre developed a friendly relationship with Russian deputy chief of staff, General Nicholas Obrutchev, who later became chief of staff (1881–1897). Probably significant in their developing friendship was the fact that Obrutchev's wife was French. In summer 1890, Boisdeffre, now a general back in France, was invited to attend the Russian maneuvers, where he discussed diplomatic possibilities with Obrutschev. The following year, Obrutschev spent the summer in France at his wife's home and met with Boisdeffre. Their meetings led to an exchange of letters between the foreign ministers of the two countries that established an identity of interests. In 1892, Boisdeffre was again invited to attend the Russian summer maneuvers. He stayed on afterward to participate in the negotiation of a secret military accord that was strictly defensive and very short on detail but was a first step toward a complete alliance.

Boisdeffre became chief of staff of the French army in 1894, serving until 1898. He negotiated the alliance with Russia in 1894 and the amendment to it in 1896.[57] Attending all the meetings with the Russians was Moulin, who had succeeded Boisdeffre as military attaché in 1891. Moulin played an active role, developing several ideas for breaking through diplomatic impasses that arose during the evolution of the relationship from an entente to an alliance. His extraordinary twenty-seven years of service in Russia, during which he acquired excellent language skills and a Russian wife, were essential for maintaining the momentum during the process. Throughout the negotiations the French government wisely deferred to Boisdeffre and Moulin, given their thorough understanding of Russia, from military capabilities to culture.[58]

France and Britain

The French military attaché in Britain, Victor Huguet (1904–1914), played a crucial role in bringing France and Britain together in a relationship that was an alliance in every sense but name. The success was based on a relationship Huguet developed with a former British military attaché in the Netherlands and Belgium, Charles Repington (1898–1902). In May 1904, the two states reached agreement on colonial issues that ended hundreds of years of brutal competition. This led to a formal understanding that they would consult on issues of joint concern. The following year, the British floated the possibility of further understandings, particularly in the event of war. When both governments fell victim to domestic difficulties, the idea languished. In December 1905, the French proposed more discussions. In the beginning, these followed two tracks, civilian and military, both unaware of what the other was doing. Meanwhile, Huget had decided that the British Army was better than he had thought. As he became better informed, he pointed out to his government that the British Army could provide critical support to the French in the event the German Army attacked France. He contacted Repington, then a military journalist for the *Times*. For weeks the two worked together, passing communications and information on their respective armies. The highest military levels supported the arrangement but at first did not inform their civilian governments. Once the military sides became convinced of the value of the discussions, they both informed their governments of the activity. Having learned much about each other, they concluded that if war should come it would be best if the two powers had a mutual understanding of capabilities and intentions. At this point the last barriers were dropped to afford frank and efficient communications that could permit them, if necessary, to join their armies on the continent to fight together against a German threat. After the talks became official and expanded in breadth and depth, Huguet and Repington continued to play their critical intermediary roles.[59]

Austria

The former military attaché in St. Petersburg, Hohenlohe, joined the Austrian diplomatic service upon his return to Vienna in 1907 and was assigned to Berlin. In 1912, he was dispatched to St. Petersburg to try to reduce tensions between Russia and Austria during the crisis of the 1912–1913 Balkan Wars. His earlier service in St. Petersburg provided a strong foundation for establishing rapport and respect in his new role. While he favored war with Serbia at this time, he later changed his view and succeeded in convincing both sides that a reduction of forces on the Austrian-Russian border would produce a better atmosphere for further discussions. Unfortunately his success was temporary: many of the key players on both sides were already fixed on war. He was appointed ambassador in July 1914 and remained in Berlin until 1918.[60]

Several Austrian military attachés in the Balkans participated in bilateral and regional diplomacy in the early twentieth century as the political situation degenerated in the face of deteriorating Turkish power and a corresponding rise in militaristic nationalism among the new Slavic states. Giesl played a variety of diplomatic roles, beginning as the military attaché in Constantinople (1893–1909). His skilled performance was recognized early, and the Austrian foreign ministry urged the general staff to make him available for ad hoc missions. For his part in the diplomacy of the war between Greece and Turkey in 1897 he was given the additional responsibility of roving military attaché to three embassies—Greece, Bulgaria, and Montenegro—in 1898. In 1907, he was attached to Austria's delegation to the Second Hague Peace Conference. In 1909, he was made Austrian ambassador to Montenegro and was made ambassador to Serbia in 1913 until his departure at the outbreak of war.[61]

Pomiankowski replaced Giesl as military attaché in Constantinople in 1909. He soon became convinced that the Turkish army was overrated and in dire need of reform: improvements made under the advice of a German mission the previous century had lapsed.[62] Pomiankowski considered a new reform program all the more important because he saw in Turkey a natural ally against the Slavic Balkan states supported by Russia. Without specific instructions from Vienna, he urged Turkish officers and politicians to lobby Austrian and German diplomats on the need for their support in helping the Turks to undertake the necessary reforms. Whether his effort had any direct effect is unclear, but in August 1913 discussions between the Turks and the Germans resulted in the dispatch of a forty-man German mission under General Otto Liman von Sanders to Constantinople.[63]

During the war Pomiankowski used his local knowledge and experience to warn Vienna away from several misconceived military plans. Within days of the war's outbreak, army headquarters in Vienna directed him to organize an operation to scuttle a ship in the Suez Canal, to disrupt the shipping of the Entente powers. The next order came shortly after hostilities began in Galicia and directed him to arrange for a landing of fifty thousand Turkish soldiers in Bessarabia to divert Russian forces attacking Lemberg (Lviv). Shortly thereafter came another demand, this time to orchestrate the landing of a force of fifty thousand Turkish soldiers on the north Black Sea coast to support the recruitment of fifty thousand Kuban cossacks for an uprising against the Russians. Pomiankowski saw past the desperation of these proposals and pointed out the facts. The high degree of security at the Suez Canal foreclosed a scuttling operation. The lack of sufficient transport meant that a landing of fifty thousand Turkish soldiers in Bessarabia would take months to complete, assuming the landings could be completed undisturbed. The Kuban cossacks were loyal to the czar; they could hardly be expected to rebel against the Russian government, and certainly not in a joint operation with Ottoman Muslims. His most persuasive point was that the Ottoman Empire was not yet at war with any of the Entente powers. Vienna deferred to Pomiankowski's judgment and withdrew the directives.[64]

Hubka's efforts in Cetinje made him more welcome at the royal palace than the ambassador himself. Partly through his mastery of the language and local dialect, he was able to get close to the king, who respected him and his position. Hubka's reporting made it clear to Vienna that Montenegro could not be won as an ally despite his ambassador's overly optimistic assurances, and he was right.[65] On August 6, 1914, Hubka's last day in Montenegro, King Nikita received him in a final audience. With formalities aside, the king whispered that his army would begin shelling the Austrian naval base at Cattaro within a few days. He assured Hubka that he was confiding this so that Hubka could warn the Austrians to move civilians out of harm's way. Hubka's relationship with the king not only raised the quality of his reporting but saved some lives as well.[66]

The Triple Alliance of 1882, like the Dual Alliance of 1879, was an exchange of promises of military support in certain contingencies. The wording was vague. In the succeeding decades, as Berlin and Vienna grew concerned about the possibility of war and prospects for success, they sought specific commitments from their third partner, Italy. They wanted to clarify just how the Italians would support their two allies in the event of war: where, when, and how much. Given the expertise required to deal with these narrow military issues, the civilian political leadership deferred the negotiations to the military principals of the leading military power: German chief of staff Helmut von Moltke (1906–1914) and his deputy Georg von Waldersee (1913–1914). The German military attachés in Vienna and Rome had already warned Berlin that the effort with Italy, like an earlier attempt with Romania, was unlikely to produce anything specific or substantial. Significantly, Moltke and Waldersee ignored their counsel. The only role for the two military attachés was to provide support for Waldersee as he shuttled among Berlin, Vienna, and Rome in 1913–1914. In the end, the Italians chose not to honor their alliance commitment in 1914 and entered the war on the side of the Entente powers in 1915.[67]

Probably the most significant diplomatic role that a German military attaché played in this period was in early August 1914, when Carl Graf von Kageneck in Vienna (1906–1917) learned that Austrian chief of staff Conrad had unilaterally and without warning deviated from the long-established understanding that in the event of war with Russia, Austria would commit all of its forces in the northeast at the Russian border. Instead, Conrad sent a large force south to confront Serbia, thereby weakening the defense against the coming Russian offensive. The solid rapport Kageneck had established with general staff officers since his arrival in 1906 facilitated inquiries that led to his discovery. On his own initiative he personally intervened and urged Conrad to change his deployment back to the original plan. At the same time, he warned Berlin of the dangerous development that triggered a series of messages from Moltke to Conrad and from Kaiser Wilhelm to Kaiser Franz Josef pressing the Austrians to return to the previously stipulated agreement. Conrad reluctantly did so. Once at the front and in communication with German forces to the north, Kageneck counseled senior German field officers on the limits of Austrian military capabilities, lest they come to grief from expecting more from the Austrians than they should. His knowledge of Austrian infirmities, apparently ignored when submitted in written form to Berlin before the war, stimulated German commanders to make allowances for the hard facts and enabled the two sides to work together despite barely suppressed mutual resentment. The insights Kageneck shared had accumulated during his eight-year tour of duty in Vienna and were consistent with information that had come down from his predecessors in the preceding decades.[68]

At the outbreak of the war, military attachés from hostile host countries were withdrawn. Many of those from allied and other states requested transfers to an active front. Undoubtedly, most were disappointed. The competition for command assignments was intense in 1914, and there was a tendency by senior officers to dismiss military diplomats as neither fish nor fowl, having served too much time with civilians and too little time commanding troops. Some found useful posts, but not the combat roles they sought. Britain and France made good choices in having military attachés Knox and Laguiche remain as liaison officers to the Russian headquarters in St. Petersburg. Some obtained positions in their home governments, where they might advise civilian military authorities on the enemy or the allies. Dawson did this for both, having served in Vienna and Paris.[69] Vagts provides a summary of the fates of many of the attachés down to the Treaty of Versailles.[70] Kageneck, the German military attaché with the Austrian general staff at the outbreak of the war, remained with it until 1917, when his long-standing request for a command on an active front was approved.[71]

In 1900, the great powers of Europe were at their apex in terms of the strength of their armies and the size of their egos. From 1900 to 1919, the role of their military attachés expanded and matured significantly. Limitations on their collection responsibilities were relaxed, and civilian diplomats learned to accept their presence and to defer to their expertise. Their highest achievement in some states was the deference they were accorded to negotiate more intimate diplomatic relationships on which their governments would depend in the event of war. By 1919, such alliances were acknowledged by many to be one, if not the main, cause of the outbreak of World War I. To eliminate the threat that military attachés were presumed to pose, the postwar treaties required the defeated states to remove the post of military attaché from their embassies abroad. Those positions were reestablished within decades.

NOTES

1   Two comprehensive treatments of the development of the role of military attaché from military officer among civilian diplomats to military diplomat are Alfred Vagts, *The Military Attaché*, (Princeton, NJ: Princeton University Press, 1967), 3–10; and Arnaud Beauvais, *Attachés Militaire, Attachés Navales, et Attachés de l'Air* (Paris: Les Presses Moderne, 1937). A brief and more recent overview is Maureen O'Connor Witter, "Sanctioned Spying—The Development of the Military Attaché in the Nineteenth Century," in *Intelligence and Statecraft—The Use and Limits of Intelligence in International Society*, Peter J. Jackson and Jennifer Siegel, eds. (New York: Praeger, 2005), 87–108.

2   For excerpts see Vagts, *The Military Attaché*, 10–14.

3   Although many states in and beyond Europe dispatched military attachés to the capitals of importance to them, this chapter will focus on the states in Eu-

rope formerly known as the Great Powers, because it was among them that the military attaché as an institution evolved rapidly in the period of 1900–1919.

4 Lothar Hilbert, "Les Attachés Militaires Francais, Leur Statut Pendant l'Entre-Deux Guerres," *Guerre Mondiales et Conflits Contemporains*, no. 215 (July 2004): 26. I am grateful to the author for making this article available to me.

5 Douglas Dawson, *A Soldier Diplomat* (London: John Murray, 1927), 155–159. See also Matthew S. Seligmann, "A Barometer of National Confidence: A British Assessment of the Role of Insecurity in the Formulation of German Military Policy before the First World War," in *The English Historical Review* 117, no. 471 (April 2002): 333–355 at 338.

6 Jennifer Siegel, "Training Thieves—The Instruction of 'Efficient Intelligence Officers,'" in Jackson and Siegel, *Intelligence and Statecraft*, 127–138. See also Gleichen's memoir, *A Guardsman's Memories* (Edinburgh: W. Blackwood & Sons, 1932). For the British Navy, see Matthew Seligmann, *Spies in Uniform: British Military and Naval Intelligence on the Eve of the First World War* (Oxford: Oxford University Press, 2006), 71.

7 Peter Malina, "Die Berichte des österr.-ung. Militärattachés in Stockholm, Oberst Eugen Straub, von der Errichtung des Postens im Mai 1913 bis Kriegserklärung Österreich-Ungarns an Serbien" (diss., Universität Wien, 1969), 151–153.

8 Stürgkh: Josef Graf Stürgkh, *Politische und militärische Erinnerungen aus meinem Leben* (Leipzig, Germany: Paul List Verlag, 1922), 101; Hubka: Josef Steiner, "Gustav Hubka—Sein Wirken als k.u.k. Militärattaché und Schriftsteller" (diss., Universität Wien, 1975), 31–33; Giesl: Eduard Ritter von Steinitz, in *Zwei Jahrzehnte im Nahen Orient—Aufzeichnungen des General der Kavallerie Baron Wladimir Giesl*, ed. Wladimir Baron (Berlin: Verlag für Kulturpolitik, 1927), 19; Pomiankowski: Joseph Pomiankowski, *Der Zusammenbruch des Ottomanischen Reiches, Erinnerungen an die Türkei aus der Zeit des Weltkrieges* (Vienna: Amalthea-Verlag, 1928), 47; Lelio Spannocchi, *Tagebuch*, in Nachlass Spannocchi, ÖS-KA Nachlass B /760, 1. Some of their reporting is published in the collection of Austrian foreign ministry documents: Ludwig Bittner and Hans Uebersberger, Österreich-Ungarns Aussenpolitik von der Bosnischen Krise 1908 bis zum Kriegsausbruch1914, Diplomatische Aktenstücke des österreichisch-*ungarischen Ministeriums des Äussern*, 9 vols. (Vienna: Österreichischer Bundesverlag für Unterricht, Wissenschaft und Kunst, 1930); and in Austrian chief of staff Franz Conrad von Hötzendorff, *Aus Meiner Dienstzeit* (Vienna: Rikola Verlag, 1921–1925). Some unpublished reports have survived in ÖS-KA, Archiv der Militärbevollmächtigten und Militäradjoints. For a description of some of the career paths of the military attachés in the Balkan states, see Günther Kronenbitter, *Krieg im Frieden, Die Führung der k. u. k. Armee und die Großmachtpolitik Österreich-Ungarns 1906–1914* (Munich: R. Oldenbourg Verlag, 2003), 254–257.

9 Prinz Kraft von Hohenlohe-Ingelfingen, *Aus Meinem Leben* (Berlin: Ernst Siegfried Mittler und Sohn, 1897), 1:243.

10 Hilbert, "Les Attachés Militaires Francais," 27.

11 "Instruction to Military Attachés, 1912," cited in William Fuller, "The Russian Empire," in Ernest R. May, *Knowing One's Enemies* (Princeton, NJ: Princeton University Press, 1984), 99–126 at 106.

12 See his memoir *La Catastrophe Austro-Hongroise, Souvenir d'Un Témoin Oculaire* (Nancy, France: Berger-Levrault, 1920), 173.

13 W. H-H. Waters, *Private and Personal, Further Experiences of a Military Attaché* (London: John Murray), 71, 121, 226.

14 See Urbanski's account, "Diplomatie und Spionage," in von Paul Lettow-Vorbeck, *Weltkriegspionage* (Munich: Verlag Justin Moser, 1931), 573–582 at 577.

15 Seligmann, *Spies in Uniform*, 104–113.

16 Edward Gleichen, *A Guardsman's Memories* (London: William Blackwood & Sons, 1932), 266–267; Waters, *Private and Personal*, 224–226.

17 For other examples of the experiences of military attachés and observers at maneuvers and actual warfare, see Vagts, *The Military Attaché*, 211–241 passim.

18 Heinz Gollwitzer, "Internationale des Schwertes: Transnationale Beziehungen im Zeitalter der 'vaterländischen' Streitkräfte," Rheinisch-Westfälische Akademie der Wissenschaften Vorträge G291 (Opladen, Germany: Westdeutscher Verlag, 1987). Also published in Hans-Christof Kraus, *Weltpolitik und deutsche Geschichte—Heinz Gollwitzer gesammelte Studien* (Göttingen, Germany: Vandenhoeck & Ruprecht, 2008), 91–114.

19 Ulrich Trumpener estimates that 73 percent of the German military attachés from 1871 to 1918 were members of the nobility. See his "The Service Attachés and Military Plenipotentiaries of Imperial Germany, 1871–1918," *International History Review* 9, no. 4 (November 1987): 621–638 at 624–625. Lamar Cecil arrived at the figure of 88 percent for the percentage of nobility among the military attachés from 1871 to 1914 in *The German Diplomatic Service, 1871–1914* (Princeton, NJ: Princeton University Press, 1976), 113–115. A vast majority of pre-1914 Austrian diplomats were from the nobility. See William D. Godsey, *Aristocratic Redoubt—The Austro-Hungarian Foreign Office on the Eve of the First World War* (West Lafayette, IN: Purdue University Press, 1999).

20 Gleichen, *A Guardsman's Memories*, 268–269.

21 Otto Hein, *Memories of Long Ago* (New York: G. P. Putnam's Sons, 1925), 177, 196–207.

22 Martchenko, *La Catastrophe Austro-Hongroise*, 173.

23 Hein, *Memories*, 164, 179.

24 Heinz Höhne, *Der Krieg im Dunkeln, Die Geschichte der deutsch-russischen Spionage* (Munich: C. Bertelsmann Verlag GmbH, 1985), 49–50.

25 Alma Hannig, "Prinz Gottfried zu Hohenlohe-Schillingsfürst (1867–1932), Ein Liebling der Kaiserhöfe," in Alma Hannig, *Die Familie Hohenlohe: Eine europäische Dynastie im 19. und 20. Jahrhundert* (Vienna: Böhlau Verlag, 2013), 229–270 at 233–234.

26 Gleichen, *A Guardsman's Memories*, 259.

27 Seligmann, *Spies in Uniform*, 93–95.

28 In November 1908. Jost Dülffer, Martin Kröger, and Rolf-Harald Wippich, *Vermiedene Kriege—Deeskalation von Konflikten der Großmächte zwischen Krimkrieg und Ersten Weltkrieg, 1865–1914* (Munich: R. Oldenbourg Verlag, 1997), 611.

29 Spannocchi, *Tagebuch*, 56, 73, 85, 108, 162, 163.

30 Hintze to Kaiser Wilhelm, December 9, 1908, in Gustav Graf von Lambsdorff, *Die Militärbevollmächtigten Kaiser Wilhelm II. Am Zarenhofe* (Schlieffen, Germany: Schlieffen Verlag, 1937), 309–315 at 314.

31 Dawson, *A Soldier Diplomat*, 134.

32 Max Egremont, *The Forgotten Land: Journeys among the Ghosts of East Prussia* (New York: Farrar, Straus & Giroux, 2011), 33–40.

33 William C. Fuller, "The Russian Empire," in *Knowing One's Enemies: Intelligence Assessment Before the Two World Wars*, ed. Ernest R. May (Princeton, NJ: Princeton University Press, 1984), 98–126 at 106, citing the Russian "Instruction to Military Attachés, 1912."

34 Peter Collmer, "Kommunikation an der Peripherie des zarischen Herrschaftsapparats-Der russische Militärattaché in Bern und seine Geheimagenten (1912/13)," in Nada Boskova et al., *Wege der Kommunikation in der Geschichte Osteuropas* (Köln, Germany: Böhlau Verlag, 2002), 180–182.

35 German Foreign Ministry Archive—Political Archive, Berlin (AA-PA), Military Attachés-Vienna (W-M), file 141, Military Report (MB) 2, January 18, 1910; MB 3, January 23, 1910; MB 4, January 26, 1910; MB 6, February 5, 1910. See also Höhne, *Der Krieg im Dunkeln*, 101–102. Martchenko does not mention the affair in his memoir/history of the period, Mitrofan Martchenko, *La Catastrophe Austro-Hongroise* (Paris: Berger-Levrault, 1920).

36 Max Ronge, *Kriegs- und Industrie-Spionage—Zwölf Jahre Kundschaftsdienst* (Vienna: Amalthea-Verlag, 1930), 47; Spannocchi, *Tagebuch*, 6.

37 Kronenbitter, *Krieg im Frieden*, 236.

38 The best assessment of the Redl case drawing on Russian intelligence files is Schindler, "Redl—Spy of the Century?," in *International Journal of Intelligence and CounterIntelligence* 8, no. 3 (2005): 483–507.

39 Peter Malina, "Die Berichte des österr.-ung. Militärattachés in Stockholm, Oberst Eugen Straub, von der Errichtung des Postens im Mai 1913 bis Kriegserklärung Österreich-Ungarns an Serbien" (diss., Universität Wien, 1969), 314–354.

40 See generally Gerhard Wanner, *Die Bedeutung der k. u. k. Gesandtschaft und*

des Militärattachements in Stockholm für die Beziehung zwischen Schweden und Österreich-Ungarn während des Ersten Weltkrieges (Bissendorf, Germany: Biblio Verlag Osnabrück, 1983).

41 Peter Schubert, *Berichte aus Bern, die Tätigkeit des k.u.k. Militärattachés in Bern während des Ersten Weltkrieges* (Bissendorf, Germany: Biblio Verlag Osnabrück, 1980). German successes are recorded in Busson von Bismarck, "Der Militärattaché im Nachrichtendienst," in Paul von Lettow-Vorbeck, *Weltkriegspionage* (Munich: Verlag Justin Moser, 1931), 104–110.

42 Pomiankowski, *Der Zusammenbruch des Ottomanischen Reiches*, 44.

43 Steiner, "Gustav Hubka," 180.

44 Nachlass Spannocchi, ÖS-KA, B/760.

45 Manfred Messerschmidt, "Die politische Geschichte der preußisch-deutschen Armee 1814–1890," *Handbuch zur deutschen Militärgeschichte 1648–1939* (Munich: Bernard & Graefe, 1975), 331–333.

46 Fuller, "The Russian Empire," 126.

47 Evgenij Sergeev, "Das Deutsche Kaiserreich aus der Sicht russischer Militär-Attachés (1900–1914)," *Forum für osteuropäische Ideen- und Zeitgeschichte*, Heft 1 (Vienna: Böhlau Verlag, 2000), 21–22.

48 Seligmann, *Spies in Uniform*, 34–38.

49 See Matthew Seligmann, "Military Diplomacy in a Military Monarchy? Wilhelm II's Relations with the British Service Attachés in Berlin, 1903–1914," in *The Kaiser*, ed. Annika Mombauer and Wilhelm Deist (Cambridge, UK: Cambridge University Press, 2006); and Matthew Seligmann, "A View from Berlin: Colonel Frederick Trench and the Development of British Perceptions of German Aggressive Intent 1906–1910," *Journal of Strategic Studies* 23, no. 2 (June 2000): 114–147. Seligmann shows how Trench's reporting was especially influential though not unbiased.

50 Maurice Vaisse, "L'evolution de la fonction d'attaché militaire en France au XXe siècle," in *Relations Internationales*, no. 32 (1982): 508–509.

51 Laguiche to Berteau, November 4, 1905, *Documents Diplomatiques Francais* (1871–1914), Series II (1901–1911), vol. 8, no. 108 (Paris: Imp. Nationale, 1937; hereafter *D. D. F.*): 145–147.

52 Moulin to General André, June 10, 1903, D. D. F. Series II, vol. 3: 291.

53 Moulin to General André, February 20, 1904, D. D. F. Series II, vol. 4, no. 301: 397–402. See also the Russian view of France at this period in Youri Korobov, "Les Relations Militaires Franco-Russes de 1870 au Lendemain de la Guerre Russo-Japonaise," *Revue Historique des Armées* 245 (2006): 104–121.

54 Karl Schünemann, "Die Stellung Österreich-Ungarns in Bismarcks Bündnispolitik," *Die Archiv für Politik und Geschichte* 6, part 1 (1926): 549–594; 7, 7, part 2 (1926): 118–152 (Berlin: Deutsche Verlagsgesellschaft für Politik und Geschichte, 1926); Egon Count Corti, *Leben und Liebe Alexanders von Battenberg* (Graz, Austria: Verlag Anton Pustet, 1950), 275.

55 See the introduction in his memoir, Carl Graf von Wedel, *Zwischen Kaiser und Kanzler* (Leipzig, Germany: Koehler & Amelang, 1943), 5–25.

56 Vagts mentions contacts between a former French military attaché and Grand Duke Nicholas in Paris in 1880 and pro-French statements by the Russian military attaché in Paris in the mid-1880s Baron Fredericks. Vagts, *The Military Attaché*, 358–359. But the ground was already being cultivated by the French embassy in St. Petersburg through the efforts of the two military attachés who would be the main players, Boisdeffre and Moulin. See D. W. Spring, "Russia and the Franco-Russian Alliance, 1905–14: Dependence or Interdependence?," in *Slavonic and East European Review* 66, no. 4 (October 1988): 564–592. A detailed study of the creation of the alliance is George Kennan's two-volume work, *The Decline of Bismarck's European Order* (Princeton, NJ: Princeton University Press, 1979), and *The Fateful Alliance: France, Russia and the Coming of the First World War* (New York: Random House, 1984).

57 A summary of some political and technical issues, e.g., the definition of the *casus belli* and the choice of wireless radio rather than carrier pigeons for communications is Muriell Avice-Hanoun's "L'Alliance Franco-Russe (1892–1914)," in Ilja Mieck and Pierre Guillen, *Deutschland-Frankreich-Rußland: Begegnungen und Konfrontationen* (Münich: R. Oldenbourg Verlag, 2000), 109–124.

58 Murielle Avice-Hanoun, "Louis-Etienne Moulin attaché militaire à Sainte-Petersbourg au temps de l'alliance franco-russe (1891–1908)," in Jean-Marc Delaunay, ed., *Aux vents des puissance* (Paris: Presses Sorbonne Nouvel, 2008), 31–39.

59 William Philpotts, "The Making of the Military Entente, 1904–1914: France, the British Army, and the Prospect of War," *English Historical Review* 127, no. 534 (2013): 1155–1185. See also Samuel R. Williamson, *The Politics of Grand Strategy: Britain and France Prepare for War 1904–1914* (Cambridge, MA: Harvard University Press, 1969). For the events preceding the effort, see Christopher Andrew, *Théophile Delcassé and the Making of the Entente Cordiale* (London: Macmillan, 1968). For the political implications of the staff talks for British diplomacy with the French, see Keith M. Wilson, "The Making and Putative Implementation of a British Foreign Policy of Gesture, December 1905 to August 1914: The Anglo-French Entente Revisited," *Canadian Journal of History* 38 (August 1996): 227–255.

60 Kronenbitter, *Krieg im Frieden*, 253. Hannig, "Prinz Gottfried zu Hohenlohe-Schillingsfurst," 229–270 especially 241–244. A third Austrian military attaché who became a diplomat during this period was Emmerich von Pflügl, who had been assistant military attaché in Constantinople (1907–1909) before he entered the diplomatic service. As a diplomat he served in Athens, Copenhagen, Belgrade, and Cairo. Godsey, *Aristocratic Redoubt*, 73–74.

61 Giesl, *Zwei Jahrzehnte im Nahen Orient*.

62 Major Wilhelm Colmar von der Goltz served in Turkey from 1883–1895 as special advisor to the Turkish army. He served again in Turkey during World War I.

63 Pomiankowski, *Der Zusammenbruch*, 35–37. Liman von Sanders remained in Turkey from 1913 to the end of the war. His postwar memoir is Otto Liman von Sanders, *Fünf Jahre Türkei* (Berlin: Scherl, 1920).

64 Pomiankowski, *Der Zusammenbruch*, 80–83.

65 Steiner,"Gustav Hubka," 181–182.

66 Steiner, 170–172. Hubka wrote his own account of his service in Cetinje, "Kritische Tage in Montenegro" in *Berliner Monatshefte*, Jahrgang 9, no. 1 (January 1931): 27–45.

67 For Romania, see Barbara Jelavich, "Romania in the First World War: The Pre-War Crisis, 1912–1914," *International Review* 14, no. 3 (August 1992): 441–451. For Italy, see Wolfgang Foerster, "Die deutsch-italienische Militärkonvention," *Berliner Monatshefte*, no. 5 (May 1927): 395–416; Günther Kronenbitter, *Krieg im Frieden* (Munich: Oldenbourg Wissenschaftsverlag, 2003), 420–425, 444–445; Georg Graf von Waldersee, "Von Deutschlands militärpolitischen Beziehung zu Italien," *Berliner Monatshefte* 7 (July 1929): 636–664.

68 Tim Hadley, *Military Diplomacy in the Dual Alliance: German Military Attaché Reporting from Vienna, 1879–1914* (Lanham, MD: Lexington, 2015).

69 Dawson, *A Soldier Diplomat*, 343–345.

70 Vagts, *The Military Attaché*, 37–48.

71 Hadley, *Military Diplomacy*, 202.

2

Strategic Influence, the Royal Navy, and the Appeasement of Japan, 1934–1937

Greg Kennedy

The idea that maritime power can be used to perform engagement and influence operations that are strategic in nature without the use of violent force is not new. In accordance with traditional principles of maritime power, as well as more recent expositions on the use of "soft power,"[1] Britain's maritime strategic policy-making elite has often sought to attempt to influence the strategic behavior of other nations through technological or expertise exchange.[2] Therefore, the tactical and operational investments in engagement and the creation of a more intimate naval relationship are expected to help ensure closer overall strategic relations, if ever tensions or differences between Britain and the other powers occurred. That such influence and engagement can then, argues this particular line of thought, be leveraged at some future crisis point for the benefit of Britain's strategic interests is a reoccurring theme in the greater literature regarding Great Britain's system of imperial defense.[3] The engagement with friendly but nonaligned, or neutral, nations was expected to add moral, physical, economic, or ethical support to Britain's strategic position.[4] The following case study from the 1930s can be instructive for contemporary UK maritime policy-makers with regard to past attempts by a British strategic policy-making elite to use maritime power in such a fashion: maritime defense engagement.

The interwar period is appropriate for such a comparative historical methodology, because of its being contextually similar in terms of a fluid and dynamic international order in which identifying friend and foe for future security and defense purposes was fraught with multiple variables hard to give exact weight to. The interwar example illustrates the point that policy-making elites must venture into such relationships with a sharp eye and wary appreciation of the possible limitations, and liabilities, that the use of maritime influence or engagement can bring through limited technical/professional interactions in the quest for effective defense engagement. Most important, it is a lesson in the need for an appreciation of the political power the target navy has in its own strategic policy-making process. Even if a sentiment of good navy-to-navy relations is created by such defense-engagement activity, there is no guarantee that this favorable professional appreciation and friendliness can be translated into any significant strategic leverage.

The relationship between Great Britain's interwar foreign policy in the 1930s and its maritime power was absolute.[5] As a key actor within the balance of power system that governed international relations in that period, Great Britain's naval, economic, fiscal, industrial, cultural, and communications power (its maritime power) was the basis of the nation's Great Power status within that system. British foreign-policy options—of whether to, how to, and where to engage, coerce, deter, or appease another state—all revolved around the effectiveness and credibility of the Empire's ability to generate and use its maritime power.[6] In particular, the linkages between the concept of appeasement and British naval power have been the subject of a number of interwar studies. The focus of these appeasement-based studies has been on a range of British strategic considerations. These have included: the limits of Great Britain's own naval power to meet threats, therefore creating an improper and incorrect reliance on diplomacy rather than military coercion to achieve the desired ends; the impact of increasing British naval power on other nations' attitudes toward Great Britain and its empire, as either a potential friend or foe; and the need to buy time through strategic accommodation in order for rearmament programs to create the naval power required to meet the challenges to imperial security created by the rise of Nazi Germany, militaristic Japan, and fascist Italy.[7] Often embedded within many of those larger methodologies regarding appeasement has been an analysis of the direct impact and influence of the Royal Navy itself as an actor in that foreign-policy-making process.[8] For today's Royal Navy (RN) and foreign and commonwealth office (FCO) practitioners, such activities and perceptions are familiar.[9]

This interwar case study contains many practical examples for Great Britain's present-day strategic thinkers and policy-makers, revealing the interconnected nature and tensions of Foreign Office (FO) and RN perceptions of threat and influence, as well as the limitations and constraints of any such defense engagement if not applied to the correct policy-making node within the target nation's policy-making system.[10] Overall, the historical debate revealed here between the FO and the admiralty regarding the nature of Japanese policy, the role of moderate political influences in Japanese policy-making, the degree of the Imperial Japanese Navy's (IJN) influence into that process, and how best to protect British strategic interests in the region during a period of fiscal restraint and austerity regarding defense spending are transferable strategic conditions that resonate with various circumstances within the current UK national-security context. As such, investigating the expectations, motivations, and outcomes of the British engagement with the IJN is a useful historical case study or lesson learned.

Arthur Marder has portrayed Anglo-Japanese naval relations in this period as growing apart rapidly. As the RN became a diminished presence in the region, Japan's naval capabilities became more powerful. With Japanese strategic focus concentrating on the Soviet Union on the Asian mainland and the growing United States Navy (USN), the primary naval threat to Japan's long-term interests, Great Britain's ability to influence its former naval ally, was diminishing rapidly.[11] That condition of British naval diminishment was the reason for a growing belief within the RN of the power of utilizing an appeasement strategy toward Japan in order to protect Britain's Far Eastern empire.[12] In the face of growing Japanese naval power and the unprepared state of Britain's naval bases in Hong Kong and Singapore to support a large battle fleet, the first sea lord, Admiral of the Fleet Alfred Ernle Montacute Chatfield, was of the opinion that, with regard to possible hostilities in the Far East, "the whole basis of our war policy were, in fact, built upon sand."[13] Therefore, appeasement for the Chatfield and the RN was about avoiding conflict while rearmament occurred. Given that preparations for the bases and ship construction would not be complete before 1941–1942, a reasonable appeasement policy toward Japan seemed a sound choice for the RN.[14] Therefore, trying to use naval diplomacy to improve overall Anglo-Japanese strategic relations was seen as being an important and ongoing mission for the service. In particular, given the RN's belief in the influence of the IJN on political events in the Japanese system of governance and decision-making, RN strategic planners believed that strategic leverage could be obtained through better relations with the IJN than through normal diplomatic efforts.[15]

The worsening of Anglo-Japanese international relations in the period following the 1932 Far Eastern Crisis saw the British foreign-policy-making elite rely on a strategy that required Britain to walk a fine line between protecting its Far Eastern interests robustly while at the same time not creating a mental map in the mind of Japanese policy-makers that Great Britain was a confirmed antagonistic power.[16] Furthermore, while Britain looked for ways to accommodate and relate to Japanese strategic objectives, the need to not create images of weakness, appeasement, or subservience in the mind of American policy-makers was also a major strategic consideration.[17] Many American politicians and government officials, such as the head of the State Department's Far Eastern Division, Stanley K. Hornbeck, were suspicious of working jointly with the British in any containment strategy that threatened to escalate regional tensions between Japan and the containing powers:

The Tory element, with the Admiralty leading, in Great Britain, keep bringing up the idea of renewing the Anglo-Japanese alliance. They ring the changes on the proposition, erroneous in fact, that Japan is the natural and effective guardian of *peace* in the Far East. They apparently either do not understand what has happened in the Far East during the past forty years (beginning with 1894) or are convinced that the disadvantages which accrued to them in consequence of the Anglo-Japanese alliance and which would accrue to them in consequence of a renewal of that alliance were and would be *less than* the damage which Japan could have done and would do (to British interests) in pursuit of a purely Japanese policy untempered by the restraining influence which Great Britain exercised and could exercise through the instrumentality of an Anglo-Japanese alliance. When they talk of Japan as a "guardian of the peace" it may be that they are fooled or it may be that they are merely trying to fool others by way of justifying a course which they would like to see pursued, in promotion, as they conceive it, of a British interest.[18]

Therefore, to cultivate better Anglo-American strategic relations that could help provide stability to the regional balance of power, British policy-makers were constantly on the lookout for situations that would present them with the opportunity to make positive overtures toward the Japanese while at the same time not arousing any suspicion in the minds of the American policy-makers that Britain might "scuttle" and appease Japan.[19] In the summer of 1934, an opportunity was thought to exist for the British to both reassure America and cooperate with Japan, therefore accommodating the requirements of both powers. The issue that arose was the possibility of naval diplomacy (defense engagement) being practiced through the RN's provision of shipbuilding and construction expertise, along with sharing technical information regarding ship-design procedures with the IJN.[20]

In December 1933, the British Ambassador to Japan, Sir Francis Lindley, informed the secretary of state for foreign affairs, Sir John Simon, that it was his belief that Japan was ready to try to make better relations with both Great Britain and the United States. In part, this was a response to fears of a possible conflict with Soviet Russia. Both aspects of his appreciation of the situation were shared by Lindley's counterpart and friend, American ambassador to Japan Joseph Grew.[21] As well, both the British military and naval attachés were of the opinion that the Japanese government was genuinely anxious to improve relations with both Western powers.[22] Lindley recognized the desire on the part of Whitehall for better Anglo-American relations in the Far East to be the cornerstone for British security in that region, but he was unconvinced that without a "hard and fast" military alliance to bind the two English-speaking nations to a common front any good would come of being overtly joined up with American policies. He told London: "I venture, therefore, most respectfully to urge that we revert to the well-tried policy of making friendly relations with Japan the cornerstone of our Far Eastern policy and that the Minister designate to China be so instructed before he leaves for his post. I am perfectly aware of all the difficulties and objections."[23] In such circumstances, commander in chief (CinC) China station, Admiral Sir Fredrick Dreyer, and the admiralty in general wished to make every reasonable effort to signal to the Japanese that Britain would defend its interests in the region, but that it was also willing to try to find room for the accommodation of

Japanese efforts to consolidate its strengthened strategic position in the Far East.[24]

By May 1934, Admiral Dreyer had been practicing this maritime diplomacy for some time. Having proposed and conducted a number of visits to various Japanese ports in the region, Dreyer was keen to continue to show the flag and network with the Japanese. His naval-defense engagement reflected his own personal belief in the historic ties between the IJN and the RN.[25] The admiralty, as well, had an overall policy of attempting to improve Anglo-Japanese naval relations, which had come under strain recently over the London Naval Treaty system, the Amau declaration, and general increases in Japanese aggression in China. Dreyer's initiative reflected a longstanding strategic desire on the part of the RN in general to improve Great Britain's strategic relationship with Japan.

Admiral Dreyer had explained his belief in the need to appease Japan to London in great detail and at great length.[26] One of the areas of interaction that he had focused on was how to continue to engage the IJN with regard to the issue of reciprocal ship visits to naval bases. Dreyer informed London that, from the moment he took command of the China Station in March 1933, he had been determined to reestablish a vigorous program of RN ship visits to Japan. Between September 11 and November 10, seventeen RN ships, in comparison to two in 1932, visited Japanese waters, the largest British attempt to use naval-defense engagement in more than twenty years.[27] Apart from the obvious display of "presence" that such visits created, Dreyer's objective for the heightened visits, including his own excursion to Japan, was to "establish personal touch with the Japanese Navy and to enable me to meet my old friends in that Navy whom I have known for many years, although I have never visited Japan before, and, to introduce our younger officers to their 'opposite numbers' in the Japanese Navy."[28] Dreyer's visit witnessed the CinC meet with the emperor, Admiral Togo, fleet admiral Prince Fushimi, and the minister of marine, Admiral Osumi, reflecting an outstanding program of high-level defense engagement all aimed at ingratiating the memories of Japan's long relationship with the RN with these key decision-makers and influencers.[29] Clearly, the senior RN admiral in the Far Eastern theater was a proponent of attempting to use naval-defense engagement to create better Anglo-Japanese strategic relations. As such, he was also a supporter of the need for London to utilize that particular RN capability to maximum effect. In early 1934, Dreyer and the RN were given an opportunity to increase their defense-engagement profile with the IJN.

On April 24, 1934, the naval attaché in Tokyo, Captain J. G. Vivian, reported on the loss of the Japanese destroyer *Tomozuru* during a large storm off the Goto Islands on March 12. One hundred of the 113 persons onboard the ship were lost. The destroyer appeared to have suffered from stability problems, as well as structural faults leading to its loss. This stability failure was a shock to the IJN leadership, in terms of its reputation as a leader in modern naval construction. The *Tomozuru*-class of vessels had been built after lessons had been learned from the loss of a similar vessel, the *Sawarabi*, in 1932, and as a result was thought to have been especially seaworthy, especially as it possessed a new stabilizing device.[30] Sixteen further vessels in that class were scheduled to be built under the IJN's 1933 building program.[31] As a result of the *Tomozuru* accident, Vivian reported, "hull construction of all destroyers and torpedo boats is stopped pending modifications to designs."[32] He also indicated that, because of the belief that construction faults were responsible for the loss of the *Tomozuru*, it was likely that major modifications in construction would have to be made to the *Mikuma*-class vessels that were underway in the construction process.[33] Vivian was already involved with the Japanese authorities regarding their search for information concerning the quality-control measures used in the RN's naval construction and acceptance procedures.

Following the loss of the *Tomozuru*, Vivian visited the place of its construction, the Maizuru Naval Dockyard, on April 24, 1934, at the behest of the Japanese naval authorities. He had been invited to attend a small conference on the incident with the admiral superintendent of the dockyard and a number of other Japanese naval officers associated with naval construction at that facility.[34] In the opening remarks by the Japanese officers, Vivian was told that the loss of the vessel had "caused what could only be described as an earthquake in naval circles" and that the accident was the result of a procurement process that was badly flawed from the time a ship was projected to the time the final design was approved.[35] It was explained to the British naval attaché that the Japanese

Naval Staff state their requirements and the Technical Departments, i.e., Constructors, Engineers, Gunnery, Torpedo, produce a design. This design is then submitted for approval to a Committee, presided over by the Vice-Minister of Marine, consisting of the heads of the Technical Departments who have been responsible for producing the design and the heads of the Naval Staff Divisions. It was understood that the Naval Staff are inclined to bring pressure on the Constructors to get what they want.[36]

Vivian was informed that it was the belief of many at the meeting that a higher authority would have to become responsible for the final acceptance of the design in the Japanese system. No matter what, however, it was recognized that the system was going to have to be changed, and as part of that transformation process the Japanese navy were anxious to know how the British procedures worked.[37]

Vivian was asked at the conference on April 20 if he could provide the Japanese with details of the RN's procurement procedures in this area, from projection to acceptance.[38] The naval attaché claimed he did not have enough information to usefully assist the Japanese at that time. He was, however, fairly certain that the request was not just a spontaneous or local event, suspecting that the ministry of marine itself had instructed the dockyard officials to ask the embarrassing question for help at such a venue so that an answer would have to be provided, even if the response was not immediate. Vivian requested that the admiralty allow him to give a rough outlined response to the Japanese. Finally, his appreciation of the opportunity presented was that a detailed provision of the information requested would be useful in helping improve strained Anglo-Japanese naval relations.[39]

Meanwhile, in response to the *Tomozuru* incident, the IJN started its far-reaching process of reform. By June 1934, a commission had been set up to investigate the designs of all new construction. This investigation included other ship types besides simply the *Tomozuru*-class of vessels. The World War I–era battleship *Fuso*, whose change over to oil-fired boilers, which was seen as a lead modernization program for other similar vessels, was to have its overall stability checked as part of the investigation.[40] The commission had also moved after its preliminary findings to have the heads of the construction, engineering, and technical departments replaced.[41] In fact, RN intelligence reported that, as a result of the capsizing of the Japanese destroyer, "the stability of all Japanese ships of recent design or recent modernisation has been investigated. The new destroyers, which carry the heaviest armament of any destroyers afloat, the new *Mogami* class cruisers, and the modernised *Fuso* and *Yamashiro* are the ships for which most concern was felt. Those destroyers under construction which are not too far advanced are being redesigned; those too far advanced for redesign are being modified."[42] By November of that year, the incident had resulted in a court of inquiry being held, with one of its findings being to set up a high technical commission to advise the navy minister on the appropriateness of warship designs: "The Commission is to consist of about five members to be chosen from Admirals (chiefly members of the Supreme Military Council), Fleet Commanders, and others having actual experience in marine warfare and operations. The qualifications required for membership of this Commission do not sound so severely 'technical' as might have been expected."[43] With such wide-ranging and deep quality-control issues preying on the minds of senior IJN leadership, a clear opportunity for RN technical expertise to gain gratitude and influence was being presented.

By July 1934, the admiralty had decided on a course of action to take with regard to the Japanese request. It had compiled the necessary documentation and was ready to begin the process of engaging in the exchanging of information. When informing the Foreign Office of the intended way ahead, the admiralty stated that for the sake of improving Anglo-Japanese relations, they were ready to supply the information requested but wanted that information to be supplied through formal channels. Therefore, the admiralty wished the Japanese ministry of marine to be provided the data through either Ambassador Sir Robert Clive himself or the naval attaché.[44] The FO had no objection to either what the Admiralty was telling the Japanese or the requested method of transmission. They instructed Ambassador Clive to proceed on July 31.[45] On September 14, Clive informed the Japanese minister for foreign affairs Koki Hirota that "in virtue of the very friendly relations which have so long existed between our two countries," Britain was "prepared exceptionally to supply the information . . . which it is hoped may be of real value to the Imperial Naval Staff as embodying the accumulated results of many years of practical experience."[46] It was the FO and admiralty's hopes that this action, along with continued requests by Dreyer to continue to increase RN ship visits to Japanese ports, would provide a formal and informal one-two diplomatic punch that would move Anglo-Japanese maritime relations onto a more favorable ground.[47] That combination did indeed produce a positive result. A return of secret information regarding ship design and construction was forthcoming from the Japanese by mid-October, and thanks for the design-procedure information provided by the RN for the IJN accompanied that data.[48]

If the story would have stopped at this point and was to be seen only through the prism of the RN-IJN relations and naval power, the perspective would be one of a successful bit of naval diplomacy, through technology information and sharing/transfer, being accomplished. However, such was not the case. The efforts to use the opportunity presented by the *Tomozuru* did not produce any significant change in Anglo-Japanese strategic relations. This was due to the lack of political influence the IJN possessed within the Japanese strategic foreign-policy-making process at that time. As well, the expectations for success symbolized a failure on the part of British policy-makers to understand the limitations of the IJN's role in the Japanese strategic decision-making system.

The IJN could not change the overall strategic direction of Japanese expansion or the aggressive nature of its policies in the region. So while there was a great deal of hope that this sharing of naval technology and know-how would improve navy-to-navy relations (perhaps allowing access to ports and shipyards), there was little evidence that the improvement of those naval relations had any significant effect on the overall strategic relationship. As well, even if better Anglo-Japanese bilateral operational relations were produced from such events, the influence of the United States on British strategic-policy formulation would also constantly be an impediment to any positive movement toward better Anglo-Japanese relations. The slightest accommodation or friendly overture to Japan ran the risk of being seen as British appeasement, a narrative that the British diplomatic and political policy-makers were careful to avoid at all costs. In particular, such small steps as the technology-sharing event could not overcome the larger issues at stake regarding the forthcoming 1935 London Naval Conference and the question of whether or not Japan would remain a part of the Washington Treaty System.

In the fall of 1934, there was little doubt that the Japanese wished for closer Anglo-Japanese strategic relations. In early October, Ambassador Clive told the FO that the Japanese government definitely favored a policy of friendship between the two nations, so much so that they wished for some sort of agreement or understanding.[49] Clive pointed out that this quest for closer relations was driven by three main factors: "fear of isolation: the desire to insure themselves in the event of relations with the Soviets becoming extremely strained: fear of Anglo-American solidarity against Japanese interests at Naval Conference."[50] Even so, this attitude of conciliation was not a true indication of Japanese attitudes, said Clive: "I cannot point to any recent case in which Japanese attitude appears to have been guided by spirit of conciliation in spite of repeated protestations of friendship."[51] Clive's lack of enthusiasm for Japan's claims of friendship were derived from Britain's leading expert on Japan, his commercial counselor, George Sansom.[52]

Sansom viewed the Japanese attempts to fabricate an Anglo-Japanese understanding and closer relations as comic and nauseating.[53] Furthermore, Sansom was adamant:

Make no mistake about it. All this is a trap. The Japanese at this moment are feeling a cold wind blowing from somewhere. I am not quite sure what their anxiety is. I think it's a combination of several things. They don't like facing Russia without one sympathizer and possible supporter. They would like to tie our hands in case events in China should so shape that they felt it necessary to take some drastic action there. They are anxious to separate us from the USA over the question of armament. And finally, I am beginning to suspect, they are getting a little nervous about their financial situation. Making every allowance for traditional like for England on the part of a number of Japanese, I still hold the opinion that their latest professions of friendship are false. In their present frame of mind the Japanese conception of friendship is give-and-take; we give and they take.[54]

Despite all the good will in the world, and as much technical assistance as the RN could reasonably provide to the IJN, the small gestures of one navy to the other did not have enough importance to shift the relationship to better ground. This was certainly proven throughout 1935 and events leading up to Japan's withdrawal from the Washington Treaty System and her abrogation of the London Naval Treaty.[55] Furthermore, Japanese intentions to use maritime power to dislodge the Anglo-American strategic presence in China would ensure that such small tactical gestures as the information exchange surrounding the *Tomozuru* affair never matured into real strategic influence or leverage.

By November 1937, less than three years after the warm exchange of pleasantries had taken place between the RN and IJN, the admiralty's assessment of conditions in the Far East at the time brought all of the various naval aspects of the situation into stark relief. It was a tale of constant deterioration and animosity. In discussions regarding the growing concerns about the stability of the situation in the Far East, the first sea lord, Admiral Chatfield, informed the British cabinet of his, and therefore the RN's, perspective on how events could be expected to proceed. In his view, the Mediterranean (Spanish Civil War) and European situation continued to demand the presence of a large portion of the RN's strength and attention. If the Japanese were to tighten the blockade controls to prevent contraband getting in to China, then the correct policy was for Great Britain to declare its neutrality, admit there was belligerency, and inform British shipping that they carried contraband to China at their own risk and without the protection of the state.[56] Most importantly, the first sea lord pointed out the differences between the European experiences for the RN in economic warfare and those that would be found in the Pacific. The case was simply one of mismatched strength: the IJN was too strong for the RN in those waters:

Naval action would only be required if the Japanese greatly exceeded their rights under International Law or used unnecessary force to exact obedience from a merchant ship. It would be, in the opinion of the Naval Staff, a mistaken policy to use our naval forces in a manner comparable to that in which they have been used in Spanish waters, i.e. to give protection on the high seas against interference by the naval forces of a nation obviously actually at war whether or not a state of war had been admitted or declared to exist. Moreover, the situation in the Far East differs widely from that obtaining on the North Coast of Spain, where a single British battleship can exercise a dominating influence, since she is, in herself, more powerful than the whole of the naval forces by which British shipping in those waters might be threatened. In the Far East, however, any Japanese threat to British shipping which might arise could be backed by the strength of the Japanese fleet.[57]

The idea of sending two capital ships to act as a deterrent was raised as well by Chatfield, but not in a positive light. His recommendation was that sending such a token force would only aggravate the Japanese to escalate their own naval activities, not deter their maritime economic warfare. If the

Japanese maritime economic warfare element of their war against China was to be nullified such that Great Britain's trading rights and access to China were ensured, then a great deal more effort—an effort resembling a full naval war in terms of its operational impact—would be required.[58] Neither the FO nor the cabinet, when this information was discussed in November of 1937, disagreed with the first sea lord's assessment or recommendation that no significant British naval reinforcements should be sent to the region.[59] As 1937 drew to a close, the Japanese revealed their growing confidence and control of the maritime environment in China with deliberate attacks on the American and British gunboats USS *Panay* and HMS *Ladybird*. At no point in this saga was any mention or use of the good will demonstrated by the RN in 1934 over the *Tomozuru* affair made at either the tactical level, between RN and IJN local commanders, or at higher operational-commander levels. Any effect at all from the defense-engagement investment was absent from the Anglo-Japanese relationship at any level.

The idea of military forces being able to conduct a separate stream of diplomacy, even in an autocracy or monarchy, is a suspect supposition. While military forces such as navies can share their expertise and knowledge, as well as use their own tools of technology, doctrine, training, education, and so on, to try to make beneficial relations with other similar institutions, the historical realities seem to be that only operational knowledge and relationships are a result. Without the ability to influence the political realm sufficiently, as even the RN could not do in the British system at this time (and certainly cannot do today), expecting too much from such naval interactions can lead to expectations that only lead to a greater sense of betrayal or tensions when they do not transpire as expected. The use of such soft or indirect power should, therefore, always be viewed with a great deal of skepticism as to its utility in the face of an aggressive, armed, and potentially hostile nation. Finally, such influencing or engagement roles should not become core business for military organizations. Using established diplomatic channels to exploit opportunities that arise through military-to-military relations is a collateral, not core, business of such organizations. Given the limited influence of militaries within most strategic-policy-making elites, and the ever shrinking expenditure on armed services in general, limiting the investment made by small, cash-strapped, manpower-light organizations on such engagement operations should be the governing rule for such resource allocation. Most important, from the strategic perspective, is for policy-making elites to expect limited value from such influence operations at best and not make strategic preparation and assessments conditional upon those sorts of operations achieving great aims.

Appendix 1: RN Memorandum—Design and Construction of H.M. Ships[60]

PART I — ADMIRALTY REGULATIONS GOVERNING
THE PROCEDURE TO BE ADOPTED IN THE PREPARATION
OF DESIGNS OF H.M. SHIPS

When the First Lord orders the design of a new ship, the First Sea Lord will, through the Assistant Chief of the Naval Staff, cause to be prepared a memorandum known as the Staff Requirements.

The Staff Requirements for any ship, or class of ship, will show the main features necessary, in the opinion of the Naval Staff, to fulfil the strategical and tactical functions for which the ship has been projected, and form the basis for preparation of a sketch design.

It will be the duty of the Director of Tactical Division to co-ordinate the opinions of the Director of plans and other divisions of the Naval Staff and to prepare the Memorandum of Staff Requirements for submission to the Assistant Chief of Naval Staff. In formulating the Staff Requirements, the divisions of the Naval Staff are to maintain close touch with the Controller's Departments to ensure that the latest advances in material are not overlooked. The Director of Personal Services is also to be kept in touch with the proposals affecting welfare.

The Assistant Chief of the Naval Staff will inform the Second Sea Lord of all proposals affecting habitability, messing and arrangements affecting discipline, and the Fourth Sea Lord of all proposals affecting the system of victualling and messing and the stowage of naval and victualling stores.

The Staff Requirements will then be discussed by the First Sea Lord, Controller, Deputy Chief of the Naval Staff and the Assistant Chief of the Naval Staff, and written instructions will be given to the Controller by the First Sea Lord.

The Controller will instruct the Director of Naval Construction to prepare a sketch design embodying the approved features and to accommodate the probable complement (plus the authorised margin for supernumeraries, etc.). The Director of Naval Construction will obtain the probable complement from the Permanent Complement Committee.

The Director of Naval Construction having obtained the probable complement and after conferring with, and obtaining the opinion in writing of, the Director of Naval Ordnance, the Director of Torpedoes and Mining and the Engineer-in-Chief, as to armament and machinery, is to prepare a sketch design for submission to the Controller, who will forward it to the Assistant Chief of the Naval Staff for the remarks of the Divisions of the Naval Staff, prior to its consideration by the First Sea Lord, Controller and the Assistant Chief of the Naval Staff in conference. The sketch design decided on will then be placed before the Board.

If Board approval is obtained, the Controller will order the design to be worked out in detail or modified with a view to its ultimate adoption.

The design will then be completed by the Director of Naval Construction in consultation with the Engineer-in-Chief, Director of Naval Ordnance, Director of Torpedoes and Mining, Director of Naval Equipment, Director of Signal Equipment, Director of Electrical Engineering, Director of Victualling, Director of Stores, Paymaster Director General, Medical Director General and the Director of Personal Services, and will be submitted to the Controller with a full and careful explanation as to the manner in which the requirements have been met and the expected qualities and capabilities of the ship.

The Controller and the Assistant Chief of the Naval Staff will then confer as to the suitability of the completed design (the latter having obtained the remarks of the Naval Staff as to whether the approved requirements have been met), any modifications in feature being placed before the First Sea Lord.

The Controller will send the design to the Secretary for circulation to the several Members of the Board before being considered at a Board Meeting.

After the final design has been approved by the Board, and has received the Board Stamp, no alteration or addition either in hull, machinery, armament, complement of men, boats or stores, or other detail, is to be permitted without the concurrence of the Board.

No deviation from the designs approved by the Board is to take place which would in any way affect the immersion of the ship when complete for service.

PART II — PROCEDURE DURING CONSTRUCTION

The Hull Specifications of all British warships contain a clause to the effect that care is to be taken that unsatisfactory conditions of stability are not reached at any time during their construction. The responsibility for this is placed with the Main Contractors, but the Hull Overseer may request the Contractors to check the stability at any time during construction. For Dockyard-built ships the responsibility rests with the Yard Officers. There are many occasions during the completion of a ship when heavy weights are landed on the weather deck causing heel, the extent of which indicates if the vessel is abnormally "tender" or not.

Every new British warship, or at least the first of a new type, is subjected to an inclining experiment shortly before proceeding on her sea trials. A Constructive Officer on the staff of the Director of Naval Construction conducts this experiment. Although usually there is insufficient time between the experiment — which is carried out when the vessel is as complete as practicable — and the sea trials to complete the calculations in full, enough is done to ensure that the stability is satisfactory in all conditions likely to occur on the trials.

Before a new contract-built ship proceeds on trials the Firm sign an application for permission to remove to vessel from their premises. In this application (Form (A) enclosed) they state the vessel is in respect of strength, stability, seaworthiness, etc., in a fit condition to leave, and that she will not, in any condition of lading be in an unsatisfactory condition as regards stability. This Form is also signed by the Naval Superintendent of the District, the Engineer Officer of the ship, the Ship Overseer, and the District Electrical Engineer, and is forwarded to the Admiralty for approval. If the stability were unsatisfactory, as shown by the results of the inclining experiment mentioned in paragraph 2, the application would not be forwarded, or if forwarded, would not be approved until such steps had been taken as would render the stability satisfactory. A second Form — (B), also enclosed — confirmatory of (A) is signed by the Contractors and Admiralty Officials on the eve of the vessel leaving for trials.

The Forms referred to do not apply to Dockyard-built ships, but the Yard Officers ensure that a new vessel proceeding on trial is satisfactory in all respects.

A Stability Statement is forwarded to the Commanding Officer of a new British warship as soon as practicable after completion and before the vessel leaves port. This Statement gives the stability in various conditions, and, if necessary, instructions as to the method of using the fuel so that the stability may not be prejudiced. In coal-fired warships these instructions were sometimes necessary, but, in oil-fired vessels they are very rarely required. If circumstances prevent the Stability Statement being completed and forwarded before the ship leaves port, the Commanding Officer is informed by letter to the same effect before he sails.

Stability Statements as supplied to British warships are referred to and examples given in several British books on Naval Architecture.

The problem of a ship's stability being an extremely intricate and highly technical one, it was decided by the Board of Admiralty many years ago that the Director of Naval Construction should be directly responsible to the Controller for the provision of adequate stability in H.M. Ships. For this reason all proposals for additions and alterations which from their nature may affect stability are required to be referred to the Director of Naval Construction before a decision is reached as to their adoption.

With these precautions there is very little risk of a ship proceeding to sea and reaching a condition in which the stability is unsatisfactory.

Appendix 2: Secret IJN Memorandum—Procedure in Connection with the Design of a New Ship

When designs are required for the construction of a new ship, the Chief of the Department of the Matériel of the Navy informs the Heads of each Section of the main features, such as the class, armament, protection, speed, cruising radius, etc. of the ship to be built and orders designs to be prepared.

The Heads of Sections Nos. 1, 2, and 3 prepare specifications of the armament, at the same time selecting the persons to have charge of the design thereof, and reporting the same to the Chief of the Department of the Matériel of the Navy.

The Head of Section No. 4 estimates the approximate horse-power required for the propulsion of the ship, selects the persons to have charge of the design and reports the same to the Chief of the Department of the Matériel of the Navy, at the same time informing the Head of Section No. 5.

The Head of Section No. 5 prepares a statement of the main features of the necessary machinery, selects the designers and reports the above to the Chief of the Department of the Matériel of the Navy.

The Chief of the Department of the Matériel of the Navy delivers the documents submitted by the Heads of Nos. 1, 2, 3, and 5 to the Head of Section No. 4 and orders the preparation of outline designs.

The Head of Section No. 4 prepares outline designs and a statement of the main features (including a table of distribution of weights in each part of the ship), which he circulates to the Heads of Sections Nos. 1, 2, 3, and 5, and, having obtained their concurrence, submits to the Chief of the Department of the Matériel of the Navy.

The Chief of the Department of the Matériel of the Navy inspects the above-mentioned drawings and documents and, when satisfied that they are adequate, orders the Chief of the Technical Research Institute to estimate and determine the most suitable model, horse-power, speed and revolutions per minute, and most suitable propelling machinery and the position thereof, etc. to accord with these designs, and delivers the results of this estimate to the Heads of Section Nos. 4 and 5.

In the event of an alteration in the outline design being required as a result of the model tests, the Head of Section No.4 exchanges the necessary papers with the Head of Section No. 5, and drafts a second outline design which he submits to the Chief of the Department of the Matériel of the Navy.

In the event of an important alteration being necessary in the particulars of a design prepared by any Department, the Head of this Department submits the particulars to the Chief of the Department of the Matériel of the Navy, who delivers them to the Heads of the Sections concerned.

When the Chief of the Department of the Matériel of the Navy has approved the outline designs he orders the Heads of each Section to proceed with the main design; as regards stores he communicates with the Director of the Bureau of Naval Stores in the Ministry of Marine and calls for an estimate of the number of fittings, consumable stores, their price and a table of weights; as regards materials to be initially supplied for standing medical equipment, he communicates with the Director of the Medial Bureau in the

Ministry of Marine, and calls for a table of weights and a rough estimate of costs.

In the initial stages of the preparation of the main design, the Heads of Sections Nos. 1, 2, 3 and 5 prepare, as early as possible, the following documents based on the outline designs and statements of main features and forward them to the Head of Section No. 4:—*The Heads of Sections Nos. 1, 2 and 3*

A general classified statement of weights connected with the armament, and diagrams showing the positions of the centres of gravity of these weights.

The Head of Section No. 5

A general classified statement of the parts of machinery, their weights and the position of their centres of gravity.

In addition, the Heads of Sections Nos. 1, 2, 3 and 4 prepare and send to the Head of Section No. 5 the following documents: a summary of the items which concern the Dockyard Engineering Section, such as types, numbers and horse-power of auxiliary machinery (ordance), the diameter of steam and exhaust pipes, etc.

The Head of Section No. 4

Drawings of parts of the hull which affect the design of the machinery, drawings of the sub-division of main machinery spaces, and also a summary of the items which concern the Dockyard Engineering Section, including types, numbers and horse-power of auxiliary machinery which come under the control of the Construction Section, the diameter of steam and exhaust pipes, etc.

When the main design drawings, statement of methods of construction and documents in connection therewith of each Section are complete, they are circulated to the other Heads of Sections concerned, and, after their concurrence has been obtained, they are submitted to the Chief of the Department of the Matériel of the Navy.

The following among the main design drawings and documents to be prepared by each Section require additional appended instructions concerning manufacture or construction: Section No. 1 Specifications of the ordnance.

Section No. 2 Specifications of torpedo equipment and navigational instruments.

Section No. 3 Specifications of electrical equipment.

Section No. 4 (1) Sheer plans, midship sections, general diagrams of fittings. (2) Statements of the methods of construction of the hull and a summary of the principal features of its design. (3) All tables of weights including those of weights connected with the hull, machinery, ordnance fittings, etc. (4) Calculations of displacement, etc. and displacement sheet and hydrostatic curves.

Section No. 5 (1) Drawings of machinery installations. (2) Specifications for manufacture of machinery and descriptions of the principal features of their design.

When the main designs have been decided on, the drafting of an authoritative decision, or instructions or discussions is dealt with by the Head of Section No. 4.

NOTES

1 Julian Corbett, *Some Principals of Maritime Strategy* (Annapolis, MD: Naval Institute Press, 1988); Joseph S. Nye, *Soft Power: The Means to Success in World Politics* (Washington, DC: Public Affairs, 2009).

2 On strategic foreign-policy-making elite, see the work of Donald C. Watt, *Personalities and Policies: Studies in the Formulation of British Foreign Policy in the Twentieth Century* (London: Greenwood, 1965), which was enhanced over the decades by others, including but not limited to Keith Neilson, "Perception and Posture in Anglo-American Relations: The Legacy of the Simon-Stimson Affair, 1932–1941," *International History Review* 29, no. 2 (2007): 313–338; Thomas G. Otte, "Introduction: Personalities and Impersonal Forces in History," in *Personalities, War and Diplomacy: Essay in International History*, ed. Thomas G. Otte and Constantine A. Pagedas (London: Routledge, 1997), 1–14; Zara Steiner, "Elitism and Foreign Policy: The Foreign Office Before the Great War," in *Shadow and Substance in British Foreign Policy 1895–1939: Memorial Essays Honoring C. J. Lowe*, ed. B. J. C. McKercher and David J. Moss (Alberta, Canada: University of Alberta Press, 1984), 19–56.

3 Greg Kennedy, "The Royal Navy and Imperial Defence, 1919–1945," in *Imperial Defence: The Old World Order, 1856–1956*, ed. Greg Kennedy (London: Routledge, 2007), 133–152.

4 Greg Kennedy, "Some Principles of Anglo-American Strategic Relations, 1900–45," in *The British Way in Warfare: Power and the International System, 1856–1956: Essays in Honour of David French*, ed. Keith Neilson and Greg Kennedy (Farnham, UK: Ashgate, 2010), 29–58.

5 Malcolm H. Murfett, "Look Back in Anger: The Western Powers and the Washington Conference of 1921–1922," in B. J. C. McKercher, ed., *Arms Limi-*

tation and Disarmament: Restraints on War, 1899–1939 (New York: Praeger, 1992), 83–104; Stephen W. Roskill, *Naval Policy Between the Wars*, vols. 1 and 2 (London: Collins, 1968), 70–75; Zara Steiner, *The Triumph of the Dark: European International History, 1933–1939* (Oxford, UK: Oxford University Press, 2011); George C. Peden, *Arms, Economics and British Strategy: From Dreadnoughts to Hydrogen Bombs* (Cambridge, UK: Cambridge University Press, 2007); Keith Neilson and T. G. Otte, *The Permanent Under-Secretary for Foreign Affairs, 1854–1946* (London: Routledge, 2009); J. Kenneth McDonald, "The Washington Conference and the Naval Balance of Power, 1921–22," in John B. Hattendorf and Robert S. Jordan, eds., *Maritime Strategy and the Balance of Power* (London: Palgrave Macmillan, 1989), 189–213; Erik Goldstein and John Maurer, eds., "Special Issue on the Washington Conference, 1921–22: Naval Rivalry, East Asian Stability and the Road to Pearl Harbor," *Diplomacy & Statecraft* 4, no. 3 (1993); Greg Kennedy, *Anglo-American Strategic Relations and the Far East, 1933–1939: Imperial Crossroads* (London: Frank Cass, 2002); Greg Kennedy, ed., *British Naval Strategy East of Suez, 1900–2000: Influences and Actions* (London: Routledge, 2005); Reynolds M. Salerno, *Vital Crossroads: Mediterranean Origins of the Second World War, 1935–1940* (Ithaca, NY: Cornell University Press, 2002).

6 John Darwin, *The Empire Project: The Rise and Fall of the British World System, 1830–1970* (Cambridge, UK: Cambridge University Press, 2009); Franklyn A. Johnson, *Defence by Committee: The British Committee of Imperial Defence, 1895–1959* (Oxford, UK: Oxford University Press, 1960); D. C. Watt, "Imperial Defence Policy and Imperial Foreign Policy, 1911–1939: A Neglected Paradox," *Journal of Commonwealth Political Studies* 12, no. 1 (1963): 12–32; D. N. Chester and F. M. G. Willson, *The Organization of British Central Government, 1914–1956* (London: George Allen & Unwin, 1957); Kennedy, ed., *Imperial Defence*; J. A. Mangan, ed., *Making Imperial Mentalities: Socialization and British Imperialism* (Manchester, UK: Manchester University Press, 1990); "The British World: Diaspora, Culture and Identity," in Carl Bridge and Kent Fedorowich, eds., Special Issue, *Journal of Imperial and Commonwealth History* 31, no. 2 (May 2003); A. Bosco and A. May, eds., *The Round Table: The Empire and Commonwealth and British Foreign Policy* (London: Lothian Foundation, 1997); Christopher Bell, *The Royal Navy, Seapower and Strategy between the Wars* (Stanford, CA: Stanford University Press, 2000); B. J. C. McKercher, *Transition of Power: Britain's Loss of Global Pre-eminence to the United States, 1930–1945* (Cambridge, UK: Cambridge University Press, 1999); Niall Ferguson, *Empire: How Britain Made the Modern World* (New York: Penguin, 2004); Walter Russell Mead, *God and Gold: Britain, America and the Making of the Modern World* (New York: Vintage, 2008); Andrew Thompson, *The Empire Strikes Back?: The Impact of*

Imperialism on Britain from the Mid-Nineteenth Century (London: Routledge, 2005); Bernard Porter, *The Absent-minded Imperialists: What the British Really Thought about Empire* (Oxford, UK: Oxford University Press, 2004).

7 Michael L. Roi, *Alternative to Appeasement: Sir Robert Vansittart and Alliance Diplomacy, 1934–1937* (Westport, CT: Praeger, 1997); Joseph A. Maiolo, *The Royal Navy and Nazi Germany, 1933–39: A Study in Appeasement and the Origins of the Second World War* (London: Macmillan, 1998); Gaines Post Jr., "Mad dogs and Englishmen: British Rearmament, Deterrence and appeasement, 1934–35," *Armed Forces and Society* 14, no. 2 (1988): 329–357; Carolyn J. Kitching, *Britain and the Geneva Disarmament Conference* (Basingstoke, UK: Palgrave Macmillan, 2003); Carolyn J. Kitching, *Britain and the Problem of International Disarmament, 1919–1934* (London: Routledge, 1999); Keith Neilson, "The Defence Requirements Sub-Committee, British Strategic Foreign Policy, Neville Chamberlain and the Path to Appeasement," *English Historical Review* 118, no. 3 (2003): 651–684; Robert Self, *Neville Chamberlain: A Biography* (Aldershot, UK: Ashgate, 2006); G. A. H. Gordon, *British Seapower and Procurement between the Wars: A Reappraisal of Rearmament* (Annapolis, MD: Naval Institute Press, 1988); Joseph Moretz, *The Royal Navy and the Capital Ship in the Interwar Period: An Operational Perspective* (London: Routledge, 2002).

8 C. I. Hamilton, "British Naval Policy, Policy-makers and Financial Control, 1860–1945," *War In History* 12, no. 1 (2005): 371–395; John Ferris, "The Last Decade of British Maritime Supremacy, 1919–1929," in *Far Flung Lines: Studies in Imperial Defence in Honour of Donald Mackenzie Schurman*, ed. Keith Neilson and Greg Kennedy (London: Frank Cass, 1996); Greg Kennedy, "Becoming Reliant on the Kindness of Strangers: Britain's Strategic Foreign Policy, Naval Arms Limitation and the Soviet Factor, 1935–1937," *War in History* 11, no. 2 (2004): 79–105; Greg Kennedy, "'Rat in Power': Neville Chamberlain and the Creation of British Foreign Policy, 1931–1939," in *Makers of British Foreign Policy. From Pitt to Thatcher*, ed. Thomas Otte (Basingstoke, UK: AIAA, 2002); David K. Varey, "The Politics of Naval Aid: The Foreign Office, the Admiralty, and Anglo-Soviet Technical Cooperation, 1936–1939," *Diplomacy and Statecraft* 14, no. 2 (2003): 50–68; Sean Greenwood, "'Caligula's Horse' Revisited: Sir Thomas Inskip as Minister for the Co-ordination of Defence, 1936–1939," *Journal of Strategic Studies* 17, no. 1 (1994): 17–38.

9 UK Ministry of Defence, *Global Strategic Trends out to 2040: The 4th Edition of Global Strategic Trends*, Development, Concepts and Doctrine Centre (DCDC), October, 2013; Royal Navy, "Future Navy Vision: The Royal Navy Today, Tomorrow and Towards 2025" (UK Government Publication, 2011); Tobias Ellwood MP, "Leveraging UK Carrier Capability: A Study into

the Preparation for and Use of the *Queen Elizabeth*-Class Carriers," Occasional Paper, Royal United Services Institute, London, September 2013; *UK's International Defence Engagement Strategy 2017* (UK Government Publication, February 2017).

10 On ideas regarding nexus and decision-making systems, see Jonathan Reed Winkler, *Nexus: Strategic Communications and American Security in World War I* (Cambridge, MA: Harvard University Press, 2008).

11 Arthur J. Marder, *Old Friends, New Enemies: Strategic Illusions, 1936–1941* (Oxford, UK: Clarendon, 1981).

12 CAB 2/6, Minutes of Meetings of the Committee of Imperial Defence (CID), TNA, Kew, London, Minutes of Meetings from November 1933–October 1937, Meeting No. 261, November 9, 1933.

13 CAB 53/4, Minutes of the Chiefs of Staff Committee (COS) Meetings, February 1932–June 1934, Meeting No. 107, February 28, 1933.

14 CAB 53/4, Minutes of COS Meeting 107; CAB 53/4, Minutes of Meeting No. 111, June 20, 1933.

15 Kennedy, *Anglo-American Strategic Relations*, chapters 3 and 4.

16 Ian Nish, *Japanese Foreign Policy in the Interwar Period* (Westport, CT: Praeger, 2002); J. Connell, *The "Office": A Study of British Foreign Policy and Its Makers, 1919–1951* (London: Wingate, 1958); Keith Neilson, *Britain, Soviet Russia and the Collapse of the Versailles Settlement, 1919–1939* (Cambridge, UK: Cambridge University Press, 2005); T. G. Otte, *The Foreign Office Mind: The Making of British Foreign Policy, 1865–1914* (Cambridge, UK: Cambridge University Press, 2011).

17 Greg Kennedy, "What Worth the Americans: Britain's Strategic Policy Making Elite's View of the US as a Far Eastern Maritime Power, 1930–1941," in *Britain's Naval Strategy East of Suez, 1900–2000: Influences and Actions*, ed. Greg Kennedy (London: Frank Cass, 2005), 90–118; Antony Best, *Britain Japan and Pearl Harbor: Avoiding War in East Asia, 1936–1941* (London: Routledge, 1995); Antony Best, "The British Empire's Image of East Asia, 1900–41: Politics, Ideology and International Order," in *Shaping British Foreign and Defence Policy in the Twentieth Century: A Tough Ask in Turbulent Times*, ed. Malcolm H. Murfett (London: Palgrave Macmillan, 2014); Ian Cowman, *Dominion or Decline: Anglo-American Naval Relations in the Pacific, 1937–1941* (Oxford, UK: Berg, 1996). This triangular relationship can be likened to the current British strategic need of remaining and assuring the United States of its resolve and future steadfast support in international affairs, while at the same time establishing a substantive relationship with the destabilizing power China in order to aid in the reconstruction of the UK's economic power. This will be an even more difficult strategic problem now post–European Union Referendum, as expectations of being able to forge individual economic rela-

tions with China resides within large parts of the UK business and financial communities.

18 Stanley K. Hornbeck Papers (hereafter SKH Papers), Hoover Institution Library, Stanford University, Stanford, CA, Chronological Day file, 1931–1946, Box 453, Folder June–December 1933, Memo by Hornbeck to Under-Secretary of State William Phillips, October 31, 1933.

19 *Papers Relating to the Foreign Relations of the United States* (hereafter *FRUS*), *The Far East*, vol. 3, 1934, dispatch from Ambassador (London) Robert Bingham to Secretary of State Cordell Hull, May 7, 1934; Keith Neilson, "Perception and Posture in Anglo-American Relations: The Legacy of the Simon-Stimson Affair, 1932–1941," *International History Review* 29, no. 2 (June 2007): 313–337; Keith Neilson, "The Royal Navy, Japan and British Strategic Foreign Policy, 1932–1934," *Journal of Military History* 75, no. 2 (2011): 505–531.

20 Greg Kennedy, "1935: A Snapshot of British Imperial Defence in the Far East," in Neilson and Kennedy, eds., *Far Flung Lines*, 190–216; F[oreign] O[ffice], The National Archives (TNA), Kew, London, 371/18184/F677/591/23, Confidential Report from Lindley to Simon, December 27, 1933.

21 FO 371/18184/F677/591/23, Confidential Report from Lindley to Simon, December 27, 1933.

22 Lindley to Simon.

23 Lindley to Simon.

24 FO 371/18186/F2996/652/23, memorandum by Dreyer to FO on Far Eastern situation, May 22, 1934.

25 Dreyer to FO, May 22, 1934; FO 371/18186/F2996/652/23, memo from Dreyer to Dickins (DNI), May 5, 1934.

26 ADM 125/72, China General Letters, Enclosure 1, Section 1, to China General Letter No. 8, January 21, 1934, 11d.

27 ADM 125/72, China General Letters, 16

28 ADM 125/72, China General Letters, 17.

29 ADM 125/72, China General Letters, 18–31a.

30 ADM 223/822, Monthly Intelligence Report, April 1934, 22–23.

31 ADM 223/822, 22–23.

32 FO 371/18183/2290/537/23, Secret dispatch from Vivian to Director of Naval Intelligence, April 24, 1934.

33 FO 371/18183/2290/537/23, Secret Dispatch.

34 FO 371/18183/F4568/537/23, Secret Report from Naval Attaché Tokyo to Director of Naval Intelligence, April 26, 1934.

35 FO 371/18183/F4568/537/23, Secret Report.

36 Secret Report.

37 Secret Report.

38 Secret Report.

39 Secret Report.
40 ADM223/822, Monthly Intelligence Report, June 1934, 29.
41 ADM223/822, Monthly Intelligence Report, June 1934, 29.
42 ADM223/822, Monthly Intelligence Report, November 1934, 39.
43 ADM223/822, Monthly Intelligence Report, November 1934, 40.
44 FO 371/18183/F4568/537/23, Secret Letter from Secretary of the Admiralty to Undersecretary of State, FO, July 24, 1934.
45 FO 371/18183/F4568/537/23, telegram from FO to Clive, July 31, 1934, July 24, 1934.
46 FO 371/18184/F5980/537/23, confidential letter from Clive to Hirota, September 14, 1934.
47 On Dreyer's further actions and FO support for them, see: FO 371/18175/F5028/233/23, all documents, August 16, 1934; FO 371/18175/F5295/233/23, all documents, August 30, 1934; FO 371/18175/F6732/233/23, all documents, November.9, 1934; FO 371/18175/F6818/233/23, all documents, November 13, 1934.
48 FO 371/18184/F7159/537/23, confidential letter from Hirota to Clive, October 16, 1934, with secret enclosure; ADM 12/1717 [Digests], "Design and Construction of Warships," MFO306, 1935.
49 FO 371/18184/F5996/591/23, very confidential telegraph from Clive to FO, October 5, 1934.
50 Very confidential telegraph.
51 Very confidential telegraph.
52 On Sansom's place in Great Britain's Far Eastern strategic policy-making process, see Greg Kennedy, "Propaganda, Strategy and the British Deterrence of Japan, 1933–1941," in Greg Kennedy and Chris Tuck, eds., *British Propaganda and Wars of Empire: Influencing Friend and Foe, 1900–2010* (Basingstoke, UK: Ashgate, 2014), 8–26.
53 FO 371/18184/F6577/591/23, letter from Sansom to Sir Edward Crow, Dept. of Overseas Trade, October 12, 1934.
54 Sansom to Crow.
55 Kennedy, "Conclusion," in *Anglo-American Strategic Relations and the Far East*, 262–269.
56 On the RN and the Spanish Civil War, see Greg Kennedy, "The Royal Navy, Intelligence and the Spanish Civil War: Lessons in Air Power, 1936–39," *Intelligence and National Security* 20, no. 2 (June 2005): 238–263; Greg Kennedy, "Anglo-American Strategic Relations and Intelligence Assessments of Japanese Air Power 1934–1941," *Journal of Military History* 74, no. 3 (July 2010): 737–773; FO 371/20979, China 1937, F8559/130/10, Most Secret FES(37)4 Cabinet Paper, Chatfield memo attached, September 23, 1937.
57 FO 371/20979, China 1937, Chatfield memo.

58 China 1937, Chatfield memo.

59 FO 371/20979, China 1937, Vansittart minute, November 4, 1937; FO 371/20979, F9710/130/10, Cabinet FES(37) 2nd Meeting, Cabinet Conclusions, November 9, 1937.

60 ADM 167/90, Board Minutes, Meetings of the Board of Admiralty, January–December 1934, Secret, February 15 and March 5, 1934.

3

Attachés in Albion
Building the Anglo-American Military Alliance, 1938–1941

Tyler Bamford

On Sunday, September 15, 1940, page four of the New York news tabloid *PM* featured the headline, "Censors Hide Heavy Damage to Vital London Areas." The article, accompanied by a dramatic photograph of a bomb-damaged room in Buckingham Palace, described in detail the damage to London's air bases, railroads, docks, and several munitions factories.[1] News of the article reached beleaguered London one week later via telegram on September 23. Subsequently, the British government initiated an investigation aimed at revealing how such highly classified information leaked to the American press. The British investigation predictably focused on the American embassy and the office of the US Army attaché. Although investigators later traced the information leak to the United States War Department in Washington, the British government registered its displeasure with the US Army's official representative in London, Brigadier General Raymond E. Lee. On October 19, the British Air Ministry revoked Lee's access to confidential memoranda that contained what one intelligence officer in the War Department referred to as "valuable detailed information not elsewhere available."[2] Anticipating the loss of this vital intelligence source, Lee turned to other close contacts in the British military who could supply him with "almost the same information."[3]

Between 1938 and 1941, US Army attachés in London repeatedly faced situations like the one that confronted Lee in October 1940. Responsible for collecting sensitive information from their British hosts and facilitating greater cooperation between Great Britain and the United States, attachés played a crucial role as midlevel intermediaries who laid the groundwork for the Anglo-American alliance. The exchanges between attachés and their contacts, however, often did not correspond to national leaders' publicly expressed attitudes of cooperation. Moreover, developments beyond attachés' control often hindered this sharing. Instead, attachés' access to intelligence was contingent on their ability to cultivate strong relationships with their British colleagues. When attachés failed to develop these connections, defense collaboration between the two nations suffered corresponding setbacks.

The military cooperation that American attachés in London encouraged during the late 1930s stemmed from their interwar role as intelligence liaisons. Since 1889, the US Army's Military Intelligence Division (MID) had stationed attachés in select European capitals.[4] These officers' primary mission was observing foreign militaries' equipment, training, and organization. Beginning in 1938, however, Adolf Hitler's aggressive international posturing elevated the strategic importance of the attachés' mission. During subsequent international crises resulting in Germany's annexation of the Sudetenland, invasion of Czechoslovakia, and invasion of Poland, American interests gradually aligned with those of Great Britain and France. To accurately plan for military and diplomatic contingencies, American military leaders ordered their attaché in London to collect increasingly sensitive details about Allied war production and unit deployments.[5] In Great Britain, this task fell to three successive army attachés: Colonel (later Brigadier General) Raymond E. Lee, Lieutenant Colonel Bradford G. Chynoweth, and Brigadier General Sherman Miles. Aided by an average of six assistant attachés, these officers reported on all developments related to the British Army and Royal Air Force and provided evaluations of Great Britain's capabilities.[6]

Though American attachés stationed in Germany and Japan have received more attention from historians than those in Allied nations, attachés in London provided invaluable information about Allied military affairs to American planners.[7] Their use of personal contacts to obtain information and navigate the British military and government bureaucracy offers a useful case study of how attachés' acquired secret military information in a nation at war. It also serves as a corrective to traditional accounts of the formation of the Anglo-American alliance that focus on formal agreements or relations at the highest levels of government. Despite the close cultural links between Great Britain and the United States, America's neutrality and its reluctance to make binding commitments made the exchange of military information a politically charged issue for British and American leaders.[8] As a result, building the foundation for an effective military partnership demanded that liaison officers form bonds of trust and mutual respect that facilitated consistent cooperation on a daily basis. The challenges attachés faced provide an important reminder that the formation and sustainment of the special relationship between the United States and Great Britain required a great deal of skill among midlevel officers and diplomats executing directives from heads of state and chiefs of staff.[9]

In 1935, Raymond Eliot Lee was a forty-nine-year-old lieutenant colonel when he first arrived in London to take up the post of military attaché. Although Lee received a degree in civil engineering from the University of Missouri, commanded an artillery regiment in World War I, and attended both the General Staff College and the National War College, he had no previous experience as an intelligence officer.[10] Nevertheless, he was a talented professional soldier who excelled as an attaché because of his vast knowledge of both military and cultural matters. Lee proved adept at making sound strategic judgments and moved comfortably through the complex social networks of London. When German designs on Czechoslovakia became public in May 1938, Lee had already been in London for almost three years. He had established strong ties with numerous high-ranking officers in the British military, thanks in no small part to his efforts to assimilate into fashionable British society. In the critical months preceding the Munich Crisis in September, Lee's contacts helped him retain access to information that the United States deemed of increasing importance even as the British became more reluctant to supply him with it.

Anticipating the difficulties of maintaining avenues of exchange with the British in an environment of heightened security, Lee informed his superiors in Washington on April 28, 1938, of the new procedures he had instituted. While Germany's annexation of Austria offered further evidence of Hitler's warlike policies in Europe, Lee reported to MID that he had initiated the practice of acquiring sensitive information through personal interviews with representatives of the British War Office. Lee correctly predicted he could maintain a steady exchange through this method of gathering information, even if the War Office tightened security and limited the release of information. He explained how information currently available in military publications and reports shared with his office would inevitably be discontinued in the event of armed conflict. This new policy also suited the War Office because it limited their liability for giving unapproved documents to Lee and eliminated the onerous task of vetting information before releasing it. Lee explained how "it is planned ultimately to transmit this information only by means of official personal interviews, either volunteered by the War Office or in response to U.S.A. requests. The War Office is therefore glad that the custom of these interviews has become so well established."[11] Not only did Lee pursue this policy in his own dealings with the British, but he encouraged it among his subordinates as well. The previous month, he commended one of his assistant air attachés for obtaining information that "would be unavailable except for [his] close relations with the Air Ministry."[12] These policies bypassed traditional channels and increased the number of potential sources, thereby expediting the flow of information between the British and the military attaché. Throughout the crises of 1938, the policy effectively supplied Lee's office with valuable intelligence.[13] Its only shortcoming emerged when Lee's tour as military attaché ended.

The importance of Lee's personality in his role as a successful attaché became apparent when his nearly four-year tour ended, and Lieutenant Colonel Bradford Chynoweth replaced him in April 1939. Lee impressed his successor as "an ideal M.A." because he possessed a "diplomatic veneer and good diplomatic discretion."[14] Unfortunately, Chynoweth had a short temper and lacked the tact necessary for diplomatic dealings. When the head of MID, Colonel Edward R. W. McCabe, wrote to Chynoweth that the London attaché post was to become available, Chynoweth had reservations about assuming the assignment. He finally relented when McCabe misleadingly assured Chynoweth that social functions were only a small part of the job.[15] In addition, Chynoweth's wife "had always dreamed of living for awhile in England."[16] After Chynoweth received his briefings in Washington, Colonel Harold R. Bull, secretary of the General Staff, "said that he and [General George C.] Marshall thought this a huge mistake. It was! But off I went to London."[17] Nevertheless, Chynoweth sailed for his new station with an open mind and resolved to fulfill his duties to the letter.

Chynoweth was the son of an infantry major and spent his early years on military bases throughout the Midwest and Great Plains regions.[18] In 1912, he graduated from West Point and began his career in the army engineers. Four years later he led a detachment of engineers as part of General John J. Pershing's Punitive Expedition into Mexico. Despite pleas for overseas service, he spent the duration of World War I in the United States and decided to resign his commission in 1919. After failing in a private business venture, Chynoweth returned to the army as a major in the infantry.[19] Before being selected for the position of attaché in 1939, his assignments included attending the Command & General Staff School, commanding an infantry battalion in Texas, and instructing the New Jersey National Guard. Chynoweth enjoyed a reputation as an intelligent and opinionated officer, but his superiors gave him only a short briefing before he sailed for London.

Several days after arriving in London, Lee introduced Chynoweth to London society at a formal ball held at Claridge's Hotel, the preferred hotel of the European aristocracy. The party arranged by Lee was both a welcoming reception for Chynoweth and a send-off for his predecessor. Chynoweth recounted that Lee duly introduced him to the "Who's Who in British society," but "the great names went in one ear and out the other."[20] Try as he might, Chynoweth could not easily blend into the company of London's upper classes. With Lee's help and some additional orientation this obstacle might have been overcome, but Chynoweth did not have these luxuries. Despite Lee's best efforts to acquaint his successor with his various British contacts and the proper methods of obtaining information, Chynoweth failed to grasp the importance of an officer's personality, as well as his skills at maintaining relationships in intelligence gathering. Lee had spent three years in London building his credibility and strong connections. These attributes could not simply be transferred to Chynoweth. Moreover, the diplomatic atmosphere in Europe deteriorated further as Chynoweth began sending regular reports, limiting the availability of intelligence from formal channels.

In May 1939, one of Chynoweth's first reports revealed the difficulties he had obtaining information after German forces invaded Czechoslovakia on March 15. On May 5, Chynoweth sent a report to MID titled "Comments on Current Events," which described some of the problems he encountered just one month after his arrival. He flatly declared, "I have little or nothing to report that cannot be seen in the newspapers."[21] He went on to describe the ways in which "secrecy is being clamped down" by the British government and military leadership.[22] The situation continued unchanged for several weeks. On May 17, he wrote: "Once more, I have practically nothing to offer. . . . They're making a great secret of everything now, and I am not *in* the secret."[23] Chynoweth recounted how censorship was being imposed on the press, and the War Office also seemed to be operating under new guidelines for information sharing. Since the newly arrived Chynoweth was still limited to operating through his official liaison within the War Office, these rules severely restricted his access.[24] While the new regulations would have made an attaché's job difficult under any circumstances, Chynoweth in particular lacked the skills to circumvent these obstacles.

Chynoweth's unfamiliarity with British customs and procedures further hindered his efforts. On June 13, 1939, Chynoweth wrote an eleven-page report that, while rambling at times, gave several insights into his perceptions of the English and why he found them so difficult. The attaché organized his report under subject headings such as "A most peculiar country," "These crazy English," and perhaps most telling of all, "Perfidious Albion."[25] In one section titled "Oriental Minds," Chynoweth claimed that the English resembled the Oriental races in "their magnificent reserve; their secrecy; their colossal indirection; their simplicity; a deep sense of majesty and pomp; an infinite patience; and a worship of prestige and tradition."[26] Chynoweth's likening of the British to one of the most denigrated races in the world at that time was the result of his utter frustration with his hosts. British officers repeatedly denied his requests for information and frequently showed him outdated equipment and meaningless parades. The British attitude toward Chynoweth appeared even more striking because, in June 1939, the British Foreign Office was carefully courting the United States through the unprecedented visit of King George VI and Queen Elizabeth to America. Thus, even as President Franklin D. Roosevelt pledged to the British full American support in the event of war with Germany, the British War Office deliberately stymied the American attaché.[27] These experiences with the English grated on Chynoweth, an officer so straightforward he once rejected the army chief of staff's offer to be his personal aide because he did not see it as beneficial to his career.[28] British officers found this self-characterized "simple-minded American with a penchant for free speech" abrasive or impulsive and accordingly withheld information from him.[29]

Chynoweth's lengthy June 13 report also narrated an incident that unfolded as a result of the attaché's unfamiliarity with British protocols. During the last week of May, he observed units of the Territorial Army and received detailed information regarding their recruitment totals and unit strength.[30] Chynoweth wrote a thorough report containing this information and his impressions of the units as well as British policy, which he generally saw in a favorable light.[31] He then sent this report to MID and forwarded a copy to the War Office as a courtesy, despite Lee's explicit warnings against such unorthodox actions.[32] On June 13, Chynoweth wrote, "The War Office acknowledged my courtesy. The Director General of the Territorials even told my assistant that it was a very nice thing to do. Since then for two weeks I have been suppressed . . . under the silence of the whole British Empire. All of my contacts disappeared from view."[33] After two weeks, some of his contacts began acknowledging him once again, and Chynoweth likened the whole affair to startling a colony of prairie dogs.[34] The unfortunate attaché concluded he had broken the cardinal British rule by being indiscreet.

The British government's preoccupation with secrecy explains this reaction to Chynoweth's distribution of his report. Though Chynoweth sent the War Office his favorable assessment of the Territorials, British officers likely thought Chynoweth's actions showed his carelessness with sensitive information. Chynoweth's unexpected action just two months after his assumption of the attaché post convinced officers in the War Office that a tactful response had to be made to ensure the attaché did not make this mistake again. After two weeks, Chynoweth's contacts reemerged, and he never repeated his mistake. The incident revealed not only the importance of forming personal ties with officers to circumvent such actions by the War Office but also how vital this trust was when dealing with the British Army's bureaucracy, which was deeply concerned with protecting sensitive information in case war broke out.

Throughout Chynoweth's tenure as attaché, he consistently encountered War Office attempts to deny him information. While his superiors urged him to obtain statistics and observations regarding British weapons, manufacturing, and unit capabilities, British officials showed Chynoweth outdated equipment and deferred his inquiries for other information. On at least one occasion, Chynoweth loosened some of these restrictions and in the process revealed the difficulties he faced compared to the other attachés in London.

The British stymied Chynoweth's requests to observe their equipment and forces until the attaché happened upon a picture published in a British newspaper. The photo showed the German military attaché examining a British antiaircraft battery in the company of General John Vereker, Viscount Gort.[35] In a report to MID dated June 20, Chynoweth described his response: "I wrote the British G-2 [chief of intelligence] a letter, whereupon he invited me to a conference where I spread my views on the table. We had a satisfactory conference."[36] One week later, Chynoweth reported that his schedule was booked with visits to British commanders, military exercises, and an antiaircraft battery on the Norfolk coast.[37] Although Chynoweth suspected this turn of events might be the result of a general loosening in British policy toward American attachés, the immediate cause was his exposure of a stark contradiction in British conduct toward attachés. Chynoweth was exasperated that a German attaché should be granted access to British facilities in the first half of 1939, while the War Office denied him the same privilege. Even though Chynoweth had requested such visits for weeks, he was virtually ignored because British officers were not willing to go out of their way to assist him. There was no official British policy that restricted this information from the American military while simultaneously granting it to Germany's attaché. Consequently, it was painfully evident to Chynoweth that the British were not governed by official regulations in their dealings with him or the other attachés. He was forced to bring these contradictions to light before the British granted him any concessions.

While Chynoweth enjoyed brief periods of success because of relaxed British policies or improved relations with British officers, his sources were still at the mercy of the larger political atmosphere. In August, he wrote in a report to MID that the return of crisis had left him with no new information. He was unable to even verify or refute rumors that the British Army had dispatched personnel to France.[38] Predictably, Chynoweth complained about the official British method of releasing information to attachés, but the War Office only promised to review its procedures. Chynoweth's description of his daily routine demonstrated the necessity of bypassing official channels using personal connections. In one of his last reports to Washington on August 29, he wrote: "I report every evening to the War Office. The liaison officer solemnly and gravely fingers over his papers, and makes an impromptu release of smattering bits of sheer nonsense. Unless there is a change, you need not count on much information from this office."[39] In the high-stakes European situation, MID needed far more than "bits of sheer nonsense" to plan for possible contingencies. Adding to Chynoweth's troubles, he angered US ambassador Joseph P. Kennedy after Chynoweth suggested that Kennedy should share any military information he acquired with Chynoweth. Kennedy replied he would not share secret information with Chynoweth, whom Kennedy did not trust.[40] In the wake of these struggles, the War Department recalled Chynoweth after only five months of sporadic success in the position of attaché.

Chynoweth's failure as a military attaché was attributable to several causes. He arrived amid a period of successive European political crises, which meant the British were less willing to share information with a country unlikely to become involved in any potential war. More important, Chynoweth's blunt personality made it difficult for him to assimilate into the social circles of British officers and build a network of strong personal contacts. Nor could he count on the parochial Ambassador Kennedy for support. As Chynoweth's successors demonstrated, developing professional relationships with British officers was the most effective tool for overcoming difficulties in acquiring information and the primary determinant of success in the position of attaché. Just days after Britain declared war on Germany on September 3, 1939, the War Department relieved Chynoweth and appointed the more experienced Brigadier General Sherman Miles to take his place.

Miles was the scion of a prominent military family.[41] His father, a Union general in the Civil War, received the Medal of Honor for his actions at Chancellorsville and later served as the last commanding general of the US Army. Miles graduated from West Point in 1905 and commenced a variety of assignments that gave him extensive experience in military intelligence-gathering. From 1914 to 1916 he served as the military attaché to Russia, and after a tour as an observer on the western front Miles was assigned to the intelligence section of the General Staff in the War Department.[42] He then spent almost three years as the military attaché in Turkey and returned to Washington to spend four years in the war-plans division of the General Staff.[43] These experiences familiarized Miles with several European armies and prepared him for a successful tour as military attaché in London.

Decades later, Chynoweth recalled the initial exchange between himself and Miles in London. The latter allegedly told Chynoweth, "Don't try to brief me because I know this game from A to Z."[44] Given his extensive experience, it is understandable why Miles looked upon Chynoweth as a novice in the attaché game. Soon after Miles arrived in London, he rearranged the attaché office to his specifications. Several of these measures, which he detailed in his first report to MID on September 11, 1939, indicated the importance he attached to cultivating personal connections between his staff and the British War Office. Miles's first recommendation in the report was that "Lt. Col. B. G. Chynoweth should be relieved by cable and directed to return to the United States by the first available transportation."[45] Miles made clear that the main reason he requested Chynoweth's reassignment was that the latter had outlived his usefulness in London. The veteran attaché found that Chynoweth's continued presence in London as an assistant attaché was "no longer necessary and is, in some measure, an embarrassment to him and to the British officers with whom he has dealt."[46] Miles wanted British officers to become accustomed to dealing with him as their primary contact, and he anticipated that Chynoweth's continued presence in London might interfere with his progress in forming these new professional relationships.

Although he requested Chynoweth's removal, Miles reaffirmed the value of his other new subordinates precisely because of their strong relations with the British. Regarding his air attaché, Colonel Martin F. Scanlon, Miles wrote that Scanlon's long tenure in London "and the contacts he has made, make him most valuable."[47] Miles also recommended to MID that another assistant attaché not be sent to any of the neutral countries in Europe "because of the secrecy which the war involves and the necessity of maintaining the utmost confidence in him on the part of his British contacts."[48] This repeated mention of contacts, and the implication that these men were not replaceable because of their success at connecting with their British counterparts, showed Miles's focus on creating a wide network of relationships that he could draw upon for his duties.

Miles wasted no time introducing himself to the most important officers in the British Army. These first interviews were crucial to the British assessment of Miles and to determining what degree of cooperation he could expect from these officers. Miles did his best to appear professional, courteous, and respectful of British positions. After a meeting with General Edmund Ironside, who had replaced Viscount Gort as the chief of the Imperial General Staff (CIGS) on September 3, Miles described the current British view of the Americans and what he could do to encourage its perpetuation. On September 19, Miles wrote to his superiors, "General [William Edmund Ironside], the Chief of the Imperial General Staff, told me yesterday that we would be regarded as 'benevolent neutrals' and that more information would be given to us than to other neutrals."[49] This news encouraged Miles because it seemed like a reversal of the British policies toward the attaché office under Gort. Despite the increased security of wartime and the prevailing British opinion that American entry into the war was unnecessary, Ironside assured Miles that the American attaché could count on as much British cooperation as was practical. Miles realized this guarantee would set the tone for his interaction with officers throughout the British Army.[50]

Miles's initial favorable exchanges with Ironside boded well for his mission. Still, he took extra precautions to maintain favorable relations, including tailoring the types of information he sought. He believed that "the continuation and strengthening of this [British] attitude depends very largely on the confidence we can inspire and on the reduction of our 'nuisance value' to a minimum."[51] As a result, he recommended that MID should not seek sensitive information that might endanger this goodwill. He thought it would be unwise to solicit certain types of information, and that he should instead wait on the British to offer it. He listed these types of information as including British war plans, unit strength, order of battle, and the locations of certain units.[52] Miles anticipated that inquiries for this information might be regarded with hostility by the British and that some of it could be acquired through observation and conversations. In the meantime, Miles proposed to focus on lessons the British learned from combat pertaining to training, deployment, and tactics. Miles's approach indicated his preference for restraint. Although MID increasingly desired the kinds of information Miles was reluctant to request, at this point in the war it was more important to Miles to establish a precedent in good relations.

Miles's cultivation of strong rapports with British officers was also important because of the limitations American policies placed on him. During

the initial months of the conflict, the War Office maintained a general attitude of openness toward the United States. In late August, the two militaries even agreed to exchange their latest fighter planes for scientific testing.
Following the outbreak of war, however, the US State Department prohibited this exchange because it might compromise American neutrality.[53]
President Franklin D. Roosevelt felt he had to limit even secret cooperation
between the two powers out of fear that the dominant isolationist faction
of the American public would learn of the efforts. For Miles, this meant
he could offer the British little in return for the valuable information they
provided him.

Despite these constraints, British CIGS, General William Ironside, aided
Miles in skirting wartime security measures. On October 22, 1939, Miles
sent a report to MID describing the outcome of a meeting two days earlier
with General Ironside. Ironside had arranged for Miles to visit one of the
largest British regional command headquarters. Ironside also gave his permission for Miles's assistant attaché to "resume his visits to arsenals and
munitions factories, which have been interrupted since the war started."[54]
Perhaps most important, Ironside gave his permission for Miles to visit the
British Expeditionary Force (BEF) in France and wrote him a personal letter of introduction to the BEF commander. Miles summed up the meeting
by writing that Ironside "was prepared to let us Americans see what we
wanted, even possibly one of their ports of embarkation."[55] Unlike Chynoweth, Miles's schedule had been full with visits to British headquarters
and military bases even prior to Ironside's intervention, but this meeting
illustrated that Ironside was prepared to give Miles aid even in contradiction to some of the newly instituted wartime policies of the British military.
The fact that Ironside offered his valuable time to the American attaché two
months into a conflict in which the British were still hurriedly mobilizing
and shipping men and equipment to France speaks volumes about the high
regard in which he held Miles. The tone of Miles's report revealed some of
the surprise the attaché experienced when informed of Ironside's generous
offers. Moreover, because not every aspect of the Anglo-American military
relationship progressed as smoothly, this exchange between the two men
stood out as exceptional.

Miles's success at gaining opportunities to observe British forces and facilities compensated for the difficulties he faced in arranging the types of

exchange sought by the US War Department and the British War Office. Before the outbreak of a second global conflict, the War Department requested that its attaché attempt to set up a regularly scheduled exchange of information pertaining to the aircraft assigned to frontline units and the structure of the British command.[56] Miles raised the topic with the Air Ministry in October, but he received a reply stating, "Unfortunately at the present moment it is not possible to employ the exchange of information which you suggest."[57] Given his earlier reports, Miles likely foresaw the response his request would generate and made it only as a formality to please his superiors. Nevertheless, this rejection displayed the difficulty of establishing regularly scheduled, systematic transfers of information.[58] Because of changing censorship guidelines, the Air Ministry could not always release the information MID requested, nor did they always have the manpower to allocate to such a task. Even when exchanges could be arranged, they often left both parties disappointed.

By February 1940, the War Department and Air Ministry agreed to a system of bartering information regarding airplane production and aircraft specifications. Just as Miles feared, however, the arrangement left both sides unhappy. In an interagency telegram, the War Department relayed Miles's comments on the agreement. He wrote that the Air Ministry frequently neglected to answer his letters and, in the exchange of material, that the British knowingly withheld information already "known to the Germans or available thru [sic] commercial firms."[59] In response, Miles advocated sharing intelligence on the "basis of mutual confidence."[60] Individuals or offices would give information to the attaché when it became available, and the attaché returned the favor. This more personal method promised a greater success rate for Miles. It avoided potentially awkward situations in which he requested information that the British could not supply or where he was forced to deny their requests. At this point in the war both the British and the Americans possessed information and technologies they refused to share. While the British restricted information pertaining to their unit deployments and weapons, the American military unequivocally declined to give details on its advanced Norden bombsight and other experimental technologies.[61] These limitations on Miles made his job more difficult but also encouraged him to seek information through informal channels.

Sherman Miles owed his success as an attaché to a variety of factors, but his emphasis on building professional relationships with key British commanders was perhaps his most vital intelligence-gathering tool. In an atmosphere of heightened British censorship and little official US aid, which made it difficult for him to acquire useful military intelligence, Miles was able to secure significant material on aircraft production, training facilities, and the BEF's deployment to France. Miles also understood the chaotic atmosphere in the War Office and did not press British officers for information he knew they would not release. In just nine months as the military attaché in London, Miles established numerous contacts that gave him the flexibility and resources he needed to acquire vital information despite the unhelpful policies of both the British and American leaderships. In early June 1940, the War Department ordered Miles back to Washington, where he assumed command of the army's intelligence division as the assistant chief of staff, or G-2. At the same time, the War Department took the unusual step of sending Brigadier General Raymond Lee back to London. Less than four days after Lee landed in London to reassume the post of military attaché, France signed an armistice with Germany, on June 22. The British military had just completed a miraculous evacuation of its forces from Dunkirk and Brest, but in the process had lost thousands of men killed or captured and nearly all the army's heavy equipment. The atmosphere in England was somber and anxious. Lee summed up British foreboding when he wrote to his wife, "it will not be long before Hitler has a go at this country."[62]

In many ways, the London that greeted Lee in June 1940 was far removed from the city he had left just over a year ago. Upon his arrival, he wrote in his journal that the "streets, shops, [and] houses are very largely deserted. London seemed dark as a pocket, with various familiar streets barricaded and barbwired."[63] While the city and the prevailing mood had undergone a great change, Lee found many old friends throughout the vast bureaucracy managing the war effort. The War Department chose to send Lee back to London because the Anglo-American relationship was becoming increasingly important, and the army needed a diplomatic officer who could interact with a complex wartime bureaucracy with no training or orientation. The British preoccupation with secrecy meant that information would be difficult to obtain, and the US military desperately needed quality reports. Nor could MID ignore the political implications of its attaché's assessments. Since US ambassador Joseph Kennedy acquired a growing reputation as a defeatist, American military and civilian leaders needed unbiased reports on Britain's strength. MID also needed an officer with extensive knowledge of the British military who could discern fact from rumor. Lee fit all these criteria, and he was familiar to the British. Many of the contacts Lee made during his first tour in London now held key posts in the British military, and they remembered him as a competent intelligence officer. Lee's ability to renew these friendships, and his overall reputation, were indispensable over the next year.

Lee's second tour in London was the most pivotal eighteen months in establishing a precedent in Anglo-American cooperation from both a diplomatic and military standpoint. The intelligence he collected in the months after France's surrender was one of the decisive tools President Roosevelt used to determine policy toward Great Britain.[64] Unsure if Britain would survive after the fall of France, policy-makers and military leaders in Washington relied heavily on Lee's assessments of the military situation. The confidence Miles and Lee had in Britain's survival encouraged Roosevelt to risk sending valuable weapons to Britain at a time when the US Army was in desperate need of that same material. Roosevelt decided to send large quantities of planes, weapons, and ammunition to Britain over the objections of senior US Army leaders who wanted to enlarge America's own forces. Sending weapons to Britain was a major security risk to the United States as long as a German invasion was possible. If Germany had conquered Britain and captured the modern American-made weapons, these same weapons could have been used against US forces.[65]

The increased importance of Lee's work meant that he contended with a host of new difficulties. Civilian officials in Washington and London constantly meddled in the business of military intelligence, and it was Lee's job to minimize the adverse impact of their decisions on the exchange of information. He depended on his good relations with key British officers and knowledge of the British military establishment. The growing number of Americans in London, including special military and political observers, also meant more opportunities for missteps that constantly threatened to derail Lee's work. Lee simultaneously contended with increased censorship in Britain and a persistent underappreciation for keeping information classified among his American colleagues in the War Department.

British military and civilian leaders rightfully doubted American security procedures for classified information prior to American entry into the war. In March 1940, British undersecretary for foreign affairs Sir Alexander Cadogan wrote to colleagues in the Treasury, the Ministry of Economic Warfare, and the Board of Trade that the Foreign Office regularly intercepted communications sent from the American embassy in London to Washington. Cadogan told his colleagues to warn members of their departments, since "what they say in confidence to members of the United States Embassy may easily get around rather quickly, even if through no indiscretion on the part of their American interlocutors, to our enemies."[66] Lee and other Americans in London observed this attitude and thought British fears were at least somewhat justified. Lee told US Navy rear admiral Robert L. Ghormley that it seemed "as if the British were afraid that anything that fell into our hands would go astray." Ghormley replied that he understood the British attitude, because his time in the Plans Department of the Navy in Washington had shown him "it was practically impossible to keep anything secret there."[67] The British also had several instances of information leaks to substantiate their fears.

The previously described incident involving the September 15, 1940, article in *PM* was perhaps the most harmful of these security breaches. The manager of *PM*, Ralph Ingersoll, damaged the Anglo-American relationship and made British authorities more reluctant to share information.[68] By describing the precise locations of the bomb damage in London, *PM* potentially gave the German Luftwaffe valuable intelligence on the effectiveness of its bombing campaign. Soon after Britain had declared war, the government instituted strict censorship and public-awareness campaigns to keep the information out of view, but no such restraints existed on American publishers. Although *PM*'s source for the article had been in Washington, Lee's office likely transmitted the information that later found its way into print. As a result, many in the British government called for limits on the classified information given to the attaché, and some officials let their own interagency struggles hinder Lee's work.[69] These personal conflicts explained how Lee's access to confidential memoranda on the production and quality of British airplanes and pilots was revoked in response to the article in *PM*.

When Lee stopped receiving Air Ministry memoranda in October 1940, he attributed the problem to an intense personal conflict between Lord Beaverbrook, William Aitken, and the Air Ministry.[70] Lord Beaverbrook was a political appointee of Winston Churchill and was serving as the minister of aircraft production when he learned that Lee was receiving reports from the Air Ministry that he himself had not seen. His protests prompted the change in the Air Ministry's policy toward Lee, but this was only his first attempt to stifle Lee's access. In December, Beaverbrook withheld information from Lee regarding captured German equipment. On one occasion, Lee alleged that Beaverbrook literally waved the papers in front of the attaché before putting them away again.[71] Fortunately for Lee, even Beaverbrook's secretary did not like his boss, whom Lee described as "one of the most shifty and evasive people in England."[72] In a friendly conversation as Lee left Beaverbrook's office, the secretary eagerly provided Lee with as much information as he could.

To circumvent the restrictions Beaverbrook imposed on him, Lee approached high-ranking friends in the British military to plead his case. Lee scheduled personal meetings with CIGS General Sir John Dill and General Hastings "Pug" Ismay, military liaison and personal confidante of Prime Minister Winston Churchill. Lee also sent a message to the Earl of Halifax, Edward Wood, the foreign secretary.[73] The next day Lord Beaverbrook telephoned Lee's office "to say he was very anxious that we should have any information which we wanted."[74] Lee speculated that Halifax told Beaverbrook "that he must be very forthcoming."[75] The outcome demonstrated that Lee had correctly judged the dynamics among the British departments.

Lee spent countless hours getting to know these high-ranking officers and officials as he dined in their apartments and shared cigars into the small hours.[76] Brigadier General Sir John Kennedy, the director of military operations, thought Lee was "a very charming and intelligent man and a good friend of ours, and he was inclined to take an optimistic and philosophical view" of British prospects.[77] Lee's friendships with British leaders encouraged them to assist Lee in obtaining information crucial to American policy-making. Lee also had leverage since British leaders were urgently requesting more weapons, aircraft, and loans from the United States. After President Roosevelt's reelection to an unprecedented third term in November 1940, he approved additional aid and arms shipments to Britain. When Lee heard a rumor the following month about an Air Ministry official who wanted to decrease the information being shared, Lee asked that he be reminded of the 3.5 billion dollar loan the United States had given Britain.[78]

In addition to the complex personal networks Lee navigated in late 1940, he also assisted the growing number of American military and civilian observers such as retired Colonel William J. Donovan. Donovan was a New York lawyer and decorated World War I veteran who had developed a personal friendship with President Roosevelt over their mutual opposition to European dictatorships. As the German bombing campaign against Britain escalated, President Roosevelt arranged to send Donovan to London as a special observer to confer with British leaders and deliver personal reports to Roosevelt on the situation in Britain. During two visits to England in July and December 1940, Donovan toured the bombed portions of London and met with prominent British military and government leaders, including Churchill. Churchill and British military leaders understood that Donovan and succeeding envoys had the ear of the president and consequently went out of their way to supply the Americans with information.[79] British leaders also appreciated the opportunity to securely get information to Roosevelt without going through the American military bureaucracy or Ambassador Kennedy. Kennedy incensed many British leaders after allegedly telling a reporter that "democracy is finished in Britain," and he resigned as ambassador in October 1940.[80]

Lee welcomed these observers and gave generously of his time and resources to assist them in their mission. Rather than viewing them as a nuisance, Lee saw these compatriots as a way to get accurate information back to the United States quickly and have it reach key policymakers.[81] As Lee realized, American leaders could not always read his detailed reports that often took more than two weeks to reach the United States via diplomatic pouch. Lee's assistance paid off when Donovan's positive assessment of British chances helped convince Roosevelt to extend more aid to Great Britain after the fall of France over Ambassador Kennedy and senior military leaders' objections. In June 1940, large numbers of observers from the US Army and US Navy also began visiting London on various intelligence and liaison assignments.[82]

Although Lee readily aided these temporary observers, their presence complicated his mission and threatened to make him irrelevant for weeks at a time. The British had been reducing Lee's access to written reports for some time, leaving interviews as the primary method of exchange.[83] The observers usually managed to get audiences with the most important individuals in the British military and government because they provided a personal link to the president. The British director of naval intelligence wrote to Admiral Sir Andrew Cunningham, "There is no doubt we can achieve infinitely more through Donovan than through any other individual."[84] Consequently, Donovan and other observers often received more current assessments than Lee, and therefore the attaché had to gain their confidence as well. Otherwise he faced a situation similar to one in February 1941 when MID asked him for intelligence that the British had supplied to Roosevelt's special envoys but not their office.[85] Just as Lee valued his personal relationships for getting accurate information, Roosevelt habitually bypassed formal bureaucratic channels in favor of personal connections at the highest level of government. His personal emissaries, however, lacked training and were unaccustomed to the censorship restrictions in Britain. British officials kept a close watch on these and other American observers and did not hesitate to point out their security indiscretions.[86] While highlighting the parallel importance of personal relationships at the highest levels of government, these observers also created the conditions for one of Lee's most serious obstacles as an attaché.[87]

In January 1941, Churchill limited the information the military freely traded with American attachés. General Ismay told Lee that Churchill "is completely rampant on the question of secrecy, and is cutting down the number of people in the British government who know anything about what is going on."[88] Churchill adopted this approach because the American observers now gave him a secure means of communication with Roosevelt, and Churchill wanted to eliminate intelligence leaks on both sides of the Atlantic. Thus, even as Churchill publicly and privately courted Roosevelt, he hindered the military attaché's efforts to promote greater openness.[89] Lee had little hope of changing the prime minister's attitude, so he depended on two of his most important contacts in the British military to retain access to strategically important intelligence. Lee often approached the new director of British military intelligence, General Francis Davidson, whom he referred to as a Scotsman of a "practical and *mediate* turn of mind."[90] After an initial private dinner during which they expressed their respective positions, Davidson agreed to look over Lee's reports and correct any inaccuracies in a way that the information could not be traced back to Davidson.[91] Lee also relied on his old friend General Ismay, who did his best to give Lee updates on the "general survey of the situation" without betraying the confidence of his superior.[92] Through these officers, Lee obtained the information he needed, including British losses and production figures, in spite of the heavy-handed political restrictions on this exchange.

Although American military cooperation with Great Britain accelerated in early 1941 with the passage of the Lend-Lease Act, extended US Navy patrols in the Atlantic, and the first Anglo-American staff talks beginning in January, Lee's acquisition of intelligence remained challenging. Officers in both armies were often unsure of restrictions and procedures for official exchanges. On June 21, Lee wrote that he had been "trying to run down some basis for the commonly accepted belief that the United States and Great Britain are on a complete exchange basis for secret and semisecret information."[93] This belief puzzled Lee, who recalled how he still struggled to get any information related to "development or operational statistics."[94] The rumor highlighted the confusion that resulted from closer ties and the different procedures followed by the myriad of departments in both governments.

Even though Churchill had determined that US entry into the war was essential by the summer of 1941, he favored a tough bargaining approach.[95] Churchill demanded that everything going to the United States from the War Office be approved by him to ensure that British military secrets were shared only in return for tangible concessions from the United States.[96] When Lee learned of this policy on July 1, 1941, he wrote in his diary: "I could get around that [policy] all right by writing up my own paper and then asking them at the War Office if they would care to discuss it. Winston Churchill doesn't have to see my estimate of the situation, and it would all come to the same thing."[97] This tactic enabled Lee to continue sending useful reports to MID, and his contacts in the War Office played an important role in aiding him, even though the spirit of their orders indicated they should not. The restrictions Lee faced even in mid-1941 also showed how more American aid to Great Britain did not make the attaché's job easier. Lee's reports were more important than ever, but the information was harder to obtain.

Still, Lee enjoyed unparalleled success as the US attaché in Great Britain. In a complex atmosphere fraught with potential political missteps, he obtained vital intelligence and helped orchestrate the increased American military presence in Britain before the United States entered the war. Key to his success was his ability to form and sustain close relationships with British officers and officials. Personal ties, astute political acumen, and recognition of his limitations all contributed to his success. His skill was such that he circumvented mandates from the prime minister himself. As a small part of the American political effort, Lee's attainments gave Roosevelt more flexibility in his policy toward Great Britain. Lee kept the US Army well-informed on Great Britain's shifting fortunes in World War II. Despite outside forces that conspired against him, Lee built relationships that his colleagues remembered years later. In 1968, General Sir Fredrick Beaumont Nesbitt, the chief of British military intelligence from 1940 to 1941, wrote: "Raymond was not only a dear friend but a trusted professional soldier as well. I knew that what I told him would never be compromised, thus we could talk with absolute candor."[98] It was relationships such at these that made Lee a successful attaché and facilitated consistent Anglo-American cooperation. After laying solid groundwork for intelligence cooperation, Lee completed his final tour as attaché and departed from London less than one week before the Japanese attacked Pearl Harbor. Like Miles, Lee too went on to lead MID during World War II, demonstrating the importance accorded both officers' experience as attachés in Britain.

Although Lee was the ideal choice for the attaché position during this crucial time, all three American attachés came to the same conclusion about Britain's chances for survival in the war. Despite Chynoweth's difficulties with the British, he respected them and firmly believed that "British morale can be looked upon as superior" to that of the other belligerents.[99] Miles similarly concluded that the "strength and spirit" of British forces meant that any German "invasion almost certainly can be repelled."[100] And Lee firmly believed the British would prevail, and the United States should enter the war as their ally.[101] These opinions put the attachés at odds with prevailing opinions in American political and military circles throughout their tenures.

Chynoweth's correct predictions about a looming war prior to September 1939 struck many as unnecessarily alarmist.[102] Once war broke out, large numbers of US Army officers and government officials regarded Lee and Miles's seemingly pro-British and prointerventionist reports with skepticism. The attachés' fellow officers supposed Lee and Miles had become too enamored of their hosts and lost their objectivity. The attachés' prognostications nonetheless proved correct and helped persuade some of their country-men to support aid to Britain. Though the attachés enjoyed different degrees of success, and none obtained all the information they sought, their efforts contributed to the formation of an effective wartime intelligence relation-ship.[103] American military attachés played a central role in gathering infor-mation, advising on government policies, and assisting American observers.

Within the larger context of Anglo-American relations during World War II, the military attachés are a telling reminder that the alliance between the two nations rested on hundreds of interpersonal connections. Moreover, these contacts did not always work toward a single goal. British and Ameri-can political officials and military officers often showed a casual disregard toward the consequences their actions had on the greater Anglo-American relationship. This prevailing attitude highlighted their parochialism and intensely personal conceptions of international relations. Roosevelt and Churchill encouraged this practice, and the resulting difficulties meant that their subordinates had to be skilled at building international relationships. The attachés embodied this reality, and their success depended heavily on their ability to earn the trust and respect of their British hosts.

NOTES

1 "Censors Hide Heavy Damage to Vital London Areas," *PM*, September 15, 1940, Foreign News section.

2 Raymond E. Lee, "1st Ind.," November 27, 1940, 2017–1270/40, 2, Box 649, Military Intelligence Division Correspondence, 1917–41, Records of the War Department General and Special Staffs, 1860–1952, Record Group (RG) 165, National Archives and Records Administration, College Park, MD (hereafter referred to as NARA).

3 James Leutze, ed., *The London Journal of General Raymond E. Lee, 1940–1941* (Boston, MA: Little, Brown, 1971), 98.

4 Bruce W. Bidwell, *History of the Military Intelligence Division, Department of the Army General Staff: 1775–1941* (Frederick, MD: University Publications of America, 1986), 54.

5 War Department planners also relied heavily on attachés' assessments when deciding on their contingency plans, because the State Department did not inform the military of foreign policy decisions. Mark A. Stoler, *Allies and Adversaries: The Joint Chiefs of Staff, The Grand Alliance, and U.S. Strategy in World War II* (Chapel Hill: University of North Carolina Press, 2000), 3.

6 These three officers served as the US Army's official liaisons to Great Britain during their assignments. While the Office of Naval Intelligence also stationed naval attachés in Great Britain, the two offices remained largely ignorant of each other's work because they answered to different agencies and usually sought different information. This also reflected the larger lack of cooperation between the US Army and Navy and the divided American defense organization. Leutze, *London Journal*, 110.

7 For examples of scholarship focused on the role of attachés, see Thomas G. Mahnken, *Uncovering Ways of War: U.S. Intelligence and Foreign Military Innovation, 1918–1941* (Ithaca, NY: Cornell University Press, 2002); Henry G. Cole, *Exposing the Third Reich: Colonel Truman Smith in Hitler's Germany* (Lexington: University Press of Kentucky, 2013); Scott Alan Koch, "Watching the Rhine: U.S. Army Military Attaché Reports and the Resurgence of the German Army, 1933–1941" (PhD diss., Duke University, 1990).

8 To avoid making any binding commitments, no American civilian leaders or top military leaders took part in the first staff talks between the United States and Great Britain that began in January 1941; Mark Skinner Watson, *Chief of Staff: Prewar Plans and Preparations* (Washington, DC: Center of Military History, United States Army, 1950), 369.

9 The idea of a special relationship existing between Great Britain and the United States is helpful in denoting the exceptionally close military cooperation between the nations during World War II, but many excellent studies have shown the two nations did not act in complete harmony or against their own national interests. Some classic studies that refute the idea of the nations' selfless collaboration are James R. Leutze, *Bargaining for Supremacy: Anglo-American Naval Collaboration, 1937–1941* (Chapel Hill: University of North Carolina Press, 1977); David Reynolds, *The Creation of The Anglo-American Alliance, 1937–1941* (London: Europa, 1981); Mark A. Stoler, *Allies and Adversaries: The Joint Chiefs of Staff, the Grand Alliance, and U.S. Strategy in World War II* (Chapel Hill: University of North Carolina Press, 2000).

10 Leutze, *London Journal*, xiii.

11 Raymond E. Lee, "Army Information and War Office Control," April 28, 1938, 9771–249/162, 2, Box 2193, Military Intelligence Division Correspondence, 1917–41, Records of the War Department General and Special Staffs, 1860–1952, RG 165, NARA.

12 Raymond E. Lee, "Exchange of Aviation Information," March 10, 1938, 9771–249/161, 1, Box 2193, Military Intelligence Division Correspondence, 1917–41, Records of the War Department General and Special Staffs, 1860–1952, RG 165, NARA.

13 There was certain information that Lee was unable to obtain from the War Office such as aircraft production figures, but the failure of subsequent at-

tachés to acquire the same information suggests that Lee's record was difficult to improve upon.

14 Bradford G. Chynoweth, *Bellamy Park* (Hicksville, NY: Exposition, 1975), 155.

15 Theodore Wilson, "'Through the Looking Glass': Bradford G. Chynoweth as United States Military Attaché in Britain, 1939," in *The U.S. Army and World War II: Selected Papers from the Army's Commemorative Conferences*, ed. Judith Bellafaire (Washington, DC: Center of Military History, United States Army, 1998), 50.

16 Chynoweth, *Bellamy Park*, 150.

17 Bradford G. Chynoweth, "Army Recollections," 38, Bradford Grethen Chynoweth Papers, US Army Heritage and Education Center, Carlisle, PA (hereafter referred to as USAHEC).

18 Chynoweth, *Bellamy Park*, 11.

19 Chynoweth, 90.

20 Chynoweth, 154.

21 Bradford G. Chynoweth, "The General Situation," May 5, 1939, 2060–1130/71, 1, Box 794, Military Intelligence Division Correspondence, 1917–41, Records of the War Department General and Special Staffs, 1860–1952, RG 165, NARA.

22 Chynoweth, "The General Situation," May 5, 1939.

23 Bradford G. Chynoweth, "The General Situation," May 17, 1939, 2060–1130/73, 1, Box 794, Military Intelligence Division Correspondence, 1917–41, Records of the War Department General and Special Staffs, 1860–1952, RG165, NARA.

24 Chynoweth, *Bellamy Park*, 158.

25 Bradford G. Chynoweth, "Great Britain—Comments on Current Events," June 13, 1939, 2060–1130/80, 2, Box 795, Military Intelligence Division Correspondence, 1917–41, Records of the War Department General and Special Staffs, 1860–1952, RG 165, NARA.

26 Chynoweth, "Great Britain," June 13, 1939, 7.

27 Peter Bell, "The Foreign Office and the 1939 Royal Visit to America: Courting the USA in an Era of Isolationism," *Journal of Contemporary History* 37, no. 4 (2002): 615.

28 Chynoweth, *Bellamy Park*, 64.

29 Chynoweth, "Great Britain," June 13, 1939, 3.

30 The Territorial Army was the British equivalent of the United States National Guard.

31 Chynoweth, "Great Britain—Comments on Current Events," May 27, 1939, 2060–1130/76, 2, Box 795, Military Intelligence Division Correspondence, 1917–41, Records of the War Department General and Special Staffs, 1860–1952, RG 165, NARA.

32 Chynoweth, "Great Britain," June 13, 1939, 3.

33 Chynoweth, "Great Britain," June 13, 1939, 33.

34 Chynoweth, "Great Britain," June 13, 1939, 33.

35 Viscount Gort, VC, later became chief of the Imperial General Staff and, upon the outbreak of World War II, was chosen to command the British Expeditionary Force in France.

36 Bradford G. Chynoweth, "Great Britain—Comments on Current Events," July 20, 1939, 2060–1130/93, 6, Box 795, Military Intelligence Division Correspondence, 1917–41, Records of the War Department General and Special Staffs, 1860–1952, RG 165, NARA.

37 Bradford G. Chynoweth, "Great Britain—Comments on Current Events," July 27, 1939, 2060–1130/94, 4, Box 795, Military Intelligence Division Correspondence, 1917–41, Records of the War Department General and Special Staffs, 1860–1952, RG 165, NARA.

38 Bradford G. Chynoweth, "Great Britain—Comments on Current Events," August 29, 1939, 2060–1130/98, 1, Box 795, Military Intelligence Division Correspondence, 1917–41, Records of the War Department General and Special Staffs, 1860–1952, Record Group 165, NARA.

39 Bradford G. Chynoweth, "Great Britain—Comments on Current Events," September 5, 1939, 2060–1130/100, 4, Box 795, Military Intelligence Division Correspondence, 1917–41, Records of the War Department General and Special Staffs, 1860–1952, RG 165, NARA.

40 Bradford G. Chynoweth, "Letter to E. R. W. McCabe," May 9, 1939, Bradford Grethen Chynoweth Papers, USAHEC.

41 Miles retired as a major general in 1946.

42 "General Miles, Intelligence Aide: Held Key Staff Job on Pearl Harbor Day—Dies at 83," *New York Times*, October 8, 1966, 26.

43 "General Miles Dies at 83," 26.

44 Chynoweth, *Bellamy Park*, 166.

45 Sherman Miles, "Office Organization," September 11, 1939, 2610-A-140/11, 1, Box 1532, Military Intelligence Division Correspondence, 1917–41, Records of the War Department General and Special Staffs, 1860–1952, RG 165, NARA.

46 Miles, "Office Organization," 1.

47 Miles, "Office Organization," 2.

48 Miles, "Office Organization," 4.

49 Sherman Miles, "Policy Regarding Information," September 19, 1939, 2610-A-152/1, 1, Box 1532; Military Intelligence Division Correspondence, 1917–41, Records of the War Department General and Special Staffs, 1860–1952, RG 165, NARA.

50 The British Army and Royal Navy each had a large measure of autonomy in determining what to share with their American counterparts. David

Zimmerman, *Top Secret Exchange: The Tizard Mission and the Scientific War* (Montreal, Canada: McGill-Queen's University Press, 1996), 31.

51 Miles, "Policy Regarding Information," 1.

52 Miles, "Policy," 2.

53 George Pirie, untitled, September 23, 1939, 2574–1463/4, 1, Box 1517, Military Intelligence Division Correspondence, 1917–41, Records of the War Department General and Special Staffs, 1860–1952, RG 165, NARA.

54 Sherman Miles, "British Attitude Towards This Office," October 22, 1939, 9771–249/171, 1, Box 2139, Military Intelligence Division Correspondence, 1917–41, Records of the War Department General and Special Staffs, 1860–1952, RG 165, NARA.

55 Miles, "British Attitude."

56 J. A. Crane, "Exchange of Aviation Information," July 12, 1939, 9771–249/168, 1, Box 2139, Military Intelligence Division Correspondence, 1917–41, Records of the War Department General and Special Staffs, 1860–1952, RG 165, NARA.

57 Sherman Miles, "1st Ind.," July 12, 1939, 9771–249/168, 2, Box 2139, Military Intelligence Division Correspondence, 1917–41, Records of the War Department General and Special Staffs, 1860–1952, RG 165, NARA.

58 In another example of this difficulty, the US Navy and British Royal Navy agreed to a quid pro quo exchange of technical information in May 1938. The arrangement soon broke down, however, when the British grew disappointed at the information obtained. Zimmerman, *Top Secret*, 32.

59 "Cr.ref.for 9771–249," February 26, 1940, 9771–249/2w, 1, Box 2193, Military Intelligence Division Correspondence, 1917–41, Records of the War Department General and Special Staffs, 1860–1952, RG 165, NARA.

60 "Cr.ref.for 9771–249."

61 The British desperately tried to acquire the bombsight. They allegedly even asked women to charm American officers for information: Sherman Miles, "unknown," February 12, 1940, 2060–1130/155, 2, Box 795, Military Intelligence Division Correspondence, 1917–41, Records of the War Department General and Special Staffs, 1860–1952, RG 165, NARA.

62 Leutze, *London Journal*, 6.

63 Raymond E. Lee, "More Than Victory: A Story of the British People, London Journal of Raymond Eliot Lee 1940–1941," June 21, 1940, Raymond E. Lee Papers, 1940–1941, USAHEC.

64 Lee's efforts to promote increased US aid to Great Britain also faced strong resistance from army and navy strategists. Stoler, *Allies and Adversaries*, 28.

65 William T. Johnsen, *The Origins of the Grand Alliance: Anglo-American Military Collaboration from the Panay Incident to Pearl Harbor* (Lexington: University Press of Kentucky, 2016), 127.

66 Alexander Cadogan to F. Leith Ross, March 18, 1940, A.1945/G, FO 371, National Archives, Kew, UK.

67 Leutze, *London Journal*, 202.

68 One of the paper's first editorials stated that *PM* was committed to supporting the war against Hitler. The paper was also unconditionally against United States entry into the conflict. Paul Milkman, *PM: A New Deal in Journalism, 1940–1948* (New Brunswick, NJ: Rutgers University Press, 1997), 61.

69 This punitive action against Lee and the US War Department seemed misplaced given the security precautions Lee followed in London and MID's request that the FBI investigate the information leak. Sherman Miles, untitled, December 11, 1940, 2017–1270/44b, 1, Box 649, Military Intelligence Division Correspondence, 1917–41, Records of the War Department General and Special Staffs, 1860–1952, RG 165, NARA.

70 Lee, "Victory," October 19, 1940.

71 Lee, "Victory," December 4, 1940.

72 Lee, "Victory," December 4, 1940.

73 Lee, "Victory," December 6, 1940.

74 Lee, "Victory," December 6, 1940.

75 Lee, "Victory," December 6, 1940.

76 Lee recorded numerous instances of frank, private conversations with key British officers in his diary. Lee lunched with General Sir John Dill on December 5, 1940. Leutze, *London Journal*, 160, 140.

77 *The Business of War: The War Narrative of Major-General Sir John Kennedy*, ed. Bernard Fergusson (London: Hutchinson, 1957), 65.

78 Lee, "Victory," December 4, 1940.

79 Harry Hopkins, another confidant of the president, visited London in January 1941 to report on the British situation for Roosevelt. Frank Costigliola, *Roosevelt's Lost Alliances: How Personal Politics Helped Start the Cold War* (Princeton, NJ: Princeton University Press, 2012), 101.

80 Associated Press, "Kennedy Quoted as Saying British 'Democracy Is Through,'" *Washington Post*, November 10, 1940.

81 Leutze, *London Journal*, 84.

82 John Victor Perowne, untitled, August 22, 1940, A1945G, FO 371, National Archives, Kew, UK.

83 Lee, "Victory," November 25, 1940.

84 Corey Ford, *Donovan of OSS* (New York: Little, Brown, 1970), 99.

85 A. H. Harris, "Memorandum to the Liaison Officer, State Department," February 15, 1941, 2083–1695/3, 2, Box 871, Military Intelligence Division Correspondence, 1917–41, Records of the War Department General and Special Staffs, 1860–1952, RG 165, NARA.

86 Leutze, *London Journal*, 138.

87 For the importance of personalities and relationships among the Allies during World War II, see Costigliola, *Lost Alliances*, 97.

88 Leutze, *London Journal*, 213.

89 Costigliola, *Lost Alliances*, 101.

90 Lee, "Victory," January 6, 1941.

91 Lee, "Victory," May 9, 1941.

92 Lee, "Victory," May 21, 1941. The British were still reluctant to give their full order of battle and unit strengths in active theaters such as the Middle East to MID. Lee was not surprised and assumed they would show the figures to a select few American officers through their mission to Washington.

93 Lee, "Victory," June 21, 1941.

94 Lee, "Victory," June 21, 1941.

95 Reynolds, *The Creation of the Anglo-American Alliance*, 117.

96 Leutze, *London Journal*, 324.

97 Leutze, *London Journal*, 324.

98 Leutze, *London Journal*, xiv.

99 Chynoweth, "Great Britain," August 29, 1939, 1.

100 Sherman Miles, "Estimate of the Situation in All Theaters of Operation, December, 1940. Confidential Lecture to Officers and 1st Class, USMA, 4 December 1940," 5, Sherman Miles Papers, The United States Military Academy Library, West Point, NY.

101 Fergusson, *Business*, 149.

102 Wilson, "Looking Glass," 63.

103 Thomas Mahnken documents the failures of American attachés in Britain to obtain information about certain technologies like radar. Mahknen, *Uncovering*, 161.

4

Military Attaché, Accidental Agent
Colonel Bonner Fellers's Defense-Engagement Mission in Cairo, 1940–1942

C. J. Jenner

The light provided by our knowledge of technological capabilities and our capacity for sophisticated strategic analysis is so dazzling as to be almost hypnotic; but it is in those shadowy regions of human understanding based on our knowledge of social development, cultural diversity, and patterns of behaviour that we have to look for the answers.
—Michael Howard and Clive Rose, "The Future of Deterrence," 1986

Bonner Frank Fellers (1896–1973) served as the US military attaché in Cairo during an epochal period when worldwide war steered the course of history. He was selected by the Department of War to initiate and direct the United States' regional defense engagement with Great Britain's armed forces. Fellers's multifaceted liaison with the British Middle East Command influenced the thinking of military and political leaders in Washington, Whitehall, Berlin, and Rome, as well as their corollary conduct of the war.

This chapter investigates Fellers's defense-engagement mission and how and why its accidental conflation with Nazi Germany's greatest signals-intelligence coup changed the strategies and war-fighting of the Allies and the Axis during the North African Campaign

(June 10, 1940–May 13, 1943) for command of the Middle East. Comprising three parts, the chapter begins with an examination of the situational context of Fellers's defense-engagement mission. We survey his career before he undertook the assignment in Cairo and then conduct a brief geostrategic analysis of the Middle East during the period when the putatively neutral United States prepared to join Great Britain and the Allied powers as a belligerent in the Second World War. The governing operational domains of Colonel Fellers's defense-engagement mission are analyzed in the chapter's second part. In the third part, we examine the intended and unintended agency of Fellers's defense-engagement operations on the course of the North African Campaign and the nascent alliances of the American and British armed forces and intelligence services. In correlation with "The UK's International Defence Engagement Strategy," the chapter's conclusion encapsulates the practical insights for contemporary defense engagement that may be drawn from Colonel Fellers's remarkable military-attaché mission.[1]

I. Operational Context

FELLERS'S CAREER IN THE US ARMY BEFORE CAIRO

Fellers was born into a Quaker family in Ridge Farm, Illinois, on February 7, 1896. After high school, he studied for two years at Earlham College (1914–1916) and then transferred to West Point. Graduating in the class of 1918, he was commissioned as a second lieutenant in the Coast Artillery Corps and the first in his class to attain the rank of general. Various junior officer assignments followed Fellers's graduation, including his first tour in the Philippines. He returned to West Point in 1924, where he taught mathematics until 1929, and in the late 1930s he returned to teach English. He married Dorothy Dysart in 1925. Following the stint as a math instructor, Fellers undertook his second tour in the Philippines in 1929. A year later, Nancy, the couple's only child, was born on the island of Corregidor.

Fellers returned with his family to the United States in 1934 to attend the Command and General Staff School at Fort Leavenworth, Kansas, where he received a promotion to captain. The school arranged for the governmental publication of Fellers's graduation thesis, "The Psychology of the Japanese Soldier" (Fort Leavenworth, 1935). Examining Japanese cultural

psychology in relation to strategic culture, the pathbreaking thesis illumi-
nated some of the key cognitive drivers of Japan's martial mindset as well
as the associated policy of national military development. Officer training
courses at West Point, the Command and General Staff School, and elsewhere incorporated Fellers's pathbreaking study as a core text.

On his third tour of duty in the Philippines, Fellers joined General
Douglas MacArthur's staff, serving as liaison officer to President Manuel
Quezon from 1937 to 1940. During this tour, Fellers aroused the ire of Ike
Eisenhower. Major Dwight "Ike" Eisenhower served as MacArthur's chief
military aide in Washington from 1933 to 1935 during the general's tenure
as army chief of staff. Thereafter, MacArthur took Eisenhower with him
to the Philippines where, with President Franklin Roosevelt's approval,
Mac-Arthur oversaw the creation of the Philippine Army. Eisenhower's
diary is full of forceful denunciations of MacArthur and his "lackey"—
Captain Bonner Fellers, the "master bootlicker" who "bows down to worship" the general.[2] Why Eisenhower is so angered by a subordinate's close
relationship with their mutual commanding officer is a pregnant question.
Notwithstanding Eisenhower's contempt for MacArthur and Fellers, the
primary sources record Bonner's consistently excellent execution of his
duties. Fellers received commendations for his work at the Philippine Army's Reserve Officer's Service School and for his intelligence and defense-
engagement assignments with President Quezon. In the eyes of President
Roosevelt, President Quezon, and the general of the army, Fellers's missions in the Philippines had served the national interests of both the United
States and the Philippines.

During the last of his three tours in the Philippines, Captain Fellers twice
crossed the Soviet Union on military intelligence missions. General Secretary Joseph Stalin's campaign of terror and political repression was then in
full force. In 1936, Fellers traveled from the west to the east, and two years
later he undertook the reverse course. Lasting for five months, the journey
in 1938 provided the US War Department with valuable intelligence on to-
talitarian communism under Stalin. President Quezon honored Fellers with
the Distinguished Service Star for his contribution to Philippine defense engagement with the United States, military intelligence liaison, and his duty
as first commandant of the Reserve Officers School of the Philippine Army.
Following Fellers's third tour in the Philippines, he traveled with his family

to Carlisle, Pennsylvania, to attend the US Army War College. Thereafter, he served another year at West Point as assistant professor of English. In 1940, he was promoted to major.

After twenty-two years of multifaceted military service, Fellers was among a very small group of American military officers with a proven operational capability across all five governing objects of present-day defense engagement: (1) he had developed knowledge on the United States' national security requirements and those of its allies and potential enemies; (2) he had repeatedly advanced America's national interest and security via defense engagement's various diplomatic, military, and security tools; (3) he had developed the military capability, capacity, and interoperability of the Philippines, an important ally of the United States; (4) he had promoted American prosperity by advancing diplomatic and economic relations with Philippines via his successful liaison work with President Quezon; and (5) he had built and maintained extraordinary access and influence with an ally by realizing the above strategic objectives.[3]

EGYPT, THE MIDDLE EAST, AND ANGLO-AMERICAN DEFENSE ENGAGEMENT

Perceived as a core national interest by the British government and the chiefs of staff, in 1940 defense of the Mediterranean and the Middle East was considered second only to the defense of Great Britain.[4] On a theater visit in August 1942, Churchill had candidly shared Britain's regional strategy with Cairo's press corps: "We are determined to fight for Egypt and the Nile Valley as if it were the soil of England itself."[5] At that time, General Ernst Rommel was poised to divide and conquer the besieged British Empire by occupying Egypt with the seemingly indomitable *Afrika Korps*, seizing control of the Suez Canal, and capturing the Middle East's vital oil resources for the Axis. Great Britain faced an equally powerful existential threat in the North Atlantic. Most of the Royal Navy's sea power was then engaged in convoying supplies from "the great arsenal of democracy" and in the destruction of Nazi Germany's rapacious U-boats and surface raiders.[6] Adolf Hitler and Vice Admiral Karl Donitz, the commander of submarines, together threatened to sever the lifelines of seaborne supply between America and Britain. By June 1941, the severity of shipping losses had prompted the British government to halt further news reporting on sunk ships to preclude public panic and loss of morale.

In Washington, before the Imperial Japanese Navy smashed the US Pacific Fleet at Pearl Harbor, President Franklin Roosevelt and the Joint Chiefs of Staff mainly agreed with the British strategy in the Middle East. Roosevelt had accepted Churchill's argument that if Nazi Germany defeated Great Britain and dismembered the British Empire, it would expose the Western hemisphere to attack and weaken the security of the United States. Beyond this direct military threat, most of Washington believed that a German victory over Great Britain would put severe constraints on the American economy. Freedom to pursue profitable international trade was perceived as the indispensable prerequisite of the Roosevelt administration's colossal American armament program. Victory over the Axis was dependent on securing the global economic primacy of the United States and effective defense engagement with Great Britain.

Simultaneously both heartfelt and self-serving, President Roosevelt's defense-engagement and Lend-Lease programs sought to fulfill Prime Minister Churchill's urgent requests for immediate rearmament of Britain's beleaguered armed forces. Enacted on March 11, 1941, the Roosevelt administration's economic policy-makers had collaborated with the influential business lobby in Congress to enable the attachment of three stringent conditions to the Lend-Lease bill: (1) British reserves must be depleted to the lowest possible level; (2) British exports are to be pegged back to less than one-third of prewar levels; and (3) the British must cease any trade discrimination against American exports.[7] President Roosevelt's defense-engagement strategy for the Allies' war for the common cause deliberately brought bankruptcy to Great Britain and fantastic prosperity to the United States. From Roosevelt's metaphoric illusion of a hosepipe lent, without thought of reward, to a neighbor whose house was burning flowed a series of tributary payments from Whitehall to Washington that ran for sixty-one years. And in addition to debilitating interest payments, America's defense-engagement strategy required Britain to release to the United States intellectual property on jet engines, aircraft design, radar, antibiotics, nuclear technology, and other field-leading defense-related research. The British government's final Lend-Lease interest payment of $83 million was made on December 31, 2006. Running from 1940 to 1942, Fellers's mission in Cairo spanned a world-changing exchange in relative power between Whitehall and Washington that was largely driven by the self-serving terms of Roosevelt's defense engagement with Britain and the other Allied powers.

In November 1941, the chief of naval operations, Admiral "Betty" Stark, had followed the enactment of the Lend-Lease programme with the first draft of the American military's "National Policy for the US." Stark advised steering a course in the common cause "toward an eventual strong offensive in the Atlantic as an ally of the British, and a defensive in the Pacific. . . . About the least that we would do for our ally would be to send strong naval light forces and aircraft to Great Britain and the Mediterranean. Probably we could not stop with a purely naval effort. The plan might ultimately require capture of the Portuguese and Spanish Islands and military and naval bases in Africa and possibly Europe; and thereafter even involve undertaking a full-scale land offensive."[8]

Excepting Winston Churchill and a few sentient Anglo-American cryptographers, signals intelligence's supreme importance to victory in war had yet to be realized properly in Whitehall or Washington. Moreover, military intelligence and defense engagement had been equally belittled before the war. Nazi Germany's blitzkrieg occupation of Europe and the Imperial Japanese Navy's smashing of the US Pacific Fleet at Pearl Harbor largely resulted from ignorance of signals intelligence and military intelligence in general. The Allies faced a real prospect of defeat in the North African Campaign and the overarching world war, which appeared to be metastasizing like a terminal cancer as the Axis conquered new territories simultaneously in the East and the West. When Colonel Fellers took up his post at the US Embassy in Cairo on October 21, 1940, three issues governed official Anglo-American thinking on defense engagement: (1) staunching the continuously spreading war, (2) formalizing a practical Allied strategy for victory, and (3) the corollary best use of limited war-fighting resources. In the Middle East, following a cryptographic revolution that occurred miraculously at the same time as Churchill became prime minister, signals intelligence proved to be the last dimension of strategic power where the British still dominated the Americans, the other Allies, and the Axis.

In the crucible of combat across North Africa and the Mediterranean, Anglo-American defense-engagement operations enabled the Allies to win their war-fighting spurs across the fields of planning, logistics, all-source intelligence, combined arms, joint operations, and grand strategy. Thus, despite the obvious differences in economic power, strategic culture, and military capability, the inaugural defense-engagement operations in North Africa demonstrated that the Allied powers could learn how to combine arms, fight in coordination with one another, and eventually win the Second World War.

THE OBJECT OF COLONEL FELLERS'S MISSION IN CAIRO

Bonner Fellers arrived in Cairo a few days after he had received his promotion to colonel. One of 125 American military attachés posted worldwide at fifty US embassy and consulate missions, the War Department had carefully selected Fellers to undertake one of the most significant and sensitive defense-engagement missions in the war. Fellers was responsible for the execution of US military diplomacy, defense engagement, and military-intelligence collection in the North African Campaign (June 10, 1940–May 13, 1943) for command of the Middle East. His governing object was to successfully represent and realize the United States' defense-engagement strategy in the theater selected for the inaugural Anglo-American war-fighting operation, cover name "Torch" (November 8–16, 1942). Fellers's exemplary execution of America's defense engagement with the British Middle East Command enabled the US War Department to begin its overt military-assistance programs in North Africa on May 11, 1942, five months after America entered the war. Colonel Fellers's mission was made easier by the warm welcome that the British Middle East Command had been ordered to give the senior operator of the United States' defense-engagement strategy in the Middle East.

Wooing Franklin Roosevelt was integral to Winston Churchill's strategy to win the war: "No lover ever studied every whim of his mistress as I did those of President Roosevelt."[9] On May 10, 1940, the day he became prime minister, Churchill launched a whole-of-government courtship of Roosevelt that included the careful cultivation of Anglophile personalities in FDR's administration. For the remainder of Roosevelt's life, Churchill would transmit, on average, one message to him every thirty-six hours. "My whole system," Churchill told Foreign Secretary Anthony Eden, "is based upon partnership with Roosevelt."[10] Influential Anglophile person-

alities in Roosevelt's administration received repeated exposure to pains-
taking cultivation operations during the MI6-led construction of a unique
military and intelligence partnership to realize Churchill's governing object: victory. Defeating the Axis was dependent on Britain harnessing the
colossal American "arsenal of democracy" to the common cause. In addition to the president, MI6 officers targeted their cultivation campaign
on Anglophile agents of influence such as Colonel Bonner Fellers; Colonel William "Wild Bill" Donovan; Roosevelt's best friend and unofficial
national security adviser, Harry Hopkins; Secretary of the Navy Frank
Knox; and Secretary of War Henry Stimson.

Churchill's zealous demands for MI6 to speed the execution of the covert
British operation to maneuver the United States into the war created problems for the senior operators of America's and Britain's defense-engagement
strategies. Colonel Fellers's counterpart in London, the avowedly Anglophile
General Raymond Lee, discovered Churchill's order that information given
to the diplomatic corps would be edited by MI6 to expedite America's entry into the war. A true believer, Lee's proven faith in the common cause increased the power of his critical report to the US War Department on MI6's
maladroit censorship operation at the behest of Churchill:

I do not believe that we can be too emphatic in pointing out that the U.S. Government must be kept promptly and fully informed of everything which has
bearing on the progress of the war.

The United States entered the last war in 1917 practically blindfolded because a great range of vital facts had been withheld from our representatives
both here and in Paris. This has never been forgotten in Washington. It must
not happen this time.

If the full support of the United States is desired, the President and his advisers are entitled to the complete and detailed picture, whether it is favourable or
not, so that they can make their decisions with their eyes open.

The whole affair is now at a point at which Congress must decide whether
the United States is to finance the rest of the war. If any impression gets about
in Washington that any facts are being withheld on this side, so that our reports
are partial, or biased, or misinformed, it is going to be too bad.[11]

An eerie precursor of the subsequent Fellers fiasco, General Lee's trenchant reporting prompted the War Department to terminate his military-

attaché assignment and recall him to Washington. Churchill and Brigadier Stewart Menzies, the chief of MI6, had sought Lee's recall because they refused to allow any foreign military attaché to impede their governing policy for victory: maneuver the United States promptly into the war. Ironically, censoring Lee for his sentient reports probably did more to impede rather than advance American defense engagement with Britain.

The immense strain under which Churchill and Menzies worked in the desperate spring of 1940 was catalytic to their self-defeating censorship of an excellent American military attaché and to their disparagement of MI6's and the Government Code and Cipher School's American counterparts. From Churchill and Menzies's standpoint, Washington did not understand sufficiently the existential threat that the Axis was presenting to Great Britain and the United States. Churchill and Menzies's solution to perceived ignorance in Washington was to engender the creation of a central American secret intelligence service. The new service's primary purpose would be to supply timely intelligence reports on the Axis powers directly to President Roosevelt and his cabinet officers.

As France fell, Churchill initiated a covert operation to realize the construction of a unique defense-engagement relationship with the United States, which he perceived as the best instrument to secure Britain's short-term survival and a long-term Allied victory. A centralized American intelligence service that held a uniquely intimate relationship with both its British progenitor and President Roosevelt was conceived as the vehicle to deliver these strategic objectives. In three years, between May 1940 and May 1943, MI6 engendered the conception and formative conduct of a cohesive American intelligence community. At Churchill and Menzies's behest, from July 14 until August 4, 1940, William Donovan undertook the first of two covert defense-engagement missions for President Roosevelt to liaise with Churchill, British government cabinet ministers, the chiefs of staff, and the heads of Britain's secret services.

William Stephenson, MI6's chief of operations in the Western hemisphere and primary interlocutor with President Roosevelt, was directed by Churchill and Menzies to serve as the senior midwife at the birth of the first central American intelligence service. "From my point of view," Stephenson said, "COI [coordinator of information] was essentially a long-term investment and for some time it required more help than it could give in return."[12] To enable Roosevelt and his advisers to act decisively in moving America to war, MI6 covertly guided the creation of COI and its legendary leader, Colonel William Donovan. Great Britain's hidden hands enabled Donovan to establish himself as America's first chief of intelligence. Director of Naval Intelligence Rear Admiral John Godfrey summarized the definitive agency of British intelligence in a classified report: "In cooperation with Mr. Stephenson . . . Donovan was persuaded to increase his personal interest in Intelligence, and details as to how U.S. Intelligence could be improved in the common cause were worked out in collaboration with him and certain other senior officers of the government. The question was also discussed with the President direct and Colonel Donovan's qualifications as coordinator of Intelligence were advocated to Mr. Roosevelt."[13]

Nine months after Colonel Fellers arrived in Cairo, President Roosevelt's executive order of July 11, 1941, authorized the creation of the Office of Coordinator of Information with Donovan as its chief. Stephenson reported to MI6 headquarters in London: "You can imagine how relieved I am after three months of battle and jockeying for position in Washington that our man [Donovan] is in a position of such importance to our efforts."[14] Major Desmond Morton, Churchill's personal secretary responsible for liaison with the British secret services, described the character of the Anglo-American intelligence relations at the outset of Fellers's defense-engagement mission:

To all intents and purposes U.S. security is being run for them at the President's request by the British. A British officer [William Stephenson] sits in Washington with Mr Edgar Hoover and General [*sic*] Bill Donovan for this purpose and reports regularly to the President. It is of course essential that this fact should not become known in view of the furious uproar it would cause if known to the Isolationists.[15]

As the chief of prewar American defense engagement in the Middle East, Colonel Bonner Fellers reported directly to Colonel William Donovan at COI and the War Department's Military Intelligence Division. Donovan and Fellers had begun to collaborate with one another a few months earlier on a secret presidential mission for Roosevelt in January 1941. During this mission, Donovan swiftly recognized the extraordinary quality of Fellers's defense engagement and military intelligence abilities, and the professional esteem in which he was uniformly held by British field commanders, staff officers, and front-line combatants. Thus, Donovan recruited Fellers into COI in July 1941, and in June 1942 he asked Fellers to serve with COI's institutional successor, the Office of Strategic Services.[16] President Franklin Roosevelt, the heads of the American intelligence services, and the newly formed Joint Chiefs of Staff received Fellers's top-secret reports on all aspects of defense engagement in the North African Campaign.[17] By July 1942, at the premature end of his mission, the White House, the Office of Strategic Services, and the War Department held Fellers's "profound knowledge of everything in the Middle East" in such high esteem that he was recommended as a future commander in chief for Egypt.[18] As we shall examine in part three, the excellent quality of Fellers's defense engagement and military-intelligence reporting to the War Department is one of the primary reasons why Churchill and the chief of MI6 secretly arranged for his prompt and premature recall to Washington.

II. Wartime Defense Engagement

BATTLEFIELD OBSERVATION AND SUPPLY OF WAR-FIGHTING MATERIEL

In October 1940, at the outset of Colonel Fellers's defense-engagement operations, the United States was officially still postured as a neutral nation. Yet when Churchill became prime minister in May, he and Roosevelt had immediately started secret war-planning talks. MI6's still officially classified in-house history of its operations in the Western hemisphere records that the first war-fighting agreement between Churchill and Roosevelt "was reached, some six months after the start of the European war, for Anglo-American cooperation in the intelligence field. The fact that it was reached at all is indication of Mr Roosevelt's remarkable clarity of vision. The fact that it had to be kept secret even from the State Department provides striking illustration of the strength of American neutrality at the time. . . . There were still comparatively few Americans—in or out of Congress—who understood that their own country would be endangered by Britain's collapse."[19] Churchill's whole-of-state strategy to transform the United States' official posture from isolation to intervention swiftly incorporated Colonel

Fellers's defense-engagement operations with the British Middle East Command.

In June 1940, Churchill and Menzies had directed William Stephenson to launch a nationwide campaign in the United States to shift public opinion from isolationism to intervention and "to assist Mr Roosevelt's own campaign for preparedness."[20] Bilateral defense-engagement operations often contributed to political-warfare campaigns, which together exerted significant agency on public opinion during the Second World War. On June 25, 1940, the Gallup polling company found that 64 percent of Americans thought it more important to stay out of the war than to help Britain fight Nazi Germany. On October 20, a few days before Fellers arrived in Cairo, public opinion had reached an even balance between intervention and neutrality. And on November 19, Gallup's polling recorded that 62 percent of Americans thought it was more important to help Britain than to remain a neutral power in war.[21]

Intelligence and military officers conducted the inaugural rounds of Anglo-American talks to formulate the Allied war plan. Roosevelt and Churchill conceived the object of these highly classified discussions: "determine the best methods by which the U.S. and British Commonwealth could defeat Germany should the United States be compelled to resort to war," and coordinate concomitant bilateral defense-engagement and military operations.[22] Colonel Bonner Fellers's attaché assignment was one of this first combined defense-engagement and military-intelligence missions to result from the seminal war-planning talks and had the same strategic object. He was tasked to operate across three domains of interrelated military attaché activity: battlefield observation, overt and covert military-intelligence collection, and defense engagement.

In tandem with Fellers's arrival in Cairo, Churchill's and the chiefs of staff's governing concern turned from the defense of Great Britain against invasion by Germans to winning the North African Campaign for command of the Middle East. London, although still subject to the nightly terrors of the *Luftwaffe*'s bombing sorties, no longer faced imminent invasion by a rampant Wehrmacht. Second only to defense of the homeland, Great Britain's dominant influence in Egypt and the Middle East are again prioritized in Whitehall as essential prerequisites to the security of the beleaguered British Empire. On a theater visit in November 1940, the British secretary of war, Anthony

Eden, put the Middle East Command under firm orders to unreservedly embrace the bright forty-four-year-old Illinoisan West Pointer, Colonel Bonner Fellers, as the senior regional operator of American defense engagement with Great Britain. Eden firmly endorsed Fellers's authority as carrying more policy-making influence with President Roosevelt, US intelligence, and the Joint Chiefs of Staff than America's ambassador to Egypt, Bert Fish.

Following military-attaché diplomatic-protocol audiences with Egypt's leaders, Fellers was personally escorted to the Allies' key positions in the desert by General Henry Maitland "Jumbo" Wilson, general officer commanding the British troops in Egypt. Finding that Colonel Fellers was a zealous advocate of the Lend-Lease program, generous defense engagement, and America's immediate entry into the war, the "Desert Rats" enthusiastically executed Eden's order to welcome the US military attaché as a career officer and an honored guest.[23] The American colonel's impressive knowledge of artillery and "colourful, downright way" made congenial company. Fellers often drove himself through the desert to the Eighth Army's forward headquarters and frontline positions in a camouflaged van that he dryly called his "hearse" and earned widespread professional respect as a combat-proven comrade-in-arms.[24] Following orders from Churchill and Eden, he was soon cleared for "full access to everything in the Eighth Army," including the most secret intelligence on British and Commonwealth regional "strengths, positions, losses, reinforcements, supply, situation, plans, morale." On some days, Fellers transmitted as many as five "detailed reports on it all to Washington."[25]

In September 1940, under pressure from Il Duce, Marshal Rodolfo Graziani, First Marquis of Neghelli, had reluctantly led the mainly unmechanized Italian Tenth Army on a misguided advance from Libya into Egypt that soon became stymied in the desert. November and December appeared to augur an auspicious change in the war's course in favor of Great Britain. On November 11, the Italian Fleet at Taranto lost half of its capital ships in a devastating attack that shifted the balance of power to the British Mediterranean Fleet. Concomitantly, British and Commonwealth forces kicked the Italians out of Egypt and back into Libya. Together, these long-sought victories were perceived as a counterbalance to the Wehrmacht's unremitting blitzkrieg stomp across Northern Europe. And on February 6, 1941, the British Army found, fixed, and destroyed the Italian Tenth Army. Holding and securing North

Africa and the Mediterranean then appeared as a real opportunity for the Allies to "turn the hinge of fate" and secure command of the Middle East.[26] But on February 12, the balance of power had changed when one of the Wehrmacht's greatest combined arms commanders flew in to Tripoli under direct orders from Adolf Hitler to destroy the British with the Afrika Korps. General Erwin Rommel instinctively mounted a swift and brutal offensive. Ripping through the unprepared British Army as it struggled to recover from bungled interventions in Greece and Crete, Rommel quickly positioned his Panzer tanks and armor to lay siege to the strategic port of Tobruk in Libya.

By February 1941, Fellers had selected and assembled a small unit of American defense-engagement operators. In accord with his mission's governing objective, he tasked his operators to determine the best methods by which the US armed forces could defeat the Wehrmacht. Observing the British military in combat during the North African Campaign gave Fellers access to a unique war-fighting laboratory, which eventually produced a practical Allied antidote to the Afrika Korps' seemingly unstoppable blitzkrieg. His initial reports to Washington had glowed with praise for Operation Compass (December 9, 1940–February 9, 1941) and other victorious British engagements with the Italian Army. But following Rommel's acceding command in North Africa, Fellers's reports during the abysmal spring and summer of 1941 unsparingly examined a series of disastrous British defeats, which put the Axis on the cusp of conquering the Middle East.

Fellers held many British officers and soldiers in high professional esteem, but he did not flinch from identifying the root cause as he perceived it of the Afrika Korps' marked superiority over the British Army:

No race possesses more fortitude and fearless determination than the British. During forty days of trying desert combat I never heard a word of complaint from officer or soldier. They will never surrender. Somehow they know they will muddle through. The British fight best against great odds. Inadequate equipment is no discouragement. They are masters at improvisation. Yet in their willingness to improvise lies a weakness for in modern war improvisation is effective only against an inadequate enemy. The British Army is not quite in phase with the tempo of high centralization and coordination demanded by a machine age.[27]

Britain's disastrous losses in Greece and Crete, which had resulted from the Royal Navy's inability to effectively shield itself from the Luftwaffe's unremitting sorties, opened Fellers's eyes to the necessity of air power superiority during naval operations. Like-minded with Churchill and the Middle East Command regarding the region's geostrategic importance, Fellers's battlefield experiences and his defense-engagement operators convinced them of the North African Campaign's decisive bearing on the outcome of the war. After six months of frontline battlefield observation, Fellers reported to Washington, "Loss of Egypt might mean loss of the war. Recommend War Department take all possible steps to alleviate existing [British] shortages in material and aircraft."[28]

In addition to his unrestricted clearance to observe combat on the battlefield, Eden's and Churchill's support facilitated Fellers's direct access to General Sir Archibald Wavell, commander in chief Middle East; Admiral Sir Andrew Cunningham, commander in chief Mediterranean Fleet; and Air Vice Marshall Sir Arthur Longmore, air commander in chief Middle East. Battlefield comradeship and professional rapport with the Allies' military leaders did not impede Fellers's ability to trenchantly examine the role of a dysfunctional command system in serial British defeats across the Middle East. Fellers's insightful defense-engagement research on the triumvirate committee of coequal commanders of the air, land, and sea services produced a stark finding:

There should be one Middle East Commander personally responsible for the success or failure of all operations. He should have under his control all means available—sea, land, and air—for the accomplishment of his mission. . . . With Crete, Britain suffered her fourth tragic major defeat and because of divided responsibility inherent within her command system she has not the slightest idea of who is responsible. The truth is that no one is responsible. It is a convenient system which protects all commanders, dilutes responsibilities, glosses over failure, provides iron clad alibis, but it won't win wars.[29]

OVERT AND COVERT MILITARY INTELLIGENCE COLLECTION

Understanding of the value and role of defense engagement and military intelligence was insufficient in the armed forces of the United States before they entered the Second World War. The situation was no better in Great Britain. Churchill's chief of staff at the Ministry of Defence, General Hastings "Pug" Ismay, wrote: "In the years before the war we lived in a world of imagination, and the preparations on which our very existence might depend had to be made on forecasts which might prove to be entirely wrong."[30]

In 1939, Washington received no reporting from professional intelligence officers posted overseas. All the War Department's foreign intelligence originated from military attachés, "estimable, socially acceptable gentlemen; few knew the essentials of intelligence work." Departmental dysfunction was exacerbated by an archaic "custom of making long service as a military attaché, rather than ability, the essential qualification." Unable "to even develop a clear plan for its own organization," endemic inadequacy blighted the Military Intelligence Division's collection, analysis, and dissemination of intelligence to policy-makers.[31]

American diplomats, military attachés, and Roosevelt's private network of presidential spies produced various haphazard and indiscriminate reports on German rearmament. Intercepted signals provided the most reliable intelligence, but exclusively on Japan. American cryptographers had first breached Japanese diplomatic traffic (cover name "Purple") in August 1940, just two months before Fellers arrived in Egypt. In 1941, a damning interagency review of contemporary defense-engagement and military-intelligence operations revealed that most US naval and military attachés "saw what was not there, did not see what was there, and in general saw without appreciation of significance."[32] There was no appreciation of intelligence's strategic power and an equally negative provision for analyzing it. The most authoritative studies of the Pearl Harbor disaster show that the problem was not a lack of intelligence on Japan but the "absence of a system to make the intelligence that was available understandable to the national-level decision makers."[33]

Washington's whole-of-government ignorance of military intelligence remained uncorrected until Colonel Donovan's presidential appointment as the United States' first coordinator of information in July 1941. The US Army's and Navy's intelligence services worked actively against one another, refusing to share information even if doing so would clearly advance the national interest. According to Eisenhower, until Donovan's appointment in 1941 "a shocking deficiency impeded all constructive planning in the field of intelligence" within the War Department.[34] The Military Intelligence Division had only one radio-intelligence company and no secure central system for the dissemination of signals intelligence to field commanders. In October 1940, Fellers was one of only eighty-two professional intelligence officers that constituted the division. Nonetheless, President Roosevelt and Colonel Donovan held Fellers in high esteem as the United States' best source of military intelligence on the Middle East and its leading regional defense-engagement operator.[35]

Fellers's defense engagement and intelligence gathering, and the excellent quality of his associated reporting to Roosevelt, Donovan, and the War Department, provided a best-practice template for a coordinator of information and then Office of Strategic Services–led policy to make the role of attachés central and systematic in the collection, analysis, and application of military intelligence.[36] Fellers's exemplary execution of his intelligence and defense-engagement mission was recognized in President Roosevelt's awarding him with the Distinguished Service Medal. The medal's citation officially notes Fellers's "uncanny ability to foresee military development," the "clarity, brevity, and accuracy" of his reports, and his extraordinary contribution to the "tactical and technical development of [the United States'] Armed Forces."[37]

MILITARY DIPLOMACY

After Churchill and the British chiefs of staff had changed their strategic priority from repulsing a German invasion to defeating the Axis in the Middle East, they sought to steer Roosevelt's mercurial attention from Great Britain's existential prospects to the Allied-Axis balance of power in North Africa. The cogent analysis of Britain's military strengths and weaknesses that Donovan had prepared for Roosevelt in July 1940 had prompted the president to commission his intelligence chief to undertake a second secret mission to determine the relative power of Britain and Germany in the Middle East and the Balkans. On December 1, 1940, Roosevelt ordered Colonel William Donovan to undertake a theater tour with three governing objects: (1) collect military intelligence on the current situation and likely developments; (2) impress on everyone he meets that the United States is resolved to see Great Britain through; and (3) provide all possible assistance to nations who are committed to confronting Nazi Germany.[38]

Stephenson traveled with Donovan to London. He briefed the chief of MI6, Brigadier Stewart Menzies; the secretary of state for foreign affairs,

Lord Halifax; and the Foreign Office's permanent undersecretary, Sir Alexander Cadogan, on Donovan's extraordinary influence with the president, Roosevelt's cabinet officers, and the Joint Chiefs of Staff. Regarding defense engagement, Stephenson advised Churchill to be candid with Donovan because he could "contribute very largely to our obtaining all that we want of the United States."[39] Churchill accepted Stephenson's analysis and gave Donovan a generous amount of undivided attention, which included a rare private lunch in the prime minister's study at 10 Downing Street. The lunch produced an agreement between Donovan and Churchill to build a special relationship: the time had come for Britain and the United States to form a comprehensive partnership across defense engagement, military intelligence, and cryptography. Moreover, North Africa and the Mediterranean was the theater where the Anglo-American alliance would turn the tables against the Axis via a pathbreaking joint operation. "It's time for both of us, your people and our own people," Donovan agreed, to analyze "the economic, political, and military implications of the Mediterranean." Churchill and Donovan agreed that Great Britain and the United States would conceive a joint plan to secure command of the Middle East and kick the Axis out of the region.[40]

Following Churchill's talks with Donovan, the Foreign Office transmitted secret signals on behalf of the prime minister to British missions and military commands in North Africa, the Mediterranean, and the Balkans. Churchill thereby informed British ambassadors and commanders that he had ordered his "best man in the Cabinet Secretariat," Lieutenant Colonel Vivian Dykes, to accompany Donovan and support the execution of his presidential defense-engagement mission. Donovan was to be received across the region as a special emissary of President Roosevelt who exerted "great influence" in Washington. Churchill emphasized that Donovan had "been taken fully into our confidence." The message records that MI6 financed Donovan's travel, and Dykes was cleared to draw on the service's secret funds.[41]

Donovan and Dykes rendezvoused with Colonel Fellers in Libya on January 11, 1941, at General Richard O'Connor's 13 Corps headquarters in the Western Desert as the British prepared to attack Tobruk. In preparation for Donovan's mission, Fellers had carefully deployed the esteem in which he was held by the British Middle East Command to prime many of the selected conferees to freely discuss Anglo-American defense engagement and the regional geostrategic situation with Roosevelt's special envoy. Admirals Cunningham and Somerville; Generals Wavell and Wilson; Air Marshalls Longmore and Tedder; Foreign Secretary Anthony Eden; and chief of the Imperial General Staff, General John Dill, all spoke candidly with Donovan and Fellers.[42] Following his discussions with Churchill, MI6 officers, Fellers, and various British commanders, Donovan was persuaded that Great Britain would survive, and Roosevelt should rapidly increase the United States' defense engagement in North Africa and join the war for the common cause. Fellers's preparatory military diplomacy before Donovan's theater tour had deliberately engendered candid knowledge-exchanging with the British High Command. Wavell on the strategic importance of the Middle East, General James Marshall-Cornwall on Turkey and the Balkans, Wilson on the North African Campaign and the Western Desert, Cunningham on the Mediterranean and the Afrika Korps' seaborn lines of supply—all the above gave Donovan and Fellers a comprehensive commander's assessment of their respective areas of operation.[43] Indeed, following the briefings from the British regional commanders, no American held more secret British military intelligence on the Middle East than Donovan and Fellers.

Churchill and the chief of MI6 had granted the two American colonels extraordinary access to a comprehensive range of British intelligence. After three months in theater, Donovan returned to Washington on March 19, 1941, laden with leather pouches containing a wealth of secret intelligence and memoranda of revelatory conversations with British commanders. Thus, Roosevelt and the War Department understood the strategic situation, the likely developments, and the required level of American defense engagement in the Middle East from London's standpoint.

Via his guided theater tour with Fellers and Dykes, Donovan had seen more of the overt and covert war in North Africa and the Mediterranean than anyone else in Washington. Britain's defense-engagement operation had convinced Donovan and Roosevelt that Fellers's knowledge of the Middle East and the regional Axis-Allies balance of power was greater than that held by any other American. Moreover, the British influence operation had persuaded Roosevelt, Donovan, and Fellers to advocate the holy trinity of Anglo-American defense engagement, at least as it was then perceived by Churchill and the British Chiefs of Staff: (1) full supply of warfighting materiel to the British in the Middle East, (2) the United States' entry into the war, and (3) the primacy of North Africa and the Mediterranean as the theater for the United States' inaugural war-fighting operation with the Allies.

III. The Most Influential American in Cairo

WASHINGTON'S CHIEF DEFENSE-ENGAGEMENT
OPERATOR IN THE MIDDLE EAST

On New Year's Day, 1942, Colonel Bonner Fellers shared a characteristically forthright observation with his luncheon companion, MI6 officer Countess Hermione Ranfurly:

I'm getting unpopular here. Not so much with your people as with the US Embassy in Cairo and in Washington; they think I am a defeatist but that's not going to stop me saying what I think about the military situation, which is my job to do. The trouble is your top brass are overconfident, which they've no right to be: your gear is still inferior to the enemy's, and you are less well led. Too many senior officers are sitting on their arses at GHQ.[44]

After fifteen months of intimate association with the British and Commonwealth armed forces in combat on the front lines in the Western Desert, and with leaders, logisticians, and intelligence officers in Middle East Command, Fellers remained a true believer in defense engagement with the British, especially now that the United States had entered the war. He readily understood that more than any other type, military-to-military "diplomacy is the art of letting someone else have your way."[45] But observing Operation Battleaxe (June 15–17, 1941) and Operation Crusader (November 18–December 30, 1941) had given Fellers practical insight into Britain's inferior doctrine and equipment relative to the Afrika Korps'.[46] Tasked with determining "the best methods by which the U.S. and British Commonwealth could defeat Germany," Washington's leading defense-engagement operator in Cairo finished his year-end assessment with the startling conclusion that the US Army should have as little to do as possible with the British Army.[47] In accord with Donovan's advocacy for unity of command and separate American and British areas of operation, Fellers's last encrypted signal to Washington in 1941 had ended with the remarkable finding that it was absolutely essential that the United States Army have its own separate theatre of operation, separate line of communication, separate base. My personal admiration for the bravery and fortitude of the British is without limit. However, British methods are lax, their attitude casual, their follow up lack[ing], their sense of coordination faulty; they cannot fully attune their army doctrine with the tempo of mechanical warfare. 15 months intimate association, of which considerable time was spent observing actual combat, compels me to report that I am positive our forces can never work in the same theatre effectively and in close harmony with the British.[48]

After the attack on Pearl Harbor on December 7, 1941, Churchill outmaneuvered those personalities in the Roosevelt administration who had sought to delay his urgent proposal for a war-planning summit in Washington. MI6 was directed to call on its network of influential Anglophiles; not long thereafter, Churchill embarked for the United States aboard HMS *Duke of York*. With his military advisers in tow, the British prime minister arrived on December 22. He was warmly welcomed and soon ensconced in the White House with Roosevelt and Harry Hopkins, the most influential presidential adviser. Cover-named "Arcadia," the first round of summit talks in Washington decided the strategic fundamentals that steered the subsequent course of the war.

Drawing heavily on Fellers's reports from Cairo, as well as the findings from Donovan's theater tour and other military intelligence sources, on Christmas Day General George Marshall, the chief of staff of the US Army, stated that each Allied theater must have one supreme commander for all air, land, and sea operations. "We cannot manage by cooperation. . . . If we could decide on a unified command now, it would be a great advance over what was accomplished during the [First] World War."[49] During the first half of the North African Campaign, Fellers's unrestricted observation of the British military's committee system of trifurcated command had enabled his trenchant investigations of the resulting serial defeats and profligate expenditure of Allied blood and treasure. The British Army was indeed "less well led" than the Afrika Korps. And its armor and armaments remained "inferior to the enemy's."[50] British crews preferred by far the more reliable American M3 tank over the British Crusader, albeit the German Panzers outgunned both with their 50 mm and 75 mm guns. Five days after his lunch with Ranfurly, Fellers transmitted a blunt report from the battlefield to the War Department: "I personally hold nothing could be more startling than the realization in battle that the German 88 mm anti-tank gun and their 47 and 50 mm guns could outrange British 2-pounder and American 37 mm guns; destroy our tanks from ranges which were perfectly safe for the German guns and tanks. It is imperative that our Army not engage the German with such inferiority in gun power."[51] Despite plentiful military intelligence reports, the British War Office had obdurately refused to acknowledge the 88s' vital role in blitzkrieg combined-arms warfare in France in 1940, and for many months after Rommel had again used them repeatedly to destroy British armored formations in North Africa two years later. A prime example of policy-makers' common willful ignorance of military intelligence is discordance with an established orthodoxy or strategy. Then and today, superior intelligence has little power in the hands of an inferior policy-maker. Fellers's recommendations that the US Army be equipped with no less than 75 mm– and preferably 90 mm–caliber armor-piercing guns did not result in a policy for more powerful armament.[52] But the corollary advent of the M3 medium tank fitted with a British turret and a 75 mm gun did enable Fellers's to make positive reports on the British Army's improved performance during the Battle of Gazala (May 267, 1942–June 21, 1942). Nonetheless, the reports to Washington that originated from Fellers's defense engagement with the Middle East Command played a significant role in Rommel's victories in the Gazala battles and the German military's occupation of the strategic port of Tobruk. Based on his unprecedented access to the most secret military intelligence on British operations, Fellers had reported to the War Department that the Eighth Army was then incapable of defeating the Afrika Korps. Moreover, Fellers advised that the British should be immediately supplied with American war-fighting materiel sufficient to enable an Allied victory over the Axis in North Africa. Ironically, Fellers's discerning defense-engagement reports on the precise "strengths, positions, losses, reinforcements, supply, situation, plans, morale etc" of the British and Commonwealth forces simultaneously magnified Roosevelt's understanding of the war and Rommel's increasing superiority over the Allied powers' commanders.[53] Churchill described this terrible time as "a long succession of misfortune and defeats in Malaya, Singapore, and Burma; Auchinleck's lost battle in the Desert, Tobruk, *unexplained, and, it seemed, inexplicable*; the rapid retreat of the Desert Army and the loss of all our conquests in Libya and Cyrenaica; four hundred miles of retrogression towards the Egyptian frontier."[54] Contrary to Churchill's account, the Government Code and Cipher School had revealed the leading cause of Britain's heavy losses in North Africa and the fall of Tobruk to him and he had personally explicated the situation to Roosevelt.

BERLIN'S *GUTE QUELLE*

According to a National Security Agency study on secret communications in the Second World War, Colonel Fellers's reports produced "Field Marshall Erwin Rommel's best source of intelligence during the battle for North Africa."[55] Rommel's intelligence officer provided a more vivid analysis of the greatest cryptographic coup of the Cipher Department of the High Command of the German Armed Forces (*Oberkommando der Wehrmacht Chiffrierabteilung*). The Cipher Department's six-month breach of the US military attaché and State Department encryption system ran from December 1941 until June 29, 1942:

Of all the code telegrams, which included some from the US Military attaché in Moscow, those sent by Colonel Fellers from Cairo were the most important. . . . In view of the great frankness between the Americans and the English, this information was not only strategically but tactically of the utmost usefulness. In fact, it was stupefying in its openness.

Colonel Fellers committed to these telegrams the most secret data on military affairs in the Middle East—things that he witnessed for himself on visits to the front line or gleaned from the headquarters in the desert or in Cairo. He was most assiduous in his inquiries and was inevitably furnished with top secret information by the British who were angling for the entry of the United States into the war. This vital information, enciphered in the Black Code, was deciphered in Germany, translated, re-coded, and was in the hands of the General Staff and Rommel only a few hours after transmission from Cairo.[56]

On January 21, 1942, with the benefit of decisive intelligence in Fellers's encrypted reports indicating that he held front-line-armor superiority and the Royal Air Force's (RAF) airpower was significantly deficient, Rommel launched the Afrika Korps on another combined-arms offensive. In a seventeen-day blitzkrieg, the Germans achieved a 400-mile advance. Fellers's detailed defense-engagement and intelligence reporting gave Rommel the ability to plan and prosecute war with comprehensive foresight on his opponent's strategy, order of battle, operational plans, tactics, and morale. From December 1941, when *Chiffrierabteilung's* cryptographers breached the US-military-attaché encryption system, Rommel exhibited an extraordinary ability to maximize Afrika Korps' advantages while simultaneously exploiting precise weaknesses in the British and Commonwealth forces.

By late June 1942, the Afrika Korps was poised to boot the British out of Egypt, punch through Palestine, and join the German forces, which would be descending from Russia following their historic victory over the Red Army. The defense of Egypt, the Suez Delta, and Britain's whole position in the Middle East had reached its nadir. Hitler and Mussolini issued orders that directed Rommel to capture Alexandria and the Nile Delta and thereby place control of the Middle East, its strategic oil reserves, and the Suez Canal in Axis hands. Unable to contain his excitement at the prospect of conquering the Middle East, Mussolini had flown to Derna with a huge entourage of flunkies that filled twelve planes. The Italian dictator's staff made detailed plans for Mussolini's triumphal parade into Cairo.[57] On June 28, 1942, Hitler had ebulliently remarked, "The capture of Alexandria would infuriate the entire English people (only the moneyed classes were interested in the fall of Singapore) and [make them] rise in a putsch against Churchill. It was only hoped that the American [military attaché] in Cairo continues to inform us so well over the English military planning through his badly enciphered cables."[58] But the day after Hitler made his triumphant observation regarding Berlin's *Gute Quelle* (Good Source), Rommel had lost sight of Fellers's extraordinarily informative reporting from Cairo. Bletchley Park's timely termination of the only instance in the war when *Chiffrierabteilung* achieved parity with the Government Code and Cipher School in the provision of strategic signals intelligence to field commanders marked an historic turn in the hinge of fate.[59] After June 29, the British Middle East Command used the fortunate reversal in the regional balance of signals-intelligence power to turn the tables on the previously indomitable Afrika Korps.

BLETCHLEY PARK'S BÊTE NOIRE

On February 18, 1942, three days after the Imperial Japanese Army's occupation of Singapore, Fellers had sent a secret signal to Washington and,
unwittingly, to Berlin and London. Unbeknown to the US War Department, though not to Roosevelt, both the British and the German signals-
intelligence services had breached the encipherment system with which
American military attachés and diplomats encrypted their classified communications with Washington. Fellers's revelatory report recorded:

Other than air attacks, Rommel is the immediate threat to the Middle East. His
tank strength is now the equal of the British. Due to intense and immediate
pressure on Malta by the German Air Force, 85 to 90 percent of Axis supplies
and reinforcements from Italy enroute Tripoli are arriving. . . . British intelligence estimates that Rommel's Panzer Divisions may be brought up to full tank
strength and that an Italian armored division may be sent to him as a reinforce-
ment. These armored units, an additional small motorized force, together with
the forces now in Cyrenaica, make possible the invasion of Egypt. . . .

To oppose Rommel in the desert the British have: 1st Armored Division
whose combat strength is at best fair; 50th British Division; Polish Brigade deficient in transport; Guards Brigade whose combat efficiency is good; 1st South
African Division which lost a complete brigade in November; 2nd South African
Division which is without transport and is holding the frontier posts. Part of the
10th Armored Division, tankless, is now enroute to the desert. All of these units
combined could not stop Rommel were he reinforced as indicated above.

Present Libyan campaign has been costly because of poor execution. Such
victories as are claimed are empty. It is estimated that the British have lost over
700 tanks and 15,000 troops. It is estimated that the British have in the Middle
East 200,000 troops organized in units, including 43,000 Egyptians who are on
active duty in the Delta and Canal areas, and including area service and supply.
Total number up to 303,000 troops in the Middle East. This figure is in 10% of
being accurate.

If American forces are to be sent into the Muslim world our government
should arrange an understanding with the local governments concerned. The
importance of maintenance of friendly relations with the Muslims, especially
in the post war period is far reaching. The Muslims possess more homogeneity

and discernment than is generally supposed. They are far more of a force than the British realize.[60]

A few days after Fellers transmitted his excoriating report on Britain's strategic situation in the Middle East, Churchill made a remarkable confession to Roosevelt: "Some time ago . . . our experts claimed to have discovered the system and constructed some table used by your diplomatic corps. From the moment when we became allies [in December 1941], I gave instructions that this work should cease. However, danger of our enemies having achieved a measure of success cannot, I am advised, be dismissed."[61]

Known as the "Black Code" from the color of its binding cover, the decision to retain the breached encryption system for all diplomatic and military-attaché communications after Churchill had disclosed its failure is indicative of a remarkable level of complacency on the part of Roosevelt and his intelligence advisers. In response to Fellers's multiple reports on his concerns regarding the Black Code's insufficient security, the War Department repeatedly instructed him to carry on using the breached encryption system.[62]

As Rommel deployed the Afrika Korps to strike a death blow against the British forces in Egypt, the Government Code and Cipher School's boffins in Hut 3 at Bletchley Park had worked around-the-clock shifts on a fraught counterintelligence hunt for the German deep-penetration agent inside Middle East headquarters. On April 13, 1942, the German Air Force received a flash warning from *Chiffrierabteilung* that indicated the secret location of the Luftwaffe's desert headquarters had been compromised. After reading a decrypt of the message in his daily Ultra box, Churchill requested clarification from Menzies: "Please report on this. How did they [*Chiffrierabteilung*] know that we had told the Army in Egypt where it [Luftwaffe headquarters] was?"[63]

Menzies replied that he had launched a counterintelligence investigation, primarily focused on identifying security weaknesses on Middle East Command. Shortly thereafter, Fellers's unfettered access to staff conferences, including brigade and divisional planning meetings, was deemed to require an official directive to outline what he could and could not be told. On April 25, the first draft of the liaison protocol noted, "It is essential to avoid giving offence to Colonel Bonner Fellers or to give the impression that information to which he is entitled is being withheld. . . . He is entitled to seek the most secret information on any subject connected with the war effort."[64] It was crucial that Fellers should not be given any cause to decrease the United States' indispensable defense engagement with the British armed forces. Nonetheless, MI8 signals-intelligence officers duly arranged a meeting with the US military attaché, ostensibly to review his security measures. "They seemed satisfied," Fellers recalled in a postwar oral history. "They didn't say anything about the code being broken, but it made me wonder why they were doing it."[65]

On April 24, Churchill received another Ultra decrypt in which Gute Quelle had revealed that the Eighth Army was not strong enough to attack Rommel before June 1, and that Malta was on the verge of collapse. Two days later, a detailed report from Gute Quelle documented British Army positions and order of battle. Through April and May, Rommel gained a wealth of secret military intelligence via his sight of Fellers's revelatory reports. The intelligence's quality was such that it would only have been accessible to a senior officer.[66] Churchill's package of Ultra signals intelligence on June 10 had contained a decrypt with a troubling cover note from Menzies: "Another long report to German Army in Africa from 'Good Source' concerning British morale, training, supplies and intentions, evidently based on the 'Good Source's' visits to British units."[67]

Dated June 4, the flagged decrypt referred to Gute Quelle's observation of British units in the desert, and it included detailed negative comparisons with American doctrine. The comparison with American doctrine was the final piece of information necessary to facilitate a back-bearing counterintelligence analysis that identified Gute Quelle as someone who held a Black Code communication clearance at the US embassy in Cairo. In the conclusion to the cover note that accompanied the June 4 decrypt, Menzies wrote, "Prime Minister, I am satisfied that the American ciphers in Cairo are compromised. I am taking action."[68] Churchill responded the following day with a brusque instruction to the MI6 chief, "Say what action? And let me know what happens."[69] On June 12, 1942, Menzies told Churchill that the Americans had initiated an investigation.[70] In a follow-up note on June 14, Menzies informed Churchill, "There are at least three American ciphers in use between Cairo and Washington, and until the Americans inform me which cipher was used for the messages in question, it is impossible to determine whether the Germans have broken a cipher, or whether there is a traitor who is betraying information and transmitting it to the enemy by a secret channel."[71]

Two days later, Menzies relayed the results of the American's counterintelligence investigation to Churchill, and included his own analysis of the situation:

Washington informs me that it is now clear that the cipher of the American military attaché in Cairo is compromised, and I have asked that this should be changed immediately to a cipher providing the highest security, but without furnishing any reason for the change-over. Should the Germans obtain any information dispatched on the new cipher, we shall then know for certain that there is a traitor in Cairo. In my opinion, the Germans have succeeded in photographing the American cipher book; as this is held at a number of stations abroad, it is impossible to determine where the treachery occurred. We cannot, moreover, rule out the possibility of a traitor in USA, where the books are printed.[72]

Churchill was angered profoundly by the Fellers fiasco. He told Menzies that regardless of the imminent second summit in Washington, unless a satisfactory answer was received from Washington, the prime minister would contact the president personally.[73] To make matters worse, at the outset of their talks in the White House on June 21 Roosevelt had handed Churchill a report on the fall of Tobruk. Commanding a German force of half the size, Rommel had captured 33,000 British and Commonwealth troops. The blow struck Churchill almost as heavily as the loss of Singapore.

Churchill's pragmatic resolution of the catastrophic breach in the US military attachés' encryption system exhibited some of his most masterful statesmanship. Bletchley Park's termination of the military intelligence that Fellers had unwittingly supplied to Rommel enabled Churchill to exert significant influence on Roosevelt's decision, against the advice of the Joint Chiefs and the War Department, to save the Eighth Army via increased defense engagement and to undertake the Allies' inaugural joint war-fighting operation in North Africa (cover name "Torch"). Following the June 21 summit meeting, during which Churchill adroitly used his cryptography-based knowledge that Gute Quelle was still supplying Rommel with Great Britain's most secret intelligence, General Marshall transmitted a flash signal to Cairo: "Our message . . . effecting changes [to Fellers's encryption system] . . . not complied with. Matter of greatest concern. Contact military attaché and direct his immediate compliance with changes."[74]

At a decisive juncture in history, the Government Code and Cipher School provided Churchill with the power to influence the outcome of a

major summit meeting, and President Roosevelt with a solution to the cost-
liest attack against secret American military communications in the Second
World War. According to Rommel's intelligence officer,

From 29 June onwards the "Good Source" fell silent. We no longer had this in-
comparable source of authentic and reliable information, which had contributed so
decisively during the first half of 1942 to our victories in North Africa. . . . In intelligence terms Rommel could be compared to a man accustomed to going around at
will and in broad daylight but suddenly forced to grope round in the pitch dark.[75]

On July 9, following sensitive consultations with British intelligence that
remain classified, Major General George Strong, chief of the US Military Intelligence Division, informed General Marshall that it was "highly desirable
that [Fellers] should come home for consultations." Washington followed
Menzies's instruction that the official record should offer no explanation for
the premature recall of the American military attaché other than "with the
reorganization of the Middle East Command it appears that Colonel Fellers'
usefulness . . . has ceased."[76] In view of the extraordinary level of the United
States' regional defense engagement and the strategic significance of the Middle East, the "usefulness" of the most knowledgeable American military attaché in the theater having abruptly "ceased" is a naked farce. With Major
General Strong's approval, following Fellers's return to Washington he was
assigned to the Office of Strategic Services where he directed military intelligence and defense-engagement preparations for Operation Torch.

CONCLUSION

Colonel Donovan and Major General Strong commissioned Fellers to produce a classified study on the main insights for American defense-engagement operations that could be drawn from his assignment in the Middle
East. The study encapsulated Fellers's military attaché work in Cairo as well
as his effective defense-engagement contributions to Operation Torch and
the Allies' crucial victory in the North African Campaign.[77]

The Great Desert Campaign began with the initial drive of the Italians from
Libya in September 1940 and continued until the rout and debacle of the Axis
forces in the fall of 1942.

At stake in these extensive operations were the Suez, the eastern Mediterranean, and the priceless Middle East. These last two goals have been fought over for thousands of years, for the Middle East, known to most as the Near East, is the true crossroads of the world. It is the bridgehead to three continents now at war, and is one of the most important strategic areas in the world.

It now has a new importance; it contains the last great oilfield outside the Western Hemisphere that is still in the hands of the Allied Nations. Our shortage of shipping necessitates the full use of the wells and refineries in the Middle East for the fuelling of our navies, supply ships, trucks and mechanised vehicles, and airplanes.

With this great bridgehead safely in our hands, not only can we supply ourselves with this lifeblood of modern war, but we can keep open our best supply route to Russia. At the same time, from airbases in northern Persia, we can bomb the rear of Hitler's armies and his supply routes to the Russian front.

Airplanes and personnel can be flown into the Middle East from America; the fuel is close at hand. Consequently, shipping requirements for this theatre are greatly reduced. As long as we hold securely the Egyptian-Libyan desert, Palestine, Syria, Iraq, and the Persian Gulf, we have a theatre from which we can achieve vital objectives, with the least expenditure of means.

It is an objective worthy of the most costly and desperate campaign. The Kaiser for a quarter century dreamed of dominating this strategic area. The British fought 4 years in World War I to gain it; and even at that time the oil there was only one of the prizes that went with its capture. Mussolini intended one day to add it to his new Italian Empire. It was in his mind when he sent Marshall Graziani lumbering across the Libyan-Egyptian border in the first phase of the great campaign. Ludendorff wrote in his memoirs that the future of the next war might be decided in North Africa, and that he who controls the great African deserts controls the Middle East.[78]

After he returned to Washington, Fellers was also ordered to give a private briefing to President Roosevelt on his military-liaison work with the British Middle East Command. Consistent with his trenchant reporting from Cairo, Fellers argued persuasively for a robust and expeditious increase in the United States' regional defense engagement with the British armed forces. According to Roosevelt's secret memorandum of conversation, "Colonel Fellers was very pessimistic as to the ability of the British to hold the

Nile Delta and the Suez Canal [without a major increase in America's defense engagement]. He had estimated that General Rommel would penetrate the British positions by the last of August."[79] Two months after the classified briefing in the White House, President Roosevelt awarded Fellers with the Distinguished Service Medal in recognition of his extraordinary contribution to the United States' defense engagement with Great Britain.

During the period of Fellers's Middle East mission, the balance of economic and military power shifted irrevocably from Whitehall to Washington, and thus transformed the United States into the prime power in the global order. Between 1940 and 1942, defense engagement ascended rapidly from the low regard in which it had previously been held to become a major element in the conception and conduct of international military relations. Fellers's defense-engagement operations changed the balance of power in the Middle East, and they exerted formative agency on the Second World War's most powerful strategic partnership. Miraculously, Churchill's prime ministership had started at the same time as a momentous and British-led revolution in cryptography and signals intelligence.[80] No war fighters had previously operated with such a comprehensive understanding of their ally's and their enemy's order of battle, logistics, dispositions, and objectives as the Allied and the Axis commanders who fought the North African Campaign for control of the Middle East. Uniquely among the 125 American military attachés posted worldwide during the war, for six months Colonel Fellers was simultaneously both Washington's and Berlin's prime defense-intelligence source on "the most secret data on military affairs in the Middle East."[81] The consequences of Fellers's witting and unwitting actions during the North African Campaign place him among the twentieth century's most influential agents of change in the significance and practice of defense engagement via military attachés.

Britain's present-day defense-engagement strategy tasks its practitioners with five governing objects: (1) develop understanding of national security requirements; (2) prevent conflict or enable victory if circumstances make it impossible to avoid conflict; (3) develop capability, capacity, and interoperability; (4) promote prosperity; and (5) build and maintain access and influence.[82] To varying degrees, Bonner Fellers contributed to the United States' realization of all the above strategic objectives. We should, however, not overlook that in doing so he came close to accidentally handing victory in the North African Campaign to the Afrika Korps. Like deterrence, defense engagement occasionally exerts its greatest influence in the more "shadowy regions of human understanding" and is potentially a double-edged sword.[83] A complex and important case study in wartime defense engagement, Fellers's remarkable military-attaché mission demonstrates the primacy of practical knowledge as an indispensable prerequisite of influential power.

NOTES

1   MoD and FCO, "UK's International Defence Engagement Strategy" (London, 2017).

2   Dwight D. Eisenhower, *Philippine Diary* [original] (January 1936–January 1940), and *Philippine Diary* [typescript] (December 1935–January 1940), Eisenhower Diaries and Memorabilia, Kevin McCann Papers, 1918–1981, Dwight D. Eisenhower Presidential Library, Abilene, KS.

3   MoD and FCO, "UK's International Defence Engagement Strategy," 10.

4   Michael Howard, *The Mediterranean Strategy in the Second World War* (London: Greenhill, 1993), 9.

5   Winston S. Churchill, statement to press corps, August 22, 1942, PREM 4/71/4, Churchill Archive, Cambridge, UK (CAC).

6   Franklin D. Roosevelt, "Fireside Chat," nationwide radio broadcast, December 29, 1940), accessed November 26, 2018, https://www.presidency.ucsb.edu/node/209416.

7   John Darwin, *The Empire Project: The Rise and Fall of the British World System, 1830–1970* (Cambridge, UK: Cambridge University Press, 2009), 511.

8   Memo, Col. J. Anderson, acting assistant chief of staff, War Plans Division (WPD), for chief of staff (CofS) Gen. George Marshall (November 12, 1940), "National Policy of U.S."; Col. Anderson prepared an analysis of CNO Adm. H. Stark's memorandum for Gen. Marshall: Memo, Col. J. Anderson, WPD to CofS, "National Policy of U.S" (November 13, 1940), WPD 4175–15, Record Group (RG) 165, US National Archives and Records Administration, College Park, MD (NARA II).

9   Martin Gilbert, *Winston S. Churchill*, vol. 8, *Never Despair, 1946–1965* (Hillsdale, MI: Hillsdale College Press, 2013), 416.

10   WSC to Eden, November 5, 1942, PREM 4, 27/1, The National Archives (TNA), Kew, UK.

11   James Leutz, ed., *The London Journal of General Raymond E. Lee, 1940–42* (Boston: Little Brown, 1971), 144–145.

12   H. Montgomery Hyde, *The Quiet Canadian: The Secret Service Story of Sir William Stephenson* (London: Constable, 1989), 155.

13 Captain John Godfrey, "Godfrey Report," 1941, ADM 223/84, TNA.

14 Hyde, *The Quiet Canadian*, 153.

15 Memorandum, Major D. Morton to Colonel E. Jacob (December 18, 1941), Item 2, Folder 463, Box 145, Churchill Papers, CAC.

16 Donovan served as coordinator of information (July 11, 1941–June 13, 1942) and director, Office of Strategic Services (June 13, 1942–October 1, 1945).

17 Maurice Matloff and Edwin M. Snell, *Strategic Planning for Coalition Warfare, 1941–1942* (Washington, DC: Center for Military History, 1990), 253.

18 Lieutenant Colonel Amoss to Major Bruce, July 20, 1942, Records of COI/ OSS, RG 226, NARA II.

19 MI6, British Security Coordination, *The Secret History of British Intelligence in the Americas, 1940–1945*, ed. William S. Stephenson (London: St. Ermin's Press, 1998), xxv.

20 MI6, *The Secret History*, 16.

21 Wayne S. Cole, *America First: The Battle against Intervention, 1940–1941* (Madison, WI: Octagon, 1953).

22 "Staff Conversations," June 1940–December 1941, PREM 3/489/1; "Anglo-American Standardisation of Arms Committee," June 1940–August 1940, PREM 3/457, TNA.

23 C. J. Jenner, "Turning the Hinge of Fate: Good Source and the UK-U.S. Intelligence Alliance, 1940–1942," *Diplomatic History* 32, no. 2 (April 2008): 187–188.

24 Hermione, Countess of Ranfurly, *To War with Whitaker* (London: William Heinemann, 1994), 117. In September 1941, the Western Desert Force was incorporated into the British Eighth Army. I use the term "Eighth Army" throughout in this chapter.

25 Sir Stewart Mitchell to Margaret Stewart, August 10, 1975, British Naval Intelligence Papers (MLBE), CAC.

26 Winston S. Churchill, *The Hinge of Fate*, vol. 4 of *The Second World War* (Boston: Cassell, 1950), 3.

27 Fellers to War Department (WD), April 30, 1941, Records of the Army Staff, Record Group 319, Entry 57, Box 218, (RG 319/57/218), NARA II.

28 Fellers to WD, April 22, 1941.

29 Fellers to WD, June 16, 1941.

30 H. L. Ismay, *The Memoirs of Lord Ismay* (London: William Heinemann, 1960), 84.

31 US Army Intelligence Center and School, *The Evolution of American Intelligence* (Fort Huachuca, AZ: 1973), 59.

32 Robin W. Winks, *Cloak & Gown: Scholars in the Secret War, 1939–1961* (1987, repr. New Haven: Yale University Press, 1996), 72.

33 US Army Intelligence Center, *Evolution of American Intelligence*, 41

34 Dwight D. Eisenhower, *Crusade in Europe* (New York: Doubleday, 1948), 32.

35 Jenner, "Turning the Hinge of Fate," 185.

36 US Army Intelligence Center, *Evolution of American Intelligence*, 42–44.
37 US Army, Service Record, Bonner Frank Fellers, US Army Center for Military History, Fort Lesley J. McNair, Washington, DC; West Point Association of Graduates Yearbook, *Bonner F. Fellers* (Class of 1918, Cullum No. 6136–1918).
38 CIA, Secret, *The Coordinator of Information and British Intelligence* (Langley, 1974), 61.
39 CIA, *Coordinator of Information and British Intelligence*, 63.
40 Donovan speech to the Empire Club of Canada (April 10, 1941), Box: 2B, WJD Papers, US Army Military History Institute, Carlisle, PA.
41 Secret, Foreign Office to Ambassador Lampson, Cairo (December 24, 1940), FO 371/24263, TNA. This message and others note that Donovan's travel expenses in theater "will be borne by His Majesty's Government, and Colonel Dykes has been told to draw in His Majesty's Embassy/Legations for funds which should be charged to the funds of the Assistant to the Oriental Secretary/ Passport Control Officer."
42 CIA, *Coordinator of Information and British Intelligence*, 66–71; Bradley F. Smith, *The Shadow Warriors* (London: Andre Deutsch, 1983), 40–54.
43 "Colonel Donovan's Mission File," Box 304, Hopkins Papers, Roosevelt Presidential Library, Hyde Park, NY.
44 Ranfurly, *To War with Whitaker*, 117.
45 Daniele Varè, *Il Diplomatico Sorridente* [The Laughing Diplomat], "La diplomazia è l'arte di permettere a qualcuno di fare a modo tuo" (Rome, 1938), 12.
46 Fellers to WD, various reports, April–December 1941, RG 319/57, boxes 218–222, NARA II.
47 "Staff Conversations," June 1940–December 1941.
48 Fellers to WD, December 31, 1941, RG 319/57/222, NARA II.
49 *Foreign Relations of the United States*, "The Conferences at Washington, 1941–1942, and Casablanca, 1943," Secret, United States Minutes, "Meeting of the United States and British Chiefs of Staff, 4 p.m.," December 25, 1945, Document 54.
50 Ranfurly, *To War with Whitaker*, 117.
51 Fellers to Military Intelligence Division (MID), January 6, 1942, RG 165/14/10, NARA II.
52 Charles M. Baily, *Faint Praise: American Tanks and Tank Destroyers during World War II* (Hamden, CT: Archon, 1983), 32–51.
53 Sir Stewart Mitchell to Margaret Stewart, August 10, 1975.
54 Italics added by writer; Winston S. Churchill, *The Second World War*, 1-vol. ed. abridged (London: Cassell, 1959), 568. "Seemingly inexplicable" is a deliciously sly reference to Ultra intelligence's ability to reveal the reason why Rommel appeared to have second sight in his battles with the British Army from December 1941 until June 29, 1942. In 1959, Ultra signals intelligence was still a highly classified secret.

55   Robert J. Hanyok, *Eavesdropping on Hell: Historical Guide to Western Communications Intelligence and the Holocaust, 1939–1945* (Fort Meade, MD: National Security Agency, 2005), 12.

56   Hans-Ott Behrendt, *Rommel's Intelligence in the Desert Campaign* (London: Irwin, 1985), 146.

57   Paolo Monelli, *Mussolini: An Intimate Life* (London: Thames & Hudson, 1953), 9–10.

58   David Kahn, *Hitler's Spies: German Military Intelligence in World War II* (Cambridge, MA: Da Capo, 2000), 195.

59   Churchill, *The Hinge of Fate*, 3.

60   Fellers to MID, February 18, 1942, RG 165/14/10, NARA II.

61   Louis Kruh, "British-American Cryptanalytic Cooperation and an Unprecedented Admission by Winston Churchill," *Cryptologia* 13, no. 2 (1989): 123–134 at 126.

62   Jenner, "Turning the Hinge of Fate," 171.

63   Churchill to Menzies, April 13, 1942, HW1/537, TNA.

64   Draft liaison protocol, April 25, 1942, WO 201/2158, TNA.

65   Bruce Norman, *Secret Warfare: The Battles of Codes and Cyphers* (Newton Abbot, UK: David & Charles, 1989), 127.

66   Menzies to Churchill, April 26, 1942, HW 1/537, TNA.

67   Menzies to Churchill, June 10, 1942, HW 1/636, TNA.

68   Menzies to Churchill, June 10, 1942.

69   Churchill to Menzies, June 11, 1942, HW 1/636, TNA.

70   Menzies to Churchill, June 12, 1942, HW 1/636, TNA.

71   Menzies to Churchill, June 14, 1942, HW1/652, TNA.

72   Menzies to Churchill, June 16, 1942, HW1/652, TNA. Menzies's analysis was partly correct: In September 1941, the Italian *Servizio Informazione Militare* (SIM) had purloined the Black Code book from the US embassy in Rome, made a copy, and then returned it without detection. *Chiffrierabteilung*'s cryptographers decrypted the Black Code in December 1941.

73   Churchill to Menzies, June 16, 1942, HW1/652, TNA. The Second Washington Conference had the cover name "Argonaut" and ran June 20–25, 1942.

74   Marshall to US Military Attaché Office, Cairo, June 21, 1942, RG 218, NARA II.

75   Behrendt, *Rommel's Intelligence*, 167, 225.

76   Strong to Marshall, July 9, 1942, appendix to "A Chronology of the Cooperation Between the SSA and the London Office of GCCS," RG 457, Box 940, File 2714, NARA II.

77   War Department, Secret, "Notes and Lessons on Operations in the Middle East," *Campaign Study* no. 5 (January 30, 1943): 1.

78   Erich Friedrich Wilhelm Ludendorff (April 9, 1865–December 20, 1937) was a German general, the victor of the Battle of Liège and the Battle of Tannenberg.

From August 1916, his appointment as quartermaster general (*Erster General-quartiermeister*) made him the leader (along with Paul von Hindenburg) of the German war efforts during World War I until his resignation in October 1918, just before the end of hostilities.

79 Matloff and Snell, *Strategic Planning for Coalition Warfare*, 297.

80 Ralph Bennett, *Ultra and Mediterranean Strategy, 1941–45* (London: Hamish Hamilton, 1989), 25.

81 Behrendt, *Rommel's Intelligence*.

82 MoD and FCO, "UK's International Defence Engagement Strategy," 30–35.

83 Michael Howard and Clive Rose, "The Future of Deterrence," *RUSI Journal* 131, no. 2 (1986): 10.

"A Word Here and a Phrase There"
Major General Maurice A. Pope and the Canadian Joint Staff Mission, Washington, 1942–1944

Douglas E. Delaney

Much useful work . . . is possible by means of informal discussion.
If we are precluded from asking direct questions [of the Combined
Chiefs of Staff] it is not necessary for us to remain completely in the
dark. Security is never absolute and what with a phase here and a
word there, together with what we are officially told, not only can
the general picture of the moment be built up but also an intelligent
forecast can be made of things that are to come.
—Major General Maurice Pope, diary, March 31, 1943

Major General Maurice Pope was in Washington a week before he received written confirmation of his mandate. He went to Washington, as
he recorded in his memoir, "without instructions and armed only with a
pencil and some blank sheets of paper" and a vague notion that he was to
learn what he could about Anglo-American strategic direction of the war
effort and keep his government informed about it. The written guidance
that he received from the Canadian Cabinet War Committee on March
11 did not much clarify how he was to do that: "Major-General Maurice
Pope [is] appointed as representative of the [Canadian Cabinet] War
Committee in Washington for the purpose of maintaining continuous
contact with the U.K.-U.S. Combined staffs and Combined Planning

Committees and to represent the War Committee before the Combined Staffs when questions affecting Canada were under consideration."[1] His task was by no means an enviable one. For one thing, he was not a member of the Combined Chiefs of Staff (CCS), and the government of Canada had as little interest in CCS membership (for fear it would lead to demands that Canada do more for the war effort) as the Americans and British had in granting it.[2] But Canadian decision-makers did want to know about strategic deliberations in which the dominion had a direct stake and, of course, they insisted on the right of representation when such matters were being discussed. Lacking any formal affiliation with the CCS, Pope, who was confirmed as the chairman of the tri-service Canadian Joint Staff Mission (CJSM) in June 1942, had to rely on less direct means for getting the job done—personal relationships, off-line discussions, and careful readings of whatever papers the CCS allowed him to see.

He was well suited to the task by training and experience, though.[3] The son of a career civil servant, Pope grew up in high political circles with high political people, whose manners and work habits rubbed off on him. His father, Sir Joseph Pope, had been private secretary to Prime Minister John A. Macdonald and, later, Canada's first undersecretary for external affairs (1909–1925); and his Francophone mother came from one of the most prominent political families in Quebec. Powerful people never awed Maurice Pope. Like his father, he pursued a life of service, only Pope the younger chose the military instead of the civil. He graduated from McGill University in 1911 with a degree in engineering, volunteered for the Canadian Expeditionary Force in 1915, served on the Western Front, and then joined the small Canadian permanent force when the war was over. In addition to his service on the Canadian general staff and in several military districts during the 1920s and 1930s, Pope also spent a good deal of time in the United Kingdom. He passed through the staff college at Camberley (1925–1927), worked in the War Office (1931–1933), and attended the Imperial Defence College (1936). He understood the British Army and had many useful and close relationships with important British Army officers, a few of whom were in Washington when he arrived, and most of whom he could tap for information and guidance when he needed it. He spoke their "language." And while his connections with the United States and its armed forces were not nearly so deep, by the spring of 1942 he had already served twelve months as the army member of the Canadian Section of the Canada-US Permanent Joint Board on Defence (PJBD), a role that allowed him to make valuable friends of several American soldiers and diplomats.

Pope's temperament was also an asset for his CJSM post. He was more staff officer than battlefield general, more diplomat than soldier. Field command was just not for him. Peers and subordinates described Pope as a "brilliant staff officer" and "great administrator," but one who had "no aspirations of field command."[4] None of his superiors seems to have considered him for formation command either, not even his primary patrons, Harry Crerar and Ken Stuart, both of whom were wartime chiefs of the general staff (CGS). Pope's rise in rank was almost entirely based on his abilities as a staff officer. The influential Jack Pickersgill, Prime Minister W. L. Mackenzie King's private secretary, described Pope as the "best educated and informed of the [Canadian] generals," capable of assimilating vast amounts of information and making sound assessments and recommendations.[5] Pope was also something of a workaholic. His diaries reveal long and occupied days, and the rare complaints that do appear in the pages tend to be about periods of inactivity: "I am not very busy, and more is the pity."[6] For someone who had to survive on scraps of information here and corners of conversations there, the penchant to work persistently was a plus. One had to be attentive to falling scraps and loose lips. Family obligations did not distract him much. Like many men of his day, he was not a particularly warm or involved family man. Bird sightings appear more frequently in his diary than do entries about his own children, who in later years remembered their father as "reserved" and "difficult," and someone around whom one had to "watch their p's and q's."[7] Even so, Pope was positively courtier-like in his professional life, and that served him well. All in all, he was practically tailor-made to his work with the CJSM in wartime Washington—intellectual, dignified, politically minded, personally reserved, polite, professionally forthright (in an inoffensive way), and fully unflappable.

The CCS with which Pope was to maintain "continuous contact" was the product of a December 1941 agreement between the United States and Great Britain to combine their strategic staffs—the American Joint Chiefs of Staff (JCS) and the British Chiefs of Staff (COS)—and do the bulk of the work in Washington.[8] (See Figure 5.1.) There, the British COS were represented by the British Joint Staff Mission (BJSM), headed by Field Marshal Sir John Dill and which kept in constant contact with Whitehall. The CCS

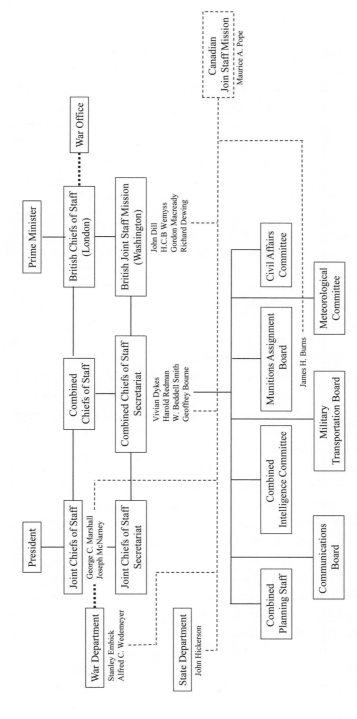

Figure 5.1. Pope's Connections to the Combined Chiefs of Staff, 1942–1944

comprised a secretariat of American and British officers, and several committees or boards that planned and set priorities for the global war effort, all in accordance with consensus guidance from the CCS. The Combined Planning Staff and the Combined Intelligence Committee were the first to be established, and they tended to drive the work of the other committees and boards—the Military Transportation Committee, the Munitions Assignment Board, the Communications Board, the Meteorological Committee, and the Civil Affairs Committee. Canada had no representation on any of them. This was not a sore spot for the Canadian government, which understood that "full and formal Canadian membership could not be obtained."[9] It simply was not practical, as Pope explained: "The possible psychological advantage that would accrue from the inclusion of the representatives of the lesser nations would be more than outweighed by the retardatory [sic] effect of such a step on the pace of the central machinery of direction."[10] Still, the Canadian government wanted, and received, Anglo-American assurances that Canada did have "the right of representation, when any question that affected Canada was under consideration." But in practice Canada was not called into the CCS often. Only once did Pope or his successor sit in on a CCS meeting, and this was on June 15, 1942, to discuss the North Atlantic Ferry Route.[11] Pope, as a result, did most of his CJSM work not at the top of the CCS but at the level of the secretariat and the subordinate committees.

His position may have been ill-defined, but he understood what he had to do: "It was clear enough to me that my task was, in some way, to establish and maintain contact with the Combined Chiefs of Staff and their subordinate committees or agencies, to the end that, above all other duties that might fall to me, I might keep Ottawa informed as to trends in the overall direction of the Allied war effort."[12] And he wasted little time in establishing the contacts and networks that would allow him to do just that.[13] His first stop after his arrival on March 6, 1942, was the Canadian Legation annex, where he met with the Canadian minister, Leighton McCarthy, whom Pope knew through his father and with whom he remembered having "many a good talk over old times, when [McCarthy] had sat in the House of Commons . . . just after the turn of the century."[14] It made sense to start at "home" before knocking on any British or American doors. McCarthy was the senior representative of the King government in Washington and he had some useful American associations of his own, not least of them his friendly relationship with President Franklin Delano Roosevelt. McCarthy also gave Pope some office space in the Legation annex. But the minister was a man of seventy-two years and waning energy in 1942, which meant that much of the initiative and hard work of the legation owed mostly to younger diplomats, starting with Hume Wrong, who was the ministerial counselor in Washington when Pope arrived. The forty-seven-year-old Wrong described McCarthy as "a nice chap, but too ignorant and too old to learn. . . . A six hour day in a four day week is about all he can handle."[15] Pope quickly surmised the same and came to the conclusion that Wrong was the de facto head of the legation, whose previous service in Washington (1927–1937) had garnered him contacts all over the city. Wrong was also the driving force behind the foreign policy approach known as the *functional principle*, whereby a middle power like Canada should have a say in those areas in which it made the greatest contribution or had the greatest stake. As Pope described it: "Hume Wrong was strongly pressing the view that the status of a country such as Canada should be closely related to its function and as our munitions production promised to reach important proportions, [for example,] so should our role in its assignment."[16] Some things were worth banging one's fist on the table, others were not; and it was important to understand which was which, as Pope did. For these and other reasons, he kept in close touch with Wrong. And when Wrong left Washington in May 1942, Pope established similarly close ties with Wrong's successor, and future Canadian prime minister, Lester "Mike" Pearson, whom he knew well from their time in London at the beginning of the war, when Pope was the chief of staff at Canadian Military Headquarters (CMHQ) and Pearson was counselor to the high commissioner.[17]

Establishing informal communication channels with British military types was, in many ways, easier than doing so with Canadian diplomats because Pope knew so many of them already, and, even with new acquaintances, he had the same military education and similar service experiences in both war and peace. At the top of the BJSM was the gentlemanly John Dill, whom Pope had first met when he hosted Dill during a 1930 visit to Quebec City. Like most people who worked with Dill, Pope admired the field marshal for his intelligence and tact: "Apart from his remarkable intelligence, which enabled him to see through the most intricate of problems, Sir John Dill had, in addition, the rare gift of understanding."[18] People liked

Dill for his fair-mindedness and even temper. His relationship with the US Army chief of staff, General George C. Marshall, is well documented and considered by many scholars to have been one of the most crucial associations of the Allied war effort.[19] Dill was good with the dominions as well. He understood them. He had served on the Canadian Corps staff for seven months during the First World War and he had instructed scores of dominion officers while at Camberley and the Imperial Defence College. Pope recalled that Dill would "invite the heads of the Dominion Missions . . . to meet with him at the start of the weekly BJSM meetings preparatory to the afternoon sessions of the [CCS], when he would tell us what he could. . . . His suave comments on men and things were a delight to hear. My feelings for him soon grew into those of affection, and I mourned him when he died [in November 1944]."[20] Pope's diary is peppered with accounts of short visits and encounters with Dill, whose assistance and counsel Pope sought when coordinating something on behalf of the Canadian COS or when matters had reached a particular impasse, but most of Pope's BJSM dealings were at a level just below Dill.

The first person he visited from the BJSM was Major General H. C. B. Wemyss, who was in charge of the British Army staff and the BJSM chief of staff. Pope and Wemyss had missed each other at Camberley (where the latter was two years ahead of Pope) and the Imperial Defence College (where he was two years behind), but they knew of each other, and Pope had met with him during an "informal and exploratory" visit to Washington in January 1942.[21] Three months later, Wemyss did Pope the great favor of furnishing the Canadian with an office in the Public Health Building, which was where the CCS held their weekly meetings and where the BJSM and the joint Anglo-American secretariat were accommodated. He also offered to provide Pope access to whatever CCS papers could be made available. Wemyss was even prepared to integrate Pope fully into the BJSM. At one of their earliest meetings, he asked Pope to fill in as the acting chief of staff for the BJSM during Wemyss's upcoming absence. But Pope demurred, ostensibly on the grounds that his duties on the PJBD consumed too much of his time, but in reality because Pope and the government he represented did not want to be "absorbed" into the British delegation. In the event, Wemyss was soon replaced by Lieutenant General Gordon N. Macready, whom Pope knew well from both Camberley and the War Office and whom Pope regarded as "the mainstay of the British Joint Staff Mission."[22] He came to rely on Macready when he needed information, or as much of a steer in the right direction as Macready could give, and Macready often vented to Pope when frustrated in his dealings with the Americans. They did not always agree—Macready tended toward centralized decision-making for the British Commonwealth and Pope guarded closely Canadian autonomy—but they only ever argued, as Pope put it, "as good and old friends."[23] Another good and old friend in the BJSM was Major General Richard "Dick" Dewing, who was Dill's deputy. Pope and Dewing had been at Camberley at the same time, and Dewing had served for two years as an instructor at the Royal Military College of Canada at Kingston (1927–1929), so they knew each other well and kept up a warm correspondence over the years. They were so close, in fact, that Dewing's wife cabled Pope shortly after their son was killed in North Africa: "Tony killed 29th May [1942]. Please help poor Dick."[24] Dewing allowed Pope to see very nearly all CCS papers that made their way to his desk, and so did another useful British contact, Brigadier Vivian Dykes, the British secretary of the CCS Secretariat.[25] Pope did not know Dykes from previous service, but, understanding that Dykes worked at the nexus of the American and British strategic staffs, Pope made Dykes one of his earliest office calls in March 1942. It helped that Pope knew one of Dykes's principal staff officers, Colonel Geoffrey Bourne,[26] from his time at CMHQ in London. Unfortunately, Dykes died in a January 1943 airplane crash and was replaced by the rigid and less accommodating Brigadier Harold Redman, but even that relationship settled into something workable.

Pope's American contacts required a bit more cultivation. The Americans, as he noted, were a little less forthcoming than the British—"while our British friends told us all they felt they could, the Americans were as mute as their highly-prized little-neck clams."[27] American reticence was not simply due to a lack of long-standing relationships or even familiarity, although that was part of it. It was also due to a strain of institutional suspicion, on the part of the American armed services, of British actions and intentions, coupled with a tendency to lump the dominions in with Britain on most matters.[28] Pope grasped these proclivities and he was prepared to work around them. He was also not without a few helpful "ins" from his time on the PJBD. First among these was Lieutenant General Stanley Embick, whom Pope described as the "'Solon' of the U.S. Army" at the time.[29]

Not a young man, the sixty-four-year-old Embick was recalled to service only days after his 1941 retirement to be chief of the Joint Strategic Survey committee on the US Joint Chiefs of Staff. He also became the senior US Army member of the PJBD, which is where Pope met him in March 1941. They worked together closely on matters pertaining to the combined US-Canadian defense of North America and they regularly dined and exchanged views on matters of Allied strategy. Embick was also close with George Marshall, which was handy. Once in Washington, Pope also got to know Embick's son-in-law, Brigadier General Alfred C. Wedemeyer, the chief of strategy and policy in the Operations Division of the War Department. The relationship with Wedemeyer was not nearly as chummy as the one with Embick, but Wedemeyer was extremely well placed. He worked directly for Dwight D. Eisenhower, who ran the Operations Division until leaving Washington in June 1942 for his appointment as Commanding General European Theatre of Operations. Another PJBD contact with whom Pope developed a very close relationship was career diplomat John D. "Jack" Hickerson. The secretary of the American section of the PJBD and the head of the State Department's Division of British Commonwealth Affairs, Hickerson had served previously in Ottawa (1925–1927), so he was well informed on Canada and sympathetic to the Canadian position. "Lunched with Hickerson" (often with Embick) appears often in Pope's diary. Finally, Pope was also acquainted with Marshall, with whom he coordinated several high-ranking visits (the Canadian chief of the general staff or the commander of First Canadian Army, for example), and Marshall's deputy, Lieutenant General Joe McNarney. Pope's networks were extensive and they proved useful. As Pearson remarked at the time, Pope has "established admirable relations with the top U.S. and U.K. Service people."[30]

He needed them. From his position on the periphery of the CCS, it was not always easy to know what was happening. In July 1942, for example, he noticed, that "a strange silence had come over the Public Health Building."[31] As he recorded in his diary and in a message to Ottawa, "During the last ten days or so there has been a good deal going on behind the scenes both here and in London under the head of strategic planning. What is in the wind I have been unable to find out and am unlikely to for yet some considerable time."[32] But he did find out. "Putting together every scrap of information that had come [his] way," and in consultation with his Australian and New Zealand counterparts, Pope came to the "fairly obvious deduction that a descent on Africa was being contemplated," which was true.[33] This was the time of the London talks about Operations Gymnast (the proposed invasion of North Africa) and Sledgehammer (a proposed operation to gain a 1942 lodgment in Northern France). To confirm his assessment, he sought out Dykes, to whom he read aloud an appraisal he had drafted for the Canadian CGS: "And though [Dykes] told me no facts his attitude to my words confirmed my hunch."[34] This was how Pope operated. This was how he *had* to operate because he was not in the CCS loop. He only learned of the January 1943 Casablanca meeting between Churchill, Roosevelt, and their military staffs, for example, when he heard it on the radio news. Sometimes Pope even had to pry information out of Ottawa. He did not even know about a similar Roosevelt-Churchill meeting at Quebec in August 1943 until the Canadian CGS contacted him in London (where Pope had been visiting CMHQ and the War Office) and ordered him to return immediately to Canada for the conference that was scheduled to take place in less than two weeks.[35] Being left out of Canadian loops could be equally challenging: "They really do not send me down very much useful gossip from Ottawa. I have to dig it out myself."[36]

Dig he did, anywhere and everywhere—at lunches, in corridor conversations, during office calls, and in the CCS papers that he was allowed to see—and he managed to assemble fairly accurate appraisals of what was happening and, more important, what was going to happen. The BJSM noticed: "Pope keeps more closely in touch with current problems than probably any of the other Dominion service representatives; he comes daily and makes touch with his various contacts in the [Public Health] building and undoubtedly gleans a lot of information which would otherwise not be available to him."[37] To start, Pope picked up entirely on Anglo-American tensions and disagreements with regard to strategy.[38] "While the political heads of the United Kingdom and the United States never weary of reiterating their complete accord as to the objects they are determined to achieve," Pope reported to Ottawa, "their respective military advisers are not of one mind as to the sequence of the steps to be taken, nor as to the weight of the operations to be put in hand."[39] Central to the disagreement was the Mediterranean theater of operations, which British military planners (and Pope) believed critical to wearing down the enemy before any "madcap venture" to cross the English Channel and engage with a still-strong German Army in Western Europe. American military planners, on the other hand, wanted to destroy quickly the German Army in Northwest Europe: "The Mediterranean and the Indian Ocean [therefore] did not commend themselves as areas of primary importance."[40] Pope confirmed these conflicting points of view in numerous one-on-one conversations with Macready, Dewing, and Dykes on the British side and Embick and Wedmeyer on the American side.[41] He also sensed that disunities internal to the American Joint Chiefs of Staff complicated matters—the US Navy, with its eyes "glued to the Pacific" and unable to appreciate the value of exploiting opportunities in the Mediterranean, and the US Army, whose principal "grievance is that the North African venture has retarded when they may come to grips with the main German armies." Pope also assessed that there was a definite "difference between the British and American military minds," which complicated combined strategy:[42] "The [British] hold that war is an art subject to broad principles rather than a science constrained by hard and fast rule. The United States High Command on the other hand always appear[s] to be loath to vary a programme or scheme of things laid down," which prevented them from taking "quick advantage of a favourable opening, such as, for example, the rapid [and recent] disintegration of Italian military strength." It should come as no surprise that Pope, schooled as he was in the British Army way of doing things, agreed completely with British strategic opinion.

Keeping in constant touch with key players was important because things in war changed rapidly. In mid-November 1943, Pope thought that the Quebec agreements to withdraw seven Anglo-American divisions from the Mediterranean and work toward a spring-1944 invasion of Northwest Europe meant that the agenda for the upcoming Tehran conference between Roosevelt, Churchill, and Soviet premier Joseph Stalin would focus mainly on political and postwar matters—until he spoke with Macready. While threatening Pope with "immediate execution" if he breathed a word to the Americans, Macready went on to indicate that the Canadian "was somewhat off the track. The old pull between the Mediterranean and the Channel is as great as ever. . . . The British see the former theatre as the one in which they and the Americans can make an effective contribution during the next number of months."[43] Pope agreed: "At best (in my view at the worst!) Overlord cannot get going for six months. Are we to twiddle our fingers for all this time without subjecting the enemy to every possible pressure?" Pope sent his assessment of the ongoing tensions and the impending delay for Overlord to the Canadian COS in Ottawa, who were in the process of increasing the size of Canada's Mediterranean contingent from a division to a corps and trying to figure out how best to involve the remainder of First Canadian Army in the invasion of Northwest Europe.[44] They undoubtedly appreciated his perspective.

Not all of Pope's projections were quite so spot-on, however. Some reflected the uncertainty of the time and circumstance in which they were made. In March 1943, for example, he best-guessed that American forces in the Pacific would move to capture the Truk Islands from the south, once they had consolidated Guadalcanal and New Guinea, in the event the Truk Islands were only attacked by air on February 17–18, 1944, and bypassed. Not until after the Quebec conference of August 1943, when the Pacific strategy became clearer and his sources began to speak more freely, did Pope piece together and report to Ottawa on the two-pronged strategy for the Pacific—the US Navy island-hopping toward Japan in the South-Central Pacific, and the US Army advancing toward the enemy home islands in the Southwest Pacific.[45] In September 1943, he predicted confidently, and wrongly as many others did, that Marshall's appointment as the supreme Allied commander for the invasion of Northwest Europe was all but a sure thing.[46] At the same time, he also passed on predictions that the German armies in Italy would not make a determined stand south of the Pisa-Rimini line and that Rome would be in Allied hands "within six weeks." Such were the hazards of making predictions on scraps of information at times when even the people making the decisions were not sure what they would do. Some inaccuracies notwithstanding, Pope's projections were still useful for giving Ottawa decision-makers an idea of what their Anglo-American allies were thinking.

As head of the CJSM, Pope also had to look out for all Canadian service interests, even those of the Royal Canadian Air Force (RCAF) and the Royal Canadian Navy. One such instance involved American and British air-force authorities determining Canada's requirements for aircraft—without consulting Canadians. Pope first learned of the problem on June 27, 1942, when Air Commodore George Walsh, the senior RCAF officer in the CJSM, advised him that an Anglo-American memorandum of agreement purported to set the strengths of air forces in Canada.[47] A perturbed Pope set out immediately to remedy the situation and assert Canada's right to be consulted. He was careful not to escalate the matter too quickly, though. His first visit, on July 1, was to Dykes, who agreed that "the matter of the insertion of strengths of C[ana]d[ia]n forces in the strategic deployment table had been badly done. There should have been prior consultation. He suggested that I should speak to the Field Marshal [Dill]," which was exactly what Pope wanted to hear.[48] It was better that he be invited to consult with Dill than to have to go over the heads of Dykes and Macready. The latter course would almost certainly have burned bridges. But because the matter was so connected with continental defense, Pope told Dykes that he would first like to speak with his American counterpart in the CCS Secretariat, Brigadier General W. Beddell Smith. Much to Pope's surprise, Smith expressed his "complete agreement that in matters of this kind there should invariably be consultations with Dominion representatives and assured me that in the future this would be done."[49] This was not the sort of response he expected from the Americans. Smith surprised Pope further when he sent the deployment table and the aircraft figures back to the Combined Staff Planning Committee with the demand that the views of Canada and the other dominions be taken into account. This was all good, but the way American planners handled the matter was irksome and more in line with what Pope understood to be the typical US view of Britain and the dominions. The American planners did not ask the Canadians what they thought. Instead, they asked the British COS in Whitehall to answer questions such as: What are the dominion air strengths? What do the dominions see as their air requirements? What is the rate of dominion aircraft production? What commitments have the British COS made to the dominions regarding air forces? And what control would the American JCS have over Canadian aircraft production?[50] The British COS answered the questionnaire and sent their responses to the BJSM, which, under Dill, endeavored to put things right. In fact, the field marshal invited the representatives of Canada and the other dominions to comment on the British COS responses, and he presided over the meeting in which they presented their thoughts and objections. As a former chief of the Imperial General Staff, and as someone who understood what the dominions would be contributing in terms of military forces and industrial output, Dill knew better than to make a pointless stand on some RAF–US Army Air Forces (USAAF) fiat for distributing aircraft. The Canadians raised eighteen objections to the British COS document, all of which Pope said could have fit under one heading: "our rejection of their right to lay down our air needs in Canada or, for that matter, anywhere else."[51] In the end, the Canadians got fourteen of the amendments they were looking for, plus an understanding that the BJSM and the British COS would be submitting only their own opinions to the CCS, not those of the dominions.

This set an important precedent and more or less resolved the immediate concern of aircraft allocation, but sometimes the British and the Americans still had to be reminded not to take decisions that directly affected the dominions without consulting the dominions. While visiting the CCS offices in October 1942, for example, Pope found out, "more or less by accident," that British joint planners "had shifted the basis of Canadian Army figures for the Strategic Deployment Table 1944." And it was full of errors as a result. Again, Pope started low and worked his way up the escalation ladder to make his point. He spoke first with Bourne, who admitted that the matter had slipped his attention and agreed with the corrections that Pope proposed. Next, Pope spoke very frankly to Dykes about "the casual way in which British Planners took it upon themselves to monkey with Canadian figures without calling us in to discuss them. . . . It should not be necessary for us to act like sleuths."[52] He made the same point to Macready a few days later and noted, not long after, that his efforts were "beginning to bear fruit." The indications were "that the B.J.S.M. is bestirring in order to see that we are consulted on questions that directly concern us."[53] He had to speak with his American colleagues in October 1942 about the "airy, not to say arrogant nonchalance" of the USAAF when it came to aircraft deployments and priorities.[54] And in June 1943, he had to put straight Redman, Dykes's rather headstrong and inflexible successor, that he would not be submitting Ottawa-bound reports on meetings with Dill for screening before they went out: "I would be damned if I would screen any of my reports through him."[55] This confrontation might have soured things, so Pope invited Redman to dinner a week later and "had a pleasant evening." He also reflected that it had done their relationship some good: "I should have done this months ago."[56]

It was not that his colleagues intentionally left Pope or the other service representatives of the CJSM out of the loop; they just forgot from time to time because they had more than enough serious strategic issues to fill their days. On the same day that Pope confronted Dykes with the matter of the Strategic Deployment Table for 1944, for example, Dykes was dealing with many weighty matters, including a Combined Staff Planning Committee paper on unity of command, ongoing Anglo-American disagreements on strategy, and the inability of the British high command to reach consensus on a strategic bombing proposal by chief of the air staff, Air Chief Marshal Sir Charles Portal.[57] Canadian concerns about counting field formations and aircraft assignments simply ranked lower in priority. Pope understood that, but it was frustrating nonetheless.

One area in which Canadians expected both higher priority and greater influence was munitions assignment. Canada had produced nearly one-third of all shells fired by the British Expeditionary Force during the First World War and, in 1942, there was every indication that Canadian factories would churn out similarly great quantities of munitions, plus other armaments, including aircraft, fighting vehicles, and motor vehicles.[58] Simply put, Canada wanted a say in how the munitions it produced would be assigned, something that was very much in line with the functional principle. Thus, in March 1942, the Cabinet War Committee decided to seek full membership on the Munitions Assignment Board (MAB) in Washington, where it would do the bulk of its assignment business.[59] First, the Canadians sought the backing of the British government before approaching the Americans—a lining up of the diplomatic ducks, as it were. The British COS and the government in Whitehall were initially reluctant to lend their support, but they eventually came around, with the help of some useful coaxing from Macready.[60] With British support thus secured, the Canadians approached the Americans. The Canadian prime minister even made a direct appeal to the president, who, according to King, agreed "that Canada ought to be represented on a [Munitions Assignment] Board which would have Britain and the U.S. on it."[61] But the whole thing got held up with Harry Hopkins, the chairman of the MAB and one of President Roosevelt's closest advisers, who resisted because he thought Canadian membership would complicate the working of the board and, worse, lead to similar demands from other dominions. A number of diplomatic efforts during the summer of 1942 eventually removed the American objections.[62] Not least of these initiatives was Pope's approach to American major general James H. Burns, the senior executive officer on the MAB. Pope proposed, at Macready's suggestion it should be noted, that Canada be granted full membership on the board, but only "when the assignment of Canadian production was under consideration."[63] Hopkins accepted the compromise and, in August, Burns sent an official letter to Pope (which Pope helped to draft), inviting Canada to join the MAB under those terms.[64] Pope was jubilant.

His happy mood soon soured, however. The project crashed on the shoals of internal Canadian jealousies and suspicions. At the heart of the issue was C. D. Howe's Ministry of Munitions and Supply and its unwillingness to cede control over how Canadian-produced munitions would be assigned. Until the establishment of the CCS and the MAB, civilians at Munitions and Supply had been solely responsible for both the procurement of American produced goods and how Canadian-made munitions were assigned. They saw no reason to give up those monopolies to the armed services. As Howe put it, "Canadian [service] orders represent only a very small fraction of production now in hand. . . . I cannot see what possible interest the three Services can have in the allocation of Canadian production ordered direct from the British Government, the U.S. Government, or, in fact, any Allied Government."[65] The trouble was that American authorities did not see it that way. Quite the contrary, they could not see what possible interest anyone but a man of military rank could have in setting priorities for various theaters and campaigns. Burns's letter had been addressed to Pope, after all, not Howe. It was a Canadian military officer for the board or nothing and, in the end, the Canadian government chose nothing. Pope thought this a badly missed opportunity. Owing to the "continuous intrigue of Munitions and Supply," as he put it, the Canadian government decided to leave the assignment of Canadian munitions to Howe's ministry and to do it from Ottawa, which, on the surface, sounds like an assertion of Canadian sovereignty, but it was not.[66] As Pope recalled ruefully, munitions-assignment meetings in Ottawa "were always attended by British and American assignment officers from Washington who, having agreed among themselves as to the appropriate disposition of our production . . . had little difficulty in inducing our Board to accept their recommendations."[67] The Canadian undersecretary for external affairs shared Pope's sense of disappointment:

"We . . . came within range of reaching what might have been a satisfactory relationship to it [the MAB]. Differences of views between our own Ministers prevented this relationship from ever being formalized."[68]

Occasionally, Pope had to take the initiative, as he did when it came to possible Canadian participation in the Pacific theater of war. He was twigged to the idea when Churchill, during a speech to a joint session of the US Congress on May 19, 1943, promised full British support in the Pacific once the war in Europe had been brought to an end. To that point, no one in Ottawa had made any mention of Canadian army troops deploying to the Far East, but surely, the politically attuned Pope thought, the Canadian government would wish to have some influence on how matters in the Pacific were resolved: "I should imagine that we, too, intend to play some part in the eventual liberation of the Pacific. . . . If this be so, I suggest that the time may already be opportune to give some thought as to how we may most effectively contribute. . . . It would be useful were we to send a fully representative number of observers to serve with Australian and New Zealand Forces in the South West and South Pacific theatres respectively."[69] The rationale was simple: "We know little, if anything, about jungle fighting and I should imagine it would be useful for us to build up a small store of knowledge and experience in this form of warfare."[70] Initially, there was little interest or enthusiasm for the idea in Ottawa, but Pope nevertheless continued to discuss tactical-technical observer missions with the British, Australian, and New Zealand staff missions in Washington, so he was ready when Canadian interest in the Pacific region gained momentum after the Quebec conference of August 1943.[71] There was soon talk of even working with American forces in the region.

Pope quickly put together an observer program that resulted in eighty-eight Canadian officers being sent to a variety of Allied forces in the Far East—twenty-three to British forces in Burma and India, fifty-five to American forces in the South-Central and Southwest Pacific areas, eleven to the Australian forces, and two to New Zealand forces.[72] As long as it was unclear *where* the Canadian government would commit the Canadian Army Pacific Force (CAPF), this shotgunning of observers all over the Pacific was actually the prudent thing to do. Concentration of the observer effort with American forces came later, toward the end of 1944, when it seemed certain that the CAPF would deploy under American operational command.[73] The program did what it was supposed to do. The observers recorded what they learned about the terrain they encountered, the equipment they used, the tactics they employed, and the allies they encountered, and they sent many detailed reports back to Ottawa.[74] All of it helped drive the training and formation of the CAPF. As an example, because observers found that the American staff system was so different than the British one in which most Canadian staff officers had been schooled, the Canadian Army hurriedly sent sixteen officers for training at American staff colleges. With workable American staff connections, the CAPF, based on the 6th Canadian Division, would be better able to plug efficiently into whichever American corps it might be attached to.[75] The war ended in August 1945, before the CAPF could be deployed, but measures to assemble a US Army–compatible division would not have been nearly so far along had Pope not anticipated the requirement for observers back in May 1943.

Pope sometimes played the role of helpful middleman. One such opportunity presented itself in early May 1943, after a conversation with Jack Hickerson. During the journey back from a PJBD meeting in Montreal, Hickerson suggested that "sooner or later the general position would be such as to enable [the United States] to drive the Japanese out of Kiska and Attu [islands in the Aleutians]. When that time came Canadian troops, in his view should participate."[76] The proposition intrigued Pope. He had never considered the Japanese threat to the West Coast to be a serious one, but he could see that there was currency in cooperating with the Americans for the capture of Attu or Kiska—political currency at home with the concerned inhabitants of British Columbia, and diplomatic currency with the United States. He duly reported the substance of his Hickerson conversation to the Canadian CGS, who took a genuine interest, making inquiries with Major General George R. Pearkes, the commander of Canada's Pacific Command, as to the feasibility of participating in Aleutian operations, and instructing Pope to discuss the scope of any such operations with Marshall. Pope poked around and confirmed that the Americans had very definite plans for the capture of both islands and, at his meeting with Marshall on May 13, he learned that an assault on Attu was already underway. Marshall attentively took note of what Pope had to say about Canadian interest in future operations and promised to consult with General John L. DeWitt, commanding general of the US Western Defense Command, about the Canadians joining in. Eleven days later, Pope received word that Marshall had "authorized General Dewitt to confer immediately with General Pearkes of the Canadian Pacific Command to work out the details of the arrangement."[77] The Americans would have preferred to leave it at that—dealing military to military—without having to bring in political authorities. That was certainly the advice that Hickerson proffered to Pope. When it came to the US Army, Hickerson pointed out, "Dealing with civilians just was not in their book."[78] They had done all their British business through Dill and, given their druthers, they would have preferred to deal only with Pope on Canadian military matters. The Canadian government did not see it that way, however, which is why Pope received a May 27 telegram with Cabinet War Committee direction that he should approach Marshall about the possibility of having the American war secretary, Harry Stimson, send an invitation for Canadian participation in Aleutian operations through the Canadian minister of national defense, J. L. Ralston.[79] Understanding American reluctance to operate in this manner, Pope took the request to the Pentagon, where he spoke with McNarney (because Marshall was out). McNarney initially balked, much as predicted, but Pope was able to convince him that no harm or snags would ensue. McNarney's only caveat was that the invitation not "go anywhere near the State Department," which was ironic because it was a State Department official (Hickerson) who had approached Pope in the first place.[80] In the end, preparations for Canadian participation in the capture of Kiska went smoothly and the 13th Canadian Infantry Brigade Group and elements of the 7th US Division assaulted the island on August 15, 1943, only to find that the Japanese had evacuated Kiska several days before the attack. Pointless as the Aleutian operations may seem in retrospect, the exercise of readying a Canadian formation for operations with the Americans yielded lessons that helped with the assembly of the CAPF, and it did send positive signals to the Americans, and to Canadian citizens, about Canada's interest in continental defense.

Pope left Washington in September 1944, having accomplished much in nineteen months. In addition to the examples outlined in this short essay, he helped administer the mutual-aid program (Canadian lend-lease), he worked on Allied chemical weapons policy, he handled urgent Canadian requests for war stocks like ball bearings and hospital ships, he helped work out command and control arrangements for the Canada-US First Special

Service Force, he supported government efforts to involve Canadian forces in Mediterranean operations in 1943, he helped smooth over command arrangements and the legal status of US forces in Newfoundland, and he spent an inordinate amount of time trying to find suitable accommodations for the expanded CJSM, which had outgrown its initial home in the Canadian Legation annex. For someone not even affiliated with the CCS, he also kept the Canadian COS and the government remarkably well informed on what the senior Allied leadership was thinking and doing. He was a well-trained and well-educated staff officer who understood what was being said—in hallways as well as in meeting rooms—and capable of anticipating requirements and making reasonable projections. He was politically adroit enough to guard the Canadian interest and sensitive enough to do so without offending his American or British allies. As he put it, he knew how "never to be in the way, and yet never out of it."[81] And he had the good sense to heed his own advice of "patience, more patience, and still more patience."[82] Getting ruffled was not part of his repertoire. The Canadian government got good service from Pope, but it must be said that this should have been the expectation. With two years at Camberley, one year at the Imperial Defence College, two years at the War Office, and a year on the PJBD, it had invested heavily in training and educating an army officer that no one seemed to think suitable for field command. In Washington, and with the CJSM, Pope found his place. Armies are complex machines that require many different officer cogs—and generals—to make them run. They cannot all be Montgomerys or Pattons. Sometimes it takes a Pope.

NOTES

1 Library and Archives Canada (LAC), RG 24, vol. 5184, Extracts from Minutes of Meeting of Cabinet War Committee held March 11, 1942. Pope's mandate was soon refined in that he was to be a representative of the Canadian chiefs of staff (COS), not the Cabinet War Committee. He reported directly to the Canadian chief of the general staff (CGS).

2 On Canadian reluctance to share in strategic decision-making, see Adrian Preston, "Canada and the Higher Direction of the Second World War, 1939–1945," *Royal United Service Institution Journal* 110, no. 637 (1965): 28–44.

3 The most thorough and authoritative study of Maurice Pope is Claude Leblanc, "Maurice A. Pope: A Study in Military Leadership" (PhD diss., Royal Military College of Canada, 2016).

4 Directorate of History and Heritage (DHH), J. L. Granatstein, *The Generals* Interviews, MGen. M. P. Bogert, Donnington, UK, September 8, 1991; N. Elliott Rodger Interview, Ottawa, May 21, 1991; and Joseph Pope (son) Interview, Toronto, March 15, 1991.

5 DHH, Granatstein, *The Generals* Interviews, J. W. Pickersgill Interview, Ottawa, May 21, 1991.

6 LAC, Maurice Arthur Pope Fonds (Pope Papers), vol. 1, Diary (Pope Diary), March 8, 1943.

7 DHH, Granatstein, *The Generals* Interviews, Joseph Pope Interview, Toronto, March 15, 1991; W. H. Pope (son) Interview, Uxbridge, Ontario, Apr 3, 1991; and Mrs. Simonne Fletcher (daughter) interview, Ottawa, May 23, 1991.

8 On the Combined Chiefs of Staff (CCS) organization, see Mark A. Stoler, *Allies and Adversaries: The Joint Chiefs of Staff, the Grand Alliance and U.S. Strategy in World War II* (Chapel Hill: University of North Carolina Press, 2000). For a Canadian perspective on the CCS, see C. P. Stacey, *Arms, Men and Governments: The War Policies of Canada 1939–1945* (Ottawa, Canada: Queen's Printer, 1970), 159–184.

9 LAC, RG 24, vol. 5184, Extracts from Minutes of Meeting of Cabinet War Committee held March 11, 1942.

10 LAC, Pope Papers, vol. 1, Pope Diary, 1943, Washington Report, March 31, 1943.

11 Stacey, *Arms, Men and Governments*, 165; and LAC, Pope Papers, vol. 1, Pope Diary, June 16, 1942. Pope's successor as chairman of the CJSM was Major General H. F. G. Letson.

12 Maurice A. Pope, *Soldiers and Politicians* (Toronto, Canada: University of Toronto Press, 1962), 184.

13 LAC, Pope Papers, vol. 1, Pope Diary, see March 6–31, 1942.

14 Pope, *Soldiers and Politicians*, 184.

15 Wrong to his sister (Marga), April 27 and June 8, 1941. Quoted in J. L. Granatstein, "Hume Wrong's Road to the Functional Principle," in *Coalition Warfare An Uneasy Accord*, ed. Keith Neilson and Roy A. Prete (Waterloo, Canada: Wilfrid Laurier University Press, 1983),

16 Pope, *Soldiers and Politicians*, 184.

17 Wrong and Pearson actually switched posts.

18 Pope, *Soldiers and Politicians*, 190.

19 On the Dill-Marshall relationship, see Alex Danchev, *Very Special Relationship: Field-Marshall Sir John Dill and the Anglo-American Alliance, 1941–44* (London: Brassey's, 1986). Dill's successor as chief of the imperial general staff (CIGS), Field Marshal Sir Alan Brooke, considered one of his "most important accomplishments during the war" that he was able to convince British prime minister Winston Churchill that Dill should be the man to head the BJSM in Washington. Arthur Bryant, *The Turn of the Tide, 1939–1943* (New York: Doubleday, 1957), 227.

20 Pope, *Soldiers and Politicians*, 191.

21 LAC, RG 24, vol. 4573, Pope to Keenleyside (assistant undersecretary for external affairs), January 24, 1942.

22 Pope, *Soldiers and Politicians*, 185.

23 Pope, 185.

24 LAC, Pope Papers, vol. 1, Pope Diary, June 16, 1942.

25 LAC, Pope Papers, vol. 1, Pope Diary, March 16, 1942, and April 11, 1942. Dykes also allowed similar access to the heads of the Australian and New Zealand missions in Washington.

26 Later, General Sir Geoffrey Bourne.

27 Pope, *Soldiers and Politicians*, 192.

28 Mark A. Stoler, "The American View of British Mediterranean Strategy, 1941–1945" in *New Aspects of Naval History* (Annapolis, MD: Naval Institute Press, 1981), 325–39. See also General Alfred C. Wedemeyer, *Wedemeyer Reports!* (New York: Henry Holt, 1958), 97–192.

29 Pope, *Soldiers and Politicians*, 162.

30 Pearson to Crerar, March 24, 1944. Quoted in LeBlanc, "Maurice A. Pope: A Study in Military Leadership," 235.

31 Pope, *Soldiers and Politicians*, 202.

32 LAC, Pope Papers, vol. 1, Pope to COS, Pope Diary, July 27, 1942.

33 Pope, *Soldiers and Politicians*, 202.

34 Pope, 202. Although Pope records the essence of this meeting in his diary entry for July 28, 1942, it cannot have taken place on that day because Dykes was still en route back from London. It likely took place sometime July 29–30, although Dykes makes no mention of it in his diary. See Alex Danchev, ed., *Establishing the Anglo-American Alliance: The Second World War Diaries of Vivian Dykes* (London: Brassey's, 1990), 182–183; and LAC, Pope Papers, vol. 1, Pope Diary, August 5, 1943.

35 LAC, Pope Diary, August 5, 1943.

36 LAC, Pope Papers, vol. 1, Pope Diary, March 16–18, 1943.

37 The National Archives (TNA), CAB 122, Joint Staff Mission to War Cabinet Offices, May 18, 1944. Also quoted in J. L. Granatstein, *The Generals: The Canadian Army's Senior Commanders in the Second World War* (Toronto, Canada: Stoddart, 1993), 215.

38 See LeBlanc, "Maurice A. Pope: A Study in Military Leadership," 239–47.

39 LAC, Pope Papers, vol. 1, Pope Diary, Washington Report, March 31, 1943.

40 Pope attributed the statement "madcap venture" to the vice-chief of the imperial general staff (VCIGS), Lieutenant General Archibald Nye, whom Pope visited at the War Office on August 5, 1943. Nye and Pope were friends who were classmates at Camberley and who served together at the War Office in the 1930s. LAC, Pope Papers, vol. 1, Pope Diary, entry for August 5, 1943; and Washington Report, March 31, 1943.

41 See for example various entries at LAC, Pope Papers, vol. 1, Pope Diary, May 4, 1942, November 11–12, 1942, January 2, 1943, May 12, 1943, November 19, 1943, April 10, 1943, and December 3, 1943.

42 LAC, Pope Papers, vol. 1, Pope Diary, The Quebec Conference, August 1943.

43 LAC, Pope Papers, vol. 1, Pope to COS, Pope Diary, November 19, 1943.

44 LAC, RG 112, vol. 33864, JS 306, under McQueen to CNS, CAS, CGS, November 19, 1943. On the negotiations for Canadian involvement in Operation Overlord, see C. P. Stacey, *The Victory Campaign: Operations in North-West Europe, 1944–1945* (Ottawa, Canada: Queen's Printer, 1966), 28–47.

45 LAC, Pope Papers, vol. 1, Pope Diary, Notes on Certain Aspects of the War Situation, September 30, 1943.

46 LAC, Pope Diary, September 30, 1943.

47 See LAC, RG 112, vol. 33864, JS 1, July 11, 1942; JS 03, July 13, 1942; Pope to NDHQ, July 14, 1942. On the matter of the Arnold-Portal-Towers Memorandum of Agreement (on air matters), see Pope, *Soldiers and Politicians*, 197–200.

48 LAC, Pope Papers, vol. 1, Pope Diary, July 1, 1942.

49 LAC, Pope Diary, July 1, 1942.

50 LAC, Pope Diary, July 1, 1942.

51 Pope, *Soldiers and Politicians*, 199.

52 LAC, Pope Papers, vol. 1, Pope Diary, October 22, 1942.

53 LAC, Pope Diary, October 29–30, 1942.

54 LAC, Pope Diary, October 29–30, 1942.

55 LAC, Pope Diary, June 17, 1943.

56 LAC, Pope Diary, June 23–24, 1943.

57 Danchev, *Establishing the Anglo-American Alliance*, 217–218.

58 In the event, Canada produced 7.9 percent of all mentions for the British Commonwealth as well as 20 percent of all motor vehicles produced by the United Kingdom, the United States, and itself. Stacey, *Arms, Men and Governments*, 167.

59 See LeBlanc, "Maurice A. Pope: A Study in Military Leadership," 252–259.

60 LAC, Pope Papers, vol. 1, Pope Diary, April 23, 1942.

61 W. L. Mackenzie King Diary, April 1942. Quoted in Stacey, *Arms, Men and Governments*, 167.

62 LAC, Pope Papers, vol. 1, Pope Diary, April 23, 1942; and June 30, 1942.

63 LAC, Pope Papers, vol. 1, Pope Diary, July 10, 1942; and August 4, 1942. See also Pope, *Soldiers and Politicians*, 201.

64 LAC, Pope Papers, vol. 1, Pope Diary, August 5–7, 1942. The letter was actually addressed to Pope.

65 Quoted in Stacey, *Arms, Men, and Governments*, 171.

66 LAC, Pope Papers, vol. 1, Pope Diary, August 21, 1942.

67 Pope, *Soldiers and Politicians*, 201. This was also Macready's impression: "There was rarely any difficulty in getting our requisitions met, or in agreeing

on a fair distribution at assignment meetings." Gordon Macready, *In the Wake of the Great* (London: William Clowes and Sons, 1965), 170.

68 Quoted in Stacey, *Arms, Men, and Governments*, 171.

69 LAC, Pope Papers, vol. 1, Pope Diary, May 24, 1943. The most authoritative source on Canadian observers in the Pacific is Andrew Brown, "Stepping in New Directions: The Canadian Army's Observer Program in the Asia Pacific Region," *Canadian Military History* 28, no. 1 (Spring 2019).

70 DHH, 314.009 (D51), Pope to Chief of the General Staff, December 18, 1943; and AHQ Report No. 16, Amendment No. 2, January 7, 1953, 1.

71 LAC, Pope Papers, vol. 1, Pope Diary, June 24, 1943; August 3 and August 10, 1943; December 14, 1943.

72 Brown, "Stepping in New Directions."

73 DHH, AHQ Report No. 16, July 15, 1947.

74 See, for example, DHH, 322.009 (713), Interim Report No. 1—Canadian Officers [on] Aust[ralian] Attachment (26 April–26 May), dated June 7, 1944; DHH, 322.009 (D714), Observations of New Zealand Expeditionary Force in the Pacific, Report No. 1, April 11, 1944; DHH, 322.009 (D142), File, Reports and Returns: Australian Jungle Warfare Liaison Letters; DHH, 322.009, Observers Reports on CWPA Attachments 1944–45, Report of Canadian Officers Attached to 27th Infantry Division, United States Army, for the Saipan Operation, 15 June to 9 July 1944, dated September 28, 1944; and DHH, 171.009 (D51), Consolidated Report of Canadian Army Officers Attached to South East Asia Command, February 12, 1945.

75 DHH, AHQ Report No. 16, July 15, 1947.

76 LAC, Pope Papers, vol. 1, Pope Diary, May 4–8, 1943. Hickerson claimed to have "no knowledge whatsoever" of any such plans, but that denial hardly seems credible. At the time, the Seventh Division of the US Army was only three days from invading Attu, and the commanding general of the US Western Defense Command, General John L. DeWitt, had already briefed Major General George R. Pearkes, the commander of Canada's Pacific Command. C. P. Stacey, *Six Years of War: The Army in Canada, Britain and the Pacific* (Ottawa, Canada: Queen's Printer, 1966), 495–500; and Galen Perras, *Stepping Stones to Nowhere: The Aleutian Islands, Alaska, and American Military Strategy, 1867–1945* (Vancouver, Canada: University of British Columbia Press, 2003).

77 LAC, Pope Papers, vol. 1, Pope Diary, Marshall to Pope, May 24, 1943.

78 Pope, *Soldiers and Politicians*, 217.

79 LAC, Pope Papers, vol. 1, Pope Diary, May 27, 1943.

80 Pope, *Soldiers and Politicians*, 218.

81 LAC, Pope Papers, vol. 1, Pope Diary, August 9, 1943.

82 Pope, *Soldiers and Politicians*, 188.

6

Japanese Military Attachés during the Second World War
Major General Makoto Onodera as a Spymaster

Ken Kotani

Introduction

The first-ever Japanese military attaché was the Japanese Imperial Army captain Kazukatsu Fukuhara, who was sent to China in February 1875. From that point until the outbreak of the Pacific War in December 1941, the number of attaché posts had been gradually increased. By 1941, the Japanese Army had military attachés in thirty-three countries, and the Japanese Navy had their naval attachés placed in twenty-five countries.[1] During the war, the army and navy left their attachés in neutral countries—such as Switzerland, Sweden, Portugal, Argentina, and Chile—and ordered them to collect information on Allied strategy and operations. Institutionally, the army and naval attachés were a part of the staff of the Japanese embassies abroad, but they tended to have their own office outside the embassies and communicated directly with the army and navy headquarters in Tokyo using military/naval-attaché cipher telegrams and radio communications. The attachés recognized that Japanese diplomatic ciphers were fragile and vulnerable to decryption by Allied code-breaking. Therefore, they were negatively disposed to sharing secret information with Japanese diplomats abroad using such methods of communication.

The military and naval attachés sent hundreds of reports to Tokyo during the war, but they did not influence the army and navy's grand strategy. Kyoichi Tachikawa points out the reasons as follows: (1) midclass officers abroad were not influential in the army or navy, (2) information and intelligence were usually neglected by the operations bureau, (3) deep-seated suspicion against foreign countries, (4) attachés were regarded as lei-surely sinecure posts in both the army and the navy.[2] Lieutenant General Hiroshi Oshima, military attaché (1934–1938) and ambassador to Germany (1939–1938, 1940–1945), was exceptionally influential in the army because he could engage with key Nazi leaders, and his pro-German reports coin-cided with the Japanese Army's grand strategy for the Tripartite Pact. How-ever, during the war it became clear that his reporting and his appreciation of events overlooked key weaknesses in German national and military power.

Oshima's reports were generally not accurate, although there were sev-eral accurate reports sent from military attachés overseas during the war. Major General Makoto Onodera, military attaché to Sweden, was one of them. Onodera became relatively well known in Japan for his intelligence contributions as a military attaché in Sweden (1940–1945), which is written about in his wife's, Yuriko Onodera's, memoir *Baruto-kai no Hotori nite (On the Edge of the Baltic Sea)*[3]; using the book, the Japanese Broadcast-ing Company (NHK) produced a TV documentary program on Onodera in 1985. In the book, Onodera is described as a splendid intelligence of-ficer but also as an unfortunate one who had been neglected by the Army General Staff. That lack of attention by the Army General Staff has subse-quently led to a common view of Onodera as an "aloof hero in Sweden," now the accepted interpretation of his impact on higher Japanese planning and assessments of the war in Europe. This chapter will attempt to rectify that "aloof" image and argue for a more nuanced understanding of the de-fense-engagement activities of this particular man.

About Makoto Onodera

Onodera's activities were highly valued and well regarded in general. Hun-garian military historian Ladislas Farago offered a fair appreciation of his work in *The Game of the Foxes*, and Farago's US counterparts also praised him as "one of the most distinguished intelligence officers" after the end of the war.[4] Hiroyasu Miyasugi wrote that the Army General Staff acted

almost immediately on some of Onodera's reports from Sweden and transferred them to the frontline troops in Southeast Asia.[5] After the war, Onodera was captured and held in Sugamo Prison, Tokyo, and interrogated
by the Strategic Services Unit of the US War Department in 1946. In 1945,
the Allied forces had already obtained information on Onodera from Karl
Heinz Krämer, a German Abwehr agent. From the information Krämer
provided, and other Japanese sources, American intelligence officials recognized that Onodera had been Japan's spymaster in Europe during the
war.[6] Onodera also wrote a memoir, *Onodera Makoto Kaisouroku*, which
is now available at the military archives in the National Institute for Defense Studies. The record of the secret telegrams between Onodera and
Tokyo, deposited at the National Archive in Kew, England, and which
were intercepted by the British Government Cypher and Code School
(GC&CS),[7] paint a clear picture of a capable and industrious intelligence
officer. The Japanese Army burnt most of its attaché reports at the end of
the war, so the GC&CS record is very critical to understanding this particular Japanese military attaché's operations during the war. In addition to
the Japanese and Allied documents, there are several intelligence reports on
Onodera in the Swedish archives. According to Bert Edström, the Swedish secrecy law was altered in 2016 and the time limit is now ninety-five
years in matters of intelligence and defense. This law has been applied to
documents that are relevant for the present project and resulted in some
Onodera-related documents in the Swedish archives not being released or
being released only partly.[8]

In Latvia and Shanghai

Onodera intended to be an intelligence officer from the time he was in the
Military Preliminary School. At that institution, he studied German eagerly
and continued his competency in that language during his time at the Army
Academy.[9] After that, he was sent to Nikolaevsk during the Siberian Intervention in 1921 and he became interested in the Russian language. He
turned his hand to mastering Russian when he was posted to the Army War
College. His proficient skills in both German and Russian enabled him to
build up his broad intelligence network afterward. However, he was a close
associate of a Japanese Army Russian specialist, Major General Toshiro

Obata, a leader of the group *Koudou-ha* (Pro-Emperor Faction).[10] Most group members had been relegated by the army mainstream to inferior posts after 1935. That persecution was the catalyst for the February 26 Incident, an attempted coup d'état by the Koudou-ha in 1936. Onodera's association with Obata and the Koudou-ha cast a dark shadow on Onodera's professional career in the army.

From 1935 to 1939, Onodera worked as a military attaché in Latvia and then concurrently in Estonia and Lithuania as well. His acquaintance with Wilhelm Saarsen, an Estonian military attaché in Latvia, led him to build up a useful network of sources among the Estonian military authorities.[11] The chief of Estonian intelligence, Colonel Richard Maasing, introduced Onodera to German admiral Wilhelm Canaris in order that the Japanese intelligence officer and the German admiral could share their views on the German-Japanese strategic relationship in Berlin. The information from Canaris via Maasing proved to be enormously advantageous to Onodera's later work in Stockholm.

After his time in Europe, Onodera returned to Japan as a Russian specialist in the Intelligence Section of the Army General Staff; he then moved to Shanghai as a staff officer in the command of the China Expeditionary Army. His duty was to collect information to help bring about an early conclusion to the Sino-Japanese war, which was the general aim of the Russian Section. He obtained information from an ex-member of the Japanese Communist Party, Tosuke Yoshida, who maintained an exceptionally good rapport with the Resisting Japan and Saving Nation Association (*Juri Jiuguohui*) and also had relations with a faction led by Chen Lifu, a Chinese anticommunist close to General Chiang Kai-shek. Onodera had tried to resolve the war directly through the Sino-Japanese summit meeting supported by the Japanese prime minister Fumimaro Konoe and Lieutenant General Masakazu Kawabe, the chief of staff of the China Expeditionary Army. However, there was no coordination between Onodera and the China Section in the Army General Staff. Onodera's activities came to be criticized by the chief of the China Section, Colonel Sadaaki Kagesa—who was plotting to build Wang Zhaoming's government in China—and Onodera was finally frustrated by Kagesa's strenuous opposition.[12]

Military Attaché in Sweden

In October 1940, Onodera was appointed military attaché in Sweden and arrived at Stockholm the next January. It seems that he was given 40,000 kroner a year as a secret fund by the Army General Staff, though in 1944 he was provided a much larger budget of 360,000 kroner to support his work.[13] According to his wife's recollection, there were three deputies to assist him in his work, and Tokyo made an extensive remittance in that year to further expand the resources at his command.[14] Onodera possessed a huge network of intelligence sources while he was in Sweden. Using the connections made during his days in the Baltic states, he established his network mainly in Swedish, Finnish, Polish, and Estonian intelligence circles. The motivating and connecting force at the base of the network was a common fear of the Soviet Union, thus ensuring that a substantial amount of information regarding Russian military and political activities would be shared. Moreover, Onodera received valuable information on the Allied forces from this network, sometimes using his extensive funding to buy information on British and American topics. Sources such as the former Soviet diplomat in Sweden, Dimitrievsky, also supplied information to Onodera.[15] Since Dimitrievsky was a White Russian, some say his cooperation with Onodera stemmed from his anti-Soviet sentiments, while others say he had covert connections with the Soviet government and was assigned to monitor Onodera's various activities.[16]

In Swedish military intelligence, Major Carl Petersén was one of Onodera's main intelligence sources. Petersén had collected an impressive range of important information from foreign diplomats and military attachés in Sweden. Onodera deepened his partnership with Petersén to get information regarding the Swedish General Staff Office, which presumably had information on Allied matters that Japan's military could find useful. Onodera also had contact with Colonel Kenpf, the chief of the Operational Department of the Swedish War Office, and with General Thoernell, the commander in chief of the Swedish Armed Forces.

As regards the Finnish intelligence sources for Onodera, Karl Heinz Krämer mentions that the Japanese attaché was able to access products produced by the Colonel Reino Hallamaa organization. The decoding department of the Finnish Defense Forces was established by Hallamaa under the chief of intelligence of the Finnish Defense Forces, Colonel Aladar Paasonen, both of whom Onodera met in the Baltic states prior to the war and with whom he reestablished contact in 1940. The Finns succeeded in breaking some Soviet codes, as well as Allied and others' codes. Moreover, Hallamaa controlled an extensive Finnish espionage ring operating mainly in Russian territory adjoining Finland and in the Baltic states, and also had contact with leaders of various Resistance groups.[17] Karl Heinz Krämer, a German Abwehr agent, reported that he regularly received the Hallamaa information through Onodera, including material from decoded telegrams to Stockholm from the Swedish diplomatic establishments abroad; copies of codebooks for diplomatic codes of various countries and for Soviet tank and antiaircraft codes; and information on Soviet military capabilities from the Finnish Defense Forces. In fact, most of the information Onodera sent to Tokyo was obtained through decoded secret Soviet communications.[18] That link to Finnish intelligence sources was not unique to Onodera.

At that time, the most accurate and informative frontline code-breaking against the Soviet Union was done by Hallamaa's decoding department in the Finnish Defense Forces, with whom Major Eiichi Hirose, the Japanese assistant military attaché to Finland, cooperated regularly and closely. Also, the Hungarian military's code-breaking organization was a great help to Major Shinta Sakurai, the Japanese attaché assigned to that nation. According to Hirose, the Imperial Japanese Army had tried to establish key centers in Europe for the decoding of Soviet secret communications in Helsinki, Budapest, and Berlin, but the activities in Hungary and Berlin came to be difficult and less useful after the start of the Soviet-German war on the Eastern Front in June 1941.[19] That dislocation of code-breaking effort was one reason why the Japanese military attaché's office in Stockholm started to decode Soviet secret communications on an ever-expanding scale.

In September 1944, Onodera received critical information concerning the US and Soviet ciphers from Hallamaa in exchange for a sizeable amount of funding along with the relocation of his organization to Sweden. That relocation operation was conducted as Operation Stella Polaris. From then on, it is estimated, Onodera injected 300,000 kroner into maintaining the operations of Hallamaa and his organization.[20] Wary, however, of the veracity and accuracy of Hallamaa's intelligence on American and Soviet forces, Onodera invited Major Sakurai from Hungary to assess the information and cross-reference the claims.

One of the most important intelligence sources for Onodera was Polish military intelligence. At the center of this relationship was Major Michał Rybikowski, a skillful intelligence officer who had served as chief of intelligence for the Second Department of the Polish Defense Forces. Rybikowski was well connected to a large intelligence network that covered Soviet Russia and most capitals around Europe. At that time, he worked under a false identity, presenting himself as one "Peter Ivanov." Ivanov was given safe haven and sheltered in the Japanese Military Attaché Office as a White Russian interpreter with a Japanese passport. Onodera inherited the Polish connection from his predecessor, Colonel Toshio Nishimura. Mrs. Onodera wrote that Rybikowski proved beyond doubt to Onodera how accurate and reliable his information was. He also confided that he collected information for the Polish general staff of the commander in chief, Tadeusz Rudnicki, thus verifying the level of intelligence he was able to access for Onodera.[21] Information from Rybicowski was code-named "Bu" Information and sent to Tokyo by Onodera. The code name was created as a reference to the Polish military attaché in Stockholm, Major Feliks Brzeskwinski, an intimate friend of Onodera and senior to Rybikowski.

The information from Rybikowski included various first-rate insights into Japan's ally Germany and some of its strategic and operational dilemmas. In mid-1940, the two most important issues, of which the Japanese leadership wished to have some visibility, were related to the difficulty of Germany's landing on the British mainland and, should such an operation ever come to pass, of a large-scale German invasion of the Soviet Union. Onodera was assured of the start of the Soviet-German war from the information passed along by Rybikowski, who reported that "the German army prepared a large number of coffins in Poland."[22] The Official War Diary of the Japanese Army General Staff also mentioned that "there are quite a few telegraphs from military attachés on signs of the outbreak of the Soviet-German War."[23]

Onodera and Rybikowski's secret activities were tolerated by the Swedish authorities so long as they were aimed at the USSR, the greatest potential threat to Sweden's security. However, in German eyes, it could not be overlooked that the military attaché of Japan as an allied country was openly cooperating with a former Polish army officer. Major Hens Wagner, the chief of the Abwehr in Stockholm, requested the extradition of Rybikowski.

However, Onodera stood his ground in the face of the German officer's pressure on the Swedish government and firmly rejected the demand. The Germans then began to pressure the Swedish Army, and in January 1944 Rybikowski was sent to the Polish government-in-exile in London. Nevertheless, Rybikowski continued to provide Onodera with valuable information via Brzeskwinski. Now the Polish source became "Bu" Information both in name and in reality.

After Rybikowski's transfer, the Polish refugee government in London continued to send secret information to Onodera. According to Noburu Okabe, Onodera was informed of the Yalta secret agreement by Rybikowski's boss, Colonel Stanisław Gano, the intelligence-section chief of the Polish government-in-exile in mid-February 1945.[24] The agreement confirmed that the Soviet Union would declare war against Japan around three months after the anticipated German surrender. The US and Great Britain agreed to the Soviets' being granted control and ownership over the southern Sakhalin and Kuril Islands in exchange for critical Russian manpower and the nation's entry into the Pacific War in time for the forecast invasion of Japan. The information was crucial for the Japanese Army's grand strategy, and Onodera urgently and carefully sent the information to Tokyo. However, Onodera's report was misfiled and did not get to the proper authorities in the Japanese Army headquarters. As a result of this poor dissemination, the Soviet Union's invasion of Manchuria on August 9, 1945, was a bolt from the blue for the Japanese Army.[25]

According to the *Sankei Shimbun* newspaper, this variety of information on Yalta, and the pending involvement of the Soviet Union in the Pacific War, was intentionally ignored by the Army General Staff. There is no evidence for the disregarding of Onodera's report, and a great many records clearly indicate that Tokyo had indeed obtained the information on the secret Yalta agreement.[26] For example, Rear Admiral Sokichi Takagi wrote, "at the Yalta Conference, [the United States, United Kingdom, and USSR] decided the time limit for the Pacific War, and unless Japan surrenders before then, [the USSR] will join the war against Japan supporting the United States and Britain."[27] Naoto Yoshimi opposed the opinion as ignorant and inferred that Onodera himself did not have confidence in the accuracy of the information, and the Army General Staff in Tokyo also doubted the report.[28] Interestingly, Onodera asked Tokyo to send him intelligence reports verifying the Yalta information, but the Army General Staff replied that it had nothing special to add to Onodera's report.[29]

Concurrently, Onodera had intentionally enlarged his Polish connections. According to Krämer, Onodera told him that he was contemplating plans that would see Polish Army troops being sent to India. Onodera also thought it possible to establish a Polish intelligence network in the United States, all of which seems to have prompted him to eagerly continue closer cooperation with the Polish.[30]

Another important intelligence source for Onodera was the former chief of intelligence of the Estonian Defense Forces, Colonel Maasing, who was exiled to Sweden for the moment. As mentioned above, Maasing's intelligence network was widespread and included Admiral Canaris. In Stockholm, Maasing directed his agents in the Baltic states and the Soviet Union to provide Onodera accurate and valuable information. In return, Onodera gave Maasing's family in Stockholm significant financial aid. Maasing also brought Onodera information from the French military attaché in Sweden, Major Pierre Albert Garnier.

Garnier was a rare resource, as he was permitted to move in the higher command levels of the Allied forces as an intelligence officer under General Charles de Gaulle. Garnier's information was sent to Tokyo as "Ma" Information, named after Maasing.[31] For example, on May 11, 1944, Onodera informed the Japanese Army General Staff about the Allied forces' plan of a massive counterattack operation in Europe to open a second front. Garnier's information, therefore, revealed the invasion of Normandy almost a month before the actual event on June 6.[32] Thus, Garnier seems to have been able to get quite delicate secret information even while the British Secret Intelligence Service and the British Security Service named him "the 27th source of information" and kept watching him in order that he not be allowed to reveal secret information.[33]

A much more important source of Onodera's intelligence was Karl Heinz Krämer of the German Abwehr. MI6 had studied Krämer's movement during the war, cooperating with GC&CS. The British Security Service had also pursued Krämer, considering Onodera one of his important intelligence sources. Actually, Krämer used the code name "Josephine" to refer to Onodera, and information from Josephine to Krämer was frequently reported to British intelligence.

Krämer and Onodera exchanged information on the Allied forces. Krämer explained that their relationship was based not only on the exchange of information but also on close cooperation, and he had a good personal impression of Onodera.[34] Krämer was given valuable information regarding the Soviet codebooks, the disposition of the Anglo-American airborne units, and so forth by Onodera. Krämer paid 10,000–20,000 kroner to Onodera as a reflection of the price he was willing to pay for the difference in both quality and quantity of the information that flowed between Onodera and Krämer.[35] Krämer obtained information about the Allied forces from the Swedish military attaché in the United Kingdom, Colonel Frank Cervell, his friend Colonel Turner of the US Army, and so on, which enabled Onodera to get critical information from London. After the war, Krämer also indicated that Onodera had his own information sources in the British War Office in London, though details remain unclear.

According to the report of the British Security Service, the information given to Krämer from Onodera contained both accurate and inaccurate assessments. For example, Onodera relayed the wrong information back to Japan about the deployment of the Allied forces' army and air troops in Britain, France, Italy, and the Far East; the exact number of Allied divisions; and the British aircraft-manufacturing capacity.[36] Possibly this reporting was influenced by Kowalewski's false information, as mentioned above.

In May 1945, Krämer was taken prisoner after the German surrender and was interrogated in the United Kingdom. The full report of Onodera's activities, based on Krämer's statement, led to the imprisonment and strict interrogation of Onodera in 1946, probably because of the deep US interest in code-breaking against the Soviets in the context of the emerging Cold War.

Onodera also had extensive plans in place to collect information about the United States. On March 13, 1945, he was introduced to Colonel Elman Kirotar by his Estonian agent. Colonel Kirotar was a brother-in-law of the chief of the Russian section of Estonian military intelligence and was familiar with information-gathering against the USSR. Estonia had a diplomatic establishment in Washington where they could issue visas to the Estonians. On July 13, Kirotar was passed a code book in stamp size, plus 18,000 Kroner and 10,000 dollars as an operating fund. He planned to gather information in order to investigate the US plans for operations against Japan and the American intentions at the Potsdam Conference, among other things. It can be inferred that Onodera was interested in what the Soviet-US relationship really was, and when, or if, the USSR would declare war against Japan. Onodera was convinced that the Soviet Union would wage war against Japan but wasn't sure of the exact timing for that. Kirotar was scheduled to leave for the United States on August 12, but the whole plan was made unnecessary by the Japanese surrender, which took place before his departure.[37]

Evaluation of Onodera's Activities

Onodera's activities revealed that the Japanese military and naval attachés' main mission during the war was to collect information on the Allies and relay that intelligence to Tokyo. Ironically, however, they were not regarded as being that important for the formulation of the Japanese grand strategy. The military attachés also faced a problem in working with the Japanese embassies abroad. This point relates to the existence of the stovepipes between the army, navy, and Ministry for Foreign Affairs representatives in the embassies. As stated above, military officers were usually reluctant to share secret information with Japanese diplomats abroad and vice versa. Onodera's relationship with the Japanese minister to Sweden, Suemasa Okamoto, was also not a smooth one during the war. Okamoto reported to Tokyo that he considered Onodera to be "an ambitious intriguer" and "not helpful but dangerous for me."[38] Okamoto did not allow Onodera to engage in information-gathering with embassy resources or consent. Therefore, Onodera was forced to devote himself to constructing his own intelligence networks and was hesitant to share any information with the minister. As far as the Yalta information is concerned, Onodera did not share that with Okamoto, but with Krämer of the German Abwehr, who then transferred it to the German Foreign Office. After a long journey, the information was passed to the Japanese ambassador Oshima in Berlin by the German foreign minister Joachim von Ribbentrop. Only then could the Japanese Ministry for Foreign Affairs obtain the crucial information on Yalta.[39] If Onodera and Okamoto had shared the information in Stockholm and sent it to Tokyo simultaneously, the senior diplomats and Army General Staff would have taken the matter more seriously and spent more time examining the information.

It has also been suggested that Onodera was part of an Allied deception plan.[40] According to Onodera, he was taught how to analyze open sources by Captain Yan Kowalewski of the Polish Army General Staff, who had visited Japan in 1923 to take charge of the class on code-breaking against Russia for the Japanese Army and Navy. Since Onodera implied to Krämer that he had intelligence sources in Spain and Portugal, and since Kowalewski was resident in Lisbon, Kowalewski's ability to supply information to Onodera cannot be denied. However, it is also true that Kowalewski worked devotedly for British intelligence during the war, so the information to Onodera from Kowalewski, if indeed such a link existed, was possibly part of the Allies' deception operations.

Hiroyasu Miyasugi points out that one of Onodera's agents, Rybikowski, was also an Allied double agent.[41] His original mission was to establish an anti-German intelligence network in Sweden, and he passed over to the Germans false information about Allied planning received from British intelligence. There is a very good possibility that Onodera was exploited as a messenger to pass that disinformation to the Germans. According to the report of the Anglo-Polish Historical Committee, it is not clear whether Onodera was aware of the "game" he was a part of.[42] Also, Rybikowski sometimes provided exaggerated information ("was too inventive") to Onodera.[43] Bert Edström points out other possible areas of deception by using Swedish documents, for example, "Maj. Carl Petersén took advantage of his positive standing with Onodera to feed him deception, when war developments had made it important for Sweden to increase collaboration with Allied intelligence services."[44] It is difficult to say exactly to what extent Onodera may have realized he was a part of such Allied deception. After the war, however, he did mention that he believed he had sometimes received false information from his sources. It can be inferred, therefore, that such worries about the veracity of his intelligence reporting caused the Japanese General Staff's attitude of diffidence regarding his reports on the Yalta Conference. On the other hand, the deception operator, Guy Liddell of the British Security Service, wrote that the information about the Allied forces exchanged between Krämer and Onodera was correct and important.[45] What is clear is that further study is required on how effectively the Allies' deception worked on Onodera.

Conclusion

During the war, Onodera had built up a considerable intelligence network. First, he formed relationships with intelligence officers of the countries that felt threatened by the Soviet Union, such as Estonia, Finland, Sweden, and Poland, and exchanged information on their common threat. Then, in exchange for that information, he obtained the leverage to create another network aimed at the Allied forces, using intelligence officers such as Garnie and Krämer. Finally, he planned to build an intelligence network in the United States using Estonian and Polish agents, but that was a bridge too far, as the final stages of the war disrupted his networks and plans. Compared with the Japanese Army, which regarded the Soviet Union as a potential enemy and could not be parted from that assumption, Onodera was sharp in his aim to gather military information on the United States in spite of his career as an expert on Soviet Russia.

Major Paul Kubara in the seventh interrogation center of the US Army recalled, "[Onodera] was diligent, deliberate and intelligent as well as skeptical. He had built up his intelligence network easily and his military information was largely accurate. The activities of Onodera could be the center of the Japanese information gathering in Europe."[46] Thus, it can be said that Onodera was highly respected by the Allies as an intelligence officer. Therefore, the United States kept watch upon Onodera even after the war. In January 1953, Onodera visited Sweden for the first time since the end of the war as a staff member of the Japan-Sweden Trading Company. The visitation was relayed by the Japanese Intelligence Office in the Cabinet Secretariat to the CIA, which started an investigation into Onodera's activities in Sweden. The Americans considered it a strong possibility that Onodera would reestablish contact with ex-agents from his wartime days in Stockholm. The chief of the Swedish Army, General Carl August Ehrensward, met with Onodera, a mere citizen, and is reported to have been highly impressed with his intelligence work during the war.[47] After his death, Onodera was also decorated by the Poles for his contribution to intelligence work.

All this speaks to Onodera's information collection having been considered excellent, with any difficulties as to its value resting with the ability of the Japanese receivers of the information to appreciate its value correctly. According to Mrs. Onodera, her husband had felt that the Germans had already turned out to be inferior to the Soviets after the outbreak of the Russo-German War in 1941 and he had sent repeated messages claiming that "Japan should not wage the war against the Allies" to the Army General Staff before Pearl Harbor, only to be ignored. The Imperial Army's inclination to accept only convenient information as well as the friction between Onodera and the Army General Staff created from his Shanghai days combined to make Onodera's activities in Stockholm a lonely battle.

Nevertheless, the Army General Staff sent Onodera's information on the US Army to the forces in the southern front for the Battle of Rabaul, and that information was also received by the Navy General Staff.[48] The Operation Department of the Navy General Staff noticed Onodera's information and remarked on some of its importance. Therefore, it cannot be said that the Navy General Staff entirely ignored Onodera's information, though further research is needed to tell how the information was evaluated and utilized by the Japanese government and also to what extent Onodera recognized the possibility of his being a part of the Allies' deception operations.

NOTES

1 Ikuhiko Hata, ed., *Nihon Riku-Kaigun Sogou Jiten* [Encyclopedia of the Japanese Army and Navy] (Tokyo: Daigaku Shuppankai, 2012), 395–400, 460–463.

2 Kyoichi Tachikawa, "Wagakuni no Senzen no Chuzaibukan Seido" [Japanese military and naval attaché system before the Pacific War], *Boei Kenkyujo Kiyo* [NID Security Studies] 17, no. 1 (October 2015): 142.

3 Yuriko Onodera, *Baruto-kai no Hotori nite* [On the edge of the Baltic Sea], (Tokyo: Kyodo Tsushinsha, 1985).

4 Ladislas Farago, *The Game of the Foxes: The Untold Story of German Espionage in the United States and Great Britain during World War II* (New York: Bantam Books, 1971), 522; Thaddeus Holt, *The Deceivers: Allied Military Deception in the Second World War* (London: Weidenfeld & Nicolson, 2004), 114.

5 Hiroyasu Miyasugi, "'Zaigai Bukan Den Joho Ichiranhyo' ni miru Senji Nihon no Joho Katsudou" [A Study of Japanese intelligence activities during the Pacific War based on the "Telegram Reports List of military Attachés Abroad"], *Seikeikenkyu* 45, no. 11 (November 2009): 454.

6 CIA library, accessed July 31, 2018, https://www.cia.gov/library/readingroom/search/site/onodera; "The Security Service personal files," KV 2/243, UK National Archives (TNA). The interrogation documents are now open at the CIA website and the documents are also open at TNA.

7 Reports of Japanese Military Attachés Decrypts, HW 35/82, TNA.

8   Bert Edström's draft paper for EAJS conference, August 8–September 2, 2017, in Lisbon.

9   Onodera Kaisouroku, The National Institute for Defense Studies Military Archives (NIDSMA), Tokyo.

10 Noboru Okabe, *Kieta Yaruta Mitsuyaku Kinkyu Den* [Disappeared secret urgent telegram on Yalta Agreement], (Tokyo: Shinchosha, 2012), 91.

11 Yuriko Onodera, *Baruto-kai no Hotori nite*, 51–55.

12 Onodera Kaisouroku, NIDSMA.

13 Major General Makoto Onodera, September 25, 1946, RG226, Entry 173, Box 10, US National Archives and Records Administration (NARA). Thanks to Professor Tetsuro Kato for the NARA documents.

14 Yuriko Onodera, *Baruto-kai no Hotori nite*, 168.

15 Onodera Kaisouroku, NIDSMA.

16 Statement handed in by Kramer, June 3, 1945, HW 2/243, TNA.

17 Onodera's source, KV2/151, TNA.

18 Reports of Japanese Military Attachés Decrypts, HW 35/82, TNA.

19 Eiichi Hirose, "Signals Intelligence Activities in Finland," *Showa Gunji Hiwa* (Secret stories of Showa period) (Tokyo: Doudai Keizai Konwakai, 1987), 74–75.

20 Progress Report on Interrogation of Major General Makoto Onodera, May 31, 1946, RG65, Box 00237, NARA; The Intentions of Japanese Intelligence Services in Europe, KV2/149, TNA.

21 Ewa Palasz Rutkowska and Andrzej Tadeusz Romer, *Nihon-Poland Kankeishi* [History of Japan-Polish relations] (Tokyo: Sairyusha, 2009), 261.

22 Rutkowska and Romer, 263.

23 Gunjisigakkai Hen (Military History Society), ed., *Daihonei Rikugunbu Sensou Shidouhan Kimitsu Sensou Nisshi* [Army's secret war diary] (Tokyo: Kinseisha, 1999), 96.

24 Okabe, *Kieta Yaruta Mitsuyaku Kinkyu Den*, 297–298.

25 Strangely enough, Onodera's report on Yalta is also missing from the GCHQ file, HW 35/111. There would be three possibilities: (1) Onodera did not send the information to Tokyo, (2) GCHQ failed to capture or decode the telegram, or (3) the British government is still keeping the record closed.

26 *Sankei Shinbun* (newspaper), August 13, 1993 (evening version), October 18, 1993 (evening version); Onodera, *Baruto-kai no Hotori nite*, 148.

27 Sokichi Takagi, "Joho Tekiroku (information summary) from 1 June to 30 June 1945," NIDSMA. Takagi obtained the information from the naval attaché report from Bern (ULTRA/ZIP/SJA/1946, June 4, 1945, HW23/351, TNA).

28 Masato Yoshimi, *Shusensi* [History of the end of the Pacific War] (Tokyo: NHK Shuppan, 2013), 94.

29 Stockholm to Tokyo, February 19, 1945, HW 35/83, TNA; "Jyokyo Handan Siryou (Intelligence Reports for Situation Estimate)," NIDSMA.

30 Karl Heinz Kramer, KV 2/148, TNA.

31 The Intentions of Japanese Intelligence Services in Europe, KV2/149, TNA.

32 Intentions of Japanese Intelligence Services.

33 The MacCallum Report on Kramer, KV 2/157, TNA.

34 Statement by Kramer, September 13, 1945, KV 2/243, TNA.

35 Karl Heinz Kramer, KV 2/148, TNA.

36 MacCallum Report on Kramer, TNA.

37 Estonian Nationals, September 28, 1945, RG65, Box 00237, Folder 0001, NARA.

38 Gaimusho hen (The MOFA edited), *Nihon Gaikou Bunsho Taiheiyou Sensou Dai 3 satsu* [Documents on Japanese foreign policy, the Pacific War, vol. 3] (Tokyo: Ministry of Foreign Affairs, 2010), 1705–1707.

39 Okabe, *Kieta Yaruta Mitsuyaku Kinkyu Den*, 55.

40 Holt, *The Deceivers*, 694.

41 Miyasugi, "'Zaigai Bukan Den Joho Ichiranhyo' ni miru Senji Nihon no Joho Katsudou," 456.

42 The Report of the Anglo-Polish Historical Committee, *Intelligence Co-Operation between Poland and Great Britain during World War II*, vol. 2 (Warsaw: Vallentine Mitchell, 2005), 293.

43 The Report of the Anglo-Polish Historical Committee, *Intelligence Co-Operation between Poland and Great Britain during World War II*, vol. 1 (London: Vallentine Mitchell, 2005), 339–340.

44 Edström's draft paper, August 8–September 2, 2017, 4.

45 Nigel West, ed., *The Guy Liddell Diaries, Vol. II: 1942–1945* (London: Routledge, 2005), 226.

46 Karl Heinz Kramer, KV 2/148, TNA.

47 Makoto Onodera, January 7, 1953, RG226, Entry 214, Box 7, NARA.

48 Japanese Estimate of Allied Order of Battle, KV2/147, TNA.

7

British Defense Engagement and Defense Advisers in Kenya after Independence

Poppy Cullen

In 2017, the British Ministry of Defence (MOD) and Foreign and Commonwealth Office (FCO) published the "UK's International Defence Engagement Strategy." The strategy highlights the importance of overseas students training in British military academies, conducting British training exercises overseas, exporting defense equipment, having access, and exercising influence. Defense attachés play a key role in this, forming a "global network" to organize defense engagement.[1] Despite being presented as "a step-change in our approach,"[2] the policies advocated are in fact reminiscent of previous policies and strategies adopted by the two departments. This can clearly be seen in the case of Kenya in the decades after its independence from the British Empire in 1963. All the above were the priorities in the defense relationship with Kenya that the British government and military pursued after independence.

This chapter explores how the British defense advisers[3] appointed to Kenya after independence encouraged and sustained the military relationship between the two countries. The defense adviser was at the center of a web of defense and military connections, underpinning the wider close relationship after independence. These defense relations were based on several interlocking areas, including arms sales from Britain to Kenya, with some funding to make such purchases possible; British training of Kenyan military personnel, in both Kenya and Britain; British personnel seconded into the Kenyan military, especially in the years immediately after independence; and British soldiers conducting training exercises in Kenya. The latter in particular was a benefit found in few other places. In all these areas, the defense adviser acted to promote the relationship. Defense advisers worked with the Kenyan military to discuss requirements and aid policies, helping to facilitate arms sales, as well as working with British companies wanting to supply arms to Kenya. They wrote reports assessing the Kenyan military's capabilities and its leading personalities as part of their attempt to maintain influence. They helped with the selection and process of sending students to Britain for training and coordinated the training team stationed in Kenya. They also helped to organize the training of British troops in Kenya. In these ways, the defense adviser acted as an important link between the two militaries and helped to ensure that Anglo-Kenyan relations remained close through the 1960s and '70s.

This chapter also addresses the wider question of how military connections between this former colony and metropole were reshaped by decolonization. About more than just temporality, the complexities brought about by the postcolonial nature of the relationship are revealed in this chapter. This could cause difficulties, notably public criticism of neocolonialism from Kenya and more widely; but it is worth emphasizing that this also brought substantial benefits for Britain. Although this was rarely the case for Britain in independent Africa, in Kenya, this chapter argues, they were able to benefit from the formerly colonial nature of their relationship. Like other colonies, Kenya's military at independence was based on the colonial force, the King's African Rifles. Unlike what was often the case elsewhere, however, Kenya continued to look to Britain for the training, equipment, and expansion of its military long after independence. Other former colonies also had British commanding officers at independence, but elsewhere they were more quickly removed.[4] In Kenya, by contrast, a British commander continued to lead the Kenya Army until 1966, the first chief of general staff (1966–1969) was British, and there were British commanders of the Kenya Navy until 1972 and the Kenya Air Force until 1973. Kenya was not the only former African colony to have a British training team; there were teams in Zambia, Malawi, Tanganyika, and Uganda, among others; but Kenya's was larger and lasted longer. In 1965, there were around three hundred personnel seconded to the training team in Kenya, compared to around fifty in Malawi.[5] And as Chester Crocker argued in 1968, Kenya was "Britain's most complete military aid relationship."[6] As the leading provider of arms and training, and with British officers commanding the different branches of the Kenyan military, this was Kenya's most important external defense relationship until at least the mid-1970s.

In some ways, of course, the decision of Kenya's President Jomo Kenyatta to pursue a close military relationship with Britain is particularly surprising given Kenya's history of Mau Mau. Britain declared a state of emergency that lasted from 1952 to 1960, and British forces conducted a brutal counterinsurgency campaign involving torture and abuses.[7] Kenyatta himself was imprisoned from 1952 until 1961 and was famously described by one British governor as "leader to darkness and death."[8] For some Kenyans, therefore, Britain has since been viewed as "an 'enemy' military" and this relationship as a form of neocolonialism.[9] Yet it is important to stress that this relationship was in many ways based on the choices of Kenyatta and his elite.[10] This is clearly demonstrated by a comparison with the alternative choices made by East Africa's other presidents, Julius Nyerere in Tanzania and Milton Obote in Uganda. Mutinies occurred in the three East African countries in January 1964, after a coup in Zanzibar, and across several companies of the formerly joint colonial force, the King's African Rifles. All three presidents called on the British to quash the mutinies, and this assistance was readily provided by Britain, where military policy intentionally retained such capabilities.[11] This was, however, an embarrassing situation for the newly independent presidents, who had to admit that they could not quell the mutinies alone and had to ask for help from the colonial power they had so recently been calling on to leave. In the aftermath of the mutinies, Nyerere and Obote acted to change the composition of their militaries and limit British influence. Kenyatta, by contrast, chose to continue to work with the British.[12] One of the complaints of the mutineers in Kenya was about the presence of British troops,[13] but Kenyatta retained British officers. Although Kenyatta was likely always inclined in this direction, and more of a "moderate" than colonial officials had supposed,[14] the mutinies further encouraged him toward this choice, and British support helped him shape an apolitical military.[15] Kenyan decisions were essential, and if Kenyatta had reacted differently, this relationship could not have been sustained.

This chapter thus highlights the exchange of benefits between the British and Kenyan armed forces, which meant that the relationship was in the interests of both governments. The chapter begins with a consideration of Britain's strategic interests in Kenya and the initial agreements at independence that set up the future relationship. It then focuses on the training team, the training facilities Kenya provided for the British military, and arms sales. The final section considers the access and influence the defense advisers had and the decline of this influence in the early 1980s.

British Military Interests in Kenya during Decolonization

The 2017 strategy focuses on strategic partnerships, and although East Africa is not mentioned among them, in the 1960s Kenya was one of Britain's strategically important defense relationships in Africa. Charles Hornsby has suggested of this military relationship that "the benefit to the British was less clear."[16] But in fact there were obvious reasons for British concern. After decolonization, Britain retained few close military relationships with former African colonies, in contrast with France.[17] Kenya was in this respect unusual for the extent of continued British influence. Kenya was also of strategic value. David French has argued that "in the run-up to independence, the British always took care to determine whether or not the colony was strategically important"; and Kenya was.[18] Hilda Nissimi has pointed out that this was especially true as the British had just built a military base there.[19] More significantly, Kenya's geographic position made her important as an air-staging point en route to Aden, and so part of the east-of-Suez role, meaning that overflying rights and access to air-staging posts were particularly valuable.[20]

Reinforcing Kenya's strategic importance were Cold War concerns. After independence, Kenya was officially nonaligned but actually closely linked to Britain. By providing military training and arms, Britain aimed to prevent socialist influence. As time passed after independence, the Cold War became increasingly prominent: Kenya was the one part of the region where Western alignment was reliable and so became the focus of British concern in East Africa. The benefits that Britain received would be hard to replace if Kenya chose to end them. In addition, Britain had an interest in Kenyan stability, especially because of Kenya's substantial European and Asian minorities. Stationing British troops in Kenya for training could potentially be useful in times of crisis.[21] There was a secret, supplementary directive for the training team that stated that "circumstances might arise under which the Team might be called upon by the British High Commissioner to assist, in so far as they are able, in the protection of British lives and property in Kenya."[22] There were wider British plans at this time for the evacuation of Europeans from East and Central Africa, for which Kenya would provide important facilities.[23] David Percox has shown how Britain's interests in security and the Cold War shaped decolonization in Kenya, but this chapter extends these arguments into the decades after formal independence.[24] With few other African countries either so strategically important or so willing to work with Britain, Kenya was crucial to British thinking about her influence and military relations with postcolonial Africa.

Given Kenya's military significance to them, British policy-makers looked to secure their interests at independence. They did not, however, aim for a formal military pact. Military agreements were common in French relations with former colonies, and the British government made one attempt to achieve this with the Anglo-Nigerian Defence Agreement, signed in October 1960 but abrogated in January 1962 after extensive Nigerian public criticism.[25] The lesson for the British government was that formal pacts would not be the best way of pursuing military links with independent Africa and that these could in fact damage their political objective of sustaining good relations with African elites.[26] Yet this does not mean that Britain was not interested in having military connections with African colonies after their independence. As Marco Wyss has argued, the Anglo-Nigerian Defence Agreement is clear evidence "that Britain, driven by its global cold war military strategy, wanted to secure its long-term interests in sub-Saharan Africa" and that it was not "for lack of trying" that this was not managed in the way that many officials had hoped.[27]

Instead of a formal defense agreement, the British government concluded a Memorandum of Intention and Understanding with Kenya in June 1964, six months after her independence, as Kenya's "golden handshake" on exiting the empire. This secured key benefits for Britain, including overflying and air-staging rights, and gave the Kenyans considerable finance and equipment, including twenty-one aircraft and the transfer of "fixed assets . . . currently valued at £6.875 million."[28] The Memorandum of Understanding also made provision for Britain to offer places on training courses in Britain and provide a training team in Kenya. Although this was not a formal defense pact, the Memorandum of Understanding offered a clear exchange of benefits. Although British methods had changed, their goal of seeking to secure defense facilities in strategically significant (former) African colonies had not. The Memorandum of Understanding was the core statement of the military relationship and continued to govern relations for many years thereafter. It was a significant part of Kenya's decolonization, a process that continued beyond the date of independence, and it was thus Britain's colonial ties with Kenya that enabled the relations that followed.

The Defense Adviser in Kenya

Prior to independence, there had been no need in Kenya for roles such as a defense adviser. After 1963, this became significant, though with so many other British military officers in Kenya, it was only in the 1970s that this position became the most important. Defense advisers had a role between soldier and diplomat, an important part of the High Commission (the Commonwealth equivalent of an embassy). Defense advisers were appointed by the military, and their central loyalty would remain to the MOD rather than the mission itself, which G. R. Berridge has argued could lead to difficulties.[29] In the Kenyan case, however, at least so far as was recorded and can be seen in the files, this did not happen. By contrast, when leaving in 1982, Defense Adviser Colonel A. N. Prestige noted, "I have particularly enjoyed working with colleagues from the FCO, for whom I have acquired a great respect."[30] Britain posted up to four defense attachés to countries, depending on their perceived importance. Kenya received two, a defense adviser and an air adviser, at the rank of colonel and wing commander.[31] They stayed in post for two to three years.

It is agreed by the few who have written about defense attachés that their role varied depending on the posting and on the nature of the wider relationship between the sending and receiving states.[32] Berridge points to their general role as one of intelligence gathering.[33] Arms sales were also significant. When relations were more difficult, however, Geoffrey Moorhouse has argued that "not much can be done except to be as friendly as possible and to find out as much as you can about local arrangements and intentions."[34] Regarding Kenya, relations with Britain were close, and the defense advisers both benefited from and had a responsibility to maintain this. The roles of the defense adviser in Kenya were explicitly laid out in a 1976 (building on earlier) directive: they were to "advise the High Commissioner on any defense relations measures which you feel could be applied in furtherance of HMG [Her Majesty's Government]'s policy . . . co-ordinating the overt collection of defense information of intelligence interest . . . the collection and reporting of such defense and commercial information as might be useful in helping the sale of British defense equipment."[35] Advising the High Commission and MOD, intelligence gathering and promoting arms sales were the key roles.

The defense adviser's job was made much easier in the decade after independence by the presence of a number of other senior British military officers based within the Kenyan military and leading Britain's training team. As Ashley Jackson has argued, "well-placed military advisers in African defense establishments and ministries offer valuable strategic insights and political-military influence in key African states."[36] This was true in Kenya, with commanders of the navy and air force, as well as training team commanders, acting as informal advisers into the early 1970s. While this was the case, defense advisers were in a position to learn much about the inner workings of the Kenyan military. Through the early 1970s, the Kenyan Defense Committee decided policy, with Kenya's leading defense figures attending, including Minister of Defense James Gichuru, Assistant Minister for Defense James Njeru, Permanent Secretary for Defense Jeremiah Kiereini, the military commanders, and often the British military adviser.[37] Brigadier J. R. Anderson, the British commander of the training team from 1969 and informal adviser to the Kenyan military, attended such meetings and then passed information to the defense adviser.[38] After he left in 1971, Colonel M. J. Harbage took over his position, attended the meetings, and instructed the defense adviser, Colonel R. M. Begbie.[39] In 1974, Begbie commented that "Colonel Harbage holds a major position of trust and respect. He is party to most aspects of their planning and seems to be entirely in their confidence."[40] These British officers, with important access and influence to the Kenyan military, thus passed the defense advisers information that would otherwise have been harder to learn. The difficulties in access that occurred after their departure are discussed at the end of this chapter.

Providing Training to Kenya

A centerpiece of the military relationship, and a crucial means of Britain gaining influence, was providing military training for the newly independent army and newly created air force and navy. After independence, Kenya immediately acted to increase the strength of the army, set up an air force and navy, and increase the speed of Africanization in the officer class. International partners who could provide training were vital: the navy and air force were new, so there were no Kenyans who could train them. Kenya received various offers. Some pilots were trained in Israel before independence.[41] The Soviet Union also offered equipment and training, with some very publicly rejected by Kenya in 1965.[42] But quite quickly, Britain became the main training partner.

The British training team in Kenya was set up in 1964 following an exchange of letters between Kenyatta and the British high commissioner, Geoffrey de Freitas. For the British, a crucial stipulation was that they would be the sole provider of training and not have to compete with others. The high commissioner initially asked that Kenya not accept training from elsewhere "without prior consultation with Britain."[43] Kenyatta refused this demand, clearly stipulating his own prerogative to make decisions.[44] De Freitas responded that "we have no wish in any way to restrict your complete freedom," but "it might be embarrassing" if another team were stationed there at the same time, and so asked "that as between partners we should be warned before any new agreement is made."[45] There was a clear shift in his language here from insisting on consultation to discussing the relationship as one of "partners." The British government aimed to show that the relationship was no longer colonial. To this Kenyatta agreed, stating that Kenya did not intend to look "elsewhere than in Britain so long as this training is given effectively."[46] This in effect gave the British what they wanted: a clear commitment from Kenyatta to have British training and to advise them if this might change. This was the basis on which the training team was set up, with a private acknowledgment from both sides that this would be, at least for the present, and so long as training was effective, the only substantial training relationship that Kenya pursued.

Once this was agreed, the establishment of a training team permanently stationed in Kenya was the key to securing British influence. As Blake

Whitaker has argued, "British military training teams, while not glamorous and seldom in the public eye, played an extremely important role in creating the military culture of the newly independent African states."[47] They meant that new recruits, as well as senior officers, would be influenced by British methods and used to working with British equipment and with British troops as allies. This in turn made Kenya more likely to buy British arms and look to Britain for overseas training. A directive issued to the training team in December 1964 highlighted that, in addition to more specific aims, "you are to be responsible for the maintenance and fostering of friendly relations which have been built up between British service personnel and personnel of the Kenya Armed Forces."[48] The training team was meant to reinforce positive connections. The team continued for longer than had been anticipated, into the 1970s. Even after it left, a series of occasional training missions continued, such as when new equipment was delivered.

The defense adviser had an important role in organizing this training as the person on the ground who negotiated with the Kenyans. In late 1968, for example, plans were made for the British Special Air Service (SAS) to go to Kenya to secretly train the Kenyan General Service Unit (GSU). The GSU was a largely Kikuyu paramilitary body within the police, intended to protect President Kenyatta. Payment for this team was disputed, and the defense adviser, Colonel Ben Dalton, negotiated this with the Kenyans. He was instructed to make the Kenyans shoulder some extra costs and in November was "optimistic that continued gentle pressure on Home Affairs on my part will extract a favourable answer in due course."[49] As this makes clear, he believed that he was in a position to exert influence and "gentle pressure" on the Kenyans to persuade them to pay more. In this he was successful, with Kenya agreeing to pay K£22,108 and Britain K£25,696 to cover the two years of SAS training.[50] Dalton was instrumental in getting the Kenyans to agree to this and was "congratulate[d]" for his efforts.[51] The defense adviser also dealt with any issues the British teams faced while in Kenya. Dalton raised concern when the lease for the house in which this SAS team was staying could not be renewed and informed the FCO that "you can rely on me to seek alternative accommodation" when necessary.[52] The defense adviser had the crucial role in arranging training before British personnel arrived in Kenya and in looking after them once they were there. He was officially their point of contact with the British government and military.

In addition, Kenyan personnel attended training courses in Britain. The defense adviser was involved in setting up this training, agreeing who would attend courses, and encouraging training institutions to allocate the desired number of places to Kenya. As one example, in 1970 Defense Adviser Colonel Brian Tayleur wrote to the FCO that "the Kenyans are most anxious to get a vacancy on the IDC [Imperial Defence College] 1971 course and I hope you will do your best to get it for them."[53] When it seemed that Kenya would not be allocated this place, Tayleur drafted a letter, sent under the high commissioner's name, to further press the case for offering this vacancy, which was eventually agreed to.[54] Tayleur also highlighted that, in not offering all the training the Kenyans wanted, Britain was losing influence, with Kenyans going to Canada for training on Chipmunk aircraft when places in Britain were not available.[55] This was increasingly true through the 1970s, as Britain could not offer enough places to meet Kenyan demand and as British training became more expensive than that offered elsewhere, most importantly in the United States and India. Monetary concerns were significant in Kenya in the late 1970s through the 1980s, and expensive courses became harder to justify. Although the British did provide some funding under their UK Military Training Assistance Scheme, this was not enough to cover Kenya's training needs, and the Kenyans increasingly looked elsewhere.[56]

British Military Training in Kenya

Another of the central roles of the defense adviser was organizing training for British troops in Kenya. That the Kenyans allowed the British military to train there was a central part of what made the defense relationship so significant from the British point of view. This was a benefit they rarely found in former African colonies. The British government was therefore more willing to offer the Kenyans training, military support, and aid in order to ensure that their access to training facilities continued. As Defense Adviser Begbie recognized in 1974, the relationship was reciprocal and "it would be realistic to accept that to a great extent our influence and interests depends on how much we are prepared to give."[57] The relationship needed to be seen to bring benefits to Kenya, not just to Britain, for the Kenyans to be willing to continue it. This mutual exchange of benefits was critical to sustaining such a close military relationship for so long after independence.

As with other significant arrangements, Kenya had agreed to allow British troops to train there in the 1964 Memorandum of Intention and Understanding. This stipulated that the Kenyan government had to agree to training exercises, so they did retain the option of refusing, and training would "initially be limited to twice a year."[58] Joint training was also encouraged. This was about capacity-building for both the British and Kenyan militaries. The British would benefit from training in other climates and terrains, having few similar facilities elsewhere. The Kenyans, when they chose to conduct joint exercises, would also benefit. The first joint-training exercise took place in August 1965. The Kenyans were keen to publicize the training to avoid speculation and announced that "joint exercises of this nature should have the effect of 'sharpening up' both armies. These are normal exercises, and there should be no cause for rumours of any nature or alarm among the public."[59] For Kenya's government, highlighting the joint nature of the exercises would show that Kenya also benefited and that this should not be seen as neocolonialism.

As would become clear in later years, however, there was ample scope for negative publicity around British training in Kenya. In 1971, what Defense Adviser Tayleur described as "an ill-informed, mischievous and sensation-seeking article" was published in the *Sunday Express* in Kenya.[60] It suggested that British troops exercising in Kenya could be used in Kenya or her neighbors if "trouble for Britons and British interests starts as a result of the South African Arms deal and requests for help are received from African Governments."[61] Britain was at this time highly criticized by African states regarding arms sales to South Africa. Luckily for the British government, such accusations were also potentially damaging to the Kenyan government, and Defence Minister Gichuru issued a statement denying them and stating that "British troops have had joint exercises with units of the Kenyan army for a long time. . . . To suggest that they have come here to quell any possible anti-British riots in Africa is nonsensical and malicious."[62] These rumors did not last. However, they made clear that Britain's ability to train in Kenya was highly dependent upon Kenyan consent to this, both from the Kenyan military and government, who were happy to offer this, and, if it was given publicity, from the wider Kenyan public, who were likely to be critical.

Alongside this training was another program designed to generate Kenyan goodwill for British training, as well as to give experience to British troops: the construction projects carried out by the Royal Engineers. As Jackson has argued, "goodwill/defence diplomacy activities of British forces visiting African countries are legion, and provide an essential support to the country's African defence architecture."[63] In 1971, British troops spent three months building a bridge, accompanied by the squadron medical officer who, Defense Adviser Tayleur reported, "did a remarkable job on the local sick. . . . The doctor's efforts plus the construction of school playing fields by the plant operators has left the British Army's image at the coast in high esteem."[64] This kind of activity encouraged Kenyans to hold a positive view of Britain and the British military. Later in the year, Tayleur asked for more of the same, requesting that medical officers in Kenya with troops "should offer medical assistance to the local population on a 'hearts and minds' basis."[65] Initially there was some dispute over who—the MOD or FCO—should pay the cost of medical supplies to do this. In response, the defense adviser and High Commission argued that "it would be very desirable politically" and would encourage support for the military-training exercise of which it was a part.[66] The MOD and FCO agreed to split the cost.[67] Providing medical care would help to militate against the kind of criticism encountered earlier in the year. As training in Kenya was valued so highly by the MOD, keeping the Kenyans onside with their activities, through hearts and minds exercises, by limiting publicity, and by conducting joint training, was key to ensuring that this remained available.

Kenya was important as a training ground because the British military had access to relatively few comparable overseas training facilities, especially after decolonization and leaving east of Suez. In 1976, the MOD argued that "apart from three battalion exercises in Canada, Kenya offers the only overseas training outlet where a UKLF [UK Land Forces] battalion can train as a complete entity and in challenging and testing terrain."[68] As this makes clear, British training opportunities were fairly limited, certainly in the conditions that Kenya could offer, and Kenya was thus highly prized by the MOD. In planning ahead for 1979–1980, ten overseas exercises were planned, of which there was one each in Belize, Bahamas/Anguilla, Bahrain, and Brunei, and the remaining six in Kenya.[69] Kenya offered a training ground where more exercises could be conducted than elsewhere. In 1981, Defense Adviser Prestige argued that "unit commanders, and their visiting superiors, all agree that more can be achieved here in a few weeks [*sic*] concentrated training than is possible elsewhere."[70] Lacking many comparable alternatives, British military planners continued to view Kenya as an important training area into the 1980s.

This was also valuable because training in Kenya was cheaper and logistically easier than training elsewhere. In 1971, the British Army Training Liaison Staff Kenya was set up to facilitate training.[71] A small staff was stationed in Kenya, working with the defense adviser, for whom organizing training remained an important part of the job.[72] Vehicles and equipment also remained in Kenya between exercises, reducing transportation costs for Britain. This made Kenya a cheaper training ground than elsewhere, offering "excellent training facilities at a minimal cost."[73] It is also important to note that the Kenyan government consistently remained willing to host such training. When, in 1978, the defense adviser asked the Kenyan Ministry of Defence for clearance for four training exercises, they raised no objections, and he "was reminded that the agreement for British units to train in Kenya was longstanding and that there was no reason to change this."[74] The Kenyan government was content for these exercises to go ahead, even though there were double the number officially agreed upon. Although it may have been expected that a self-consciously postcolonial country would be reluctant to authorize this, in fact the Kenyan military and government continued to welcome the British presence. There were also financial advantages from British training and visits: in 1982, Defense Adviser Prestige pointed out that "British forces in Kenya spend some £2m per annum, which is a good boost to their economy."[75] Another potential benefit for Kenya was the good relations this engendered, and the possibility therefore of assistance if Kenya were to be attacked. In 1967, the Bamburi Understanding was made between Britain and Kenya, promising British consultation in case of a Somali attack.[76] This was allowed to fade in the late 1970s, but Kenya's government still felt threatened by socialist neighbors with much larger armies, and successive British defense advisers noted that Kenya would be unable to resist an attack without assistance from allies. Prestige speculated in 1982 that this was one reason for Kenya's "obliging" attitude to both the British and, by that time, the Americans, in terms of training, visits, and facilities.[77]

Arms Sales

The defense adviser also had a crucial role in encouraging arms sales. Britain remained Kenya's major arms supplier after independence, providing much equipment as well as military aid. Defense sales were one of Britain's aims in Kenya and important as part of a longer-term relationship: arms required training and future spare parts and could be hard to combine with equipment from others, leading to an extended relationship. Daniel Branch has pointed to Britain's importance in Kenya's one serious conflict during this period: the *shifta* conflict in the northeast of Kenya, on Somalia's border, lasting until 1967.[78] During this time, Britain was Kenya's major supplier, and Kenyan attempts to find other suppliers had limited success. This began to change during the 1970s.

Defense advisers had a role in promoting British arms sales and in ensuring their successful delivery and training. In June 1971, Kenya wanted to buy 105 mm Light Guns from Britain, an order that went through the defense adviser.[79] Defense advisers then pushed for orders to arrive in a timely manner, as a frequent complaint of the Kenyans was that equipment was slow to arrive.[80] The Light Guns were a case in point: still in 1981, a decade after this order had been arranged, they were held up as an example of supply problems, having been very delayed in arriving and thereby caused Kenyan "disappointments."[81] Problems with slow delivery or equipment not working as promised did not encourage the reputation of British manufactures or assist future sales. If, on the other hand, British equipment arrived on time, it was much more likely that the Kenyan military would retain a good impression of British equipment. Offering training with the delivery of new equipment also helped the Kenyans to integrate it and ensured that it was viewed positively. Defense Adviser Prestige argued in 1981 that "having sold to the Kenyan army large quantities of British equipment, we have an obligation to see that it is trained on the use and management of such equipment. Failure to do so will result, in the long term, in the Kenyans going elsewhere for further arms purchases, and in a loss of our influence here."[82] He wanted to forestall any potential criticism about the equipment they had provided and instead aimed to ensure that British arms made a favorable impression.

The defense adviser was also the key point of contact for British companies wanting to sell to Kenya. In 1981, having made large previous orders and facing difficulties of absorption, the Kenyans were not in the market for further defense purchases. Nonetheless, "it is a rare day when no arms salesman calls to see the Defence Adviser; on average I see about 20 a month, which consumes a lot of my time."[83] Prestige gave advice to them and promoted products to the Kenyans, so that when they did look to purchase equipment in the future they would have British equipment in mind. When, in the following year, the Kenya Department of Defence requested that no new salesmen be brought to see them, Prestige continued to "send, two or three times a week, literature and brochures."[84] He was not willing to lose out on possible sales. Promoting arms sales was a key part of the remit of the defense adviser.

Advice and Influence

In addition to organizing training and arms sales, a crucial part of the defense adviser's work was intelligence gathering and being in a position to advise and influence the Kenyan military. The defense advisers provided a comprehensive view of the Kenyan military through their reports, sent to the MOD, FCO, and other relevant missions. These reports provided the British government with a wealth of information on the Kenyan military, its equipment, its abilities, and its personnel. The defense advisers concerned themselves with understanding the leading Kenyan military officers' personalities, strengths and weaknesses, and promotions and structural changes, as well as the ethnic balance of the military and its resultant tensions, such as over Asian officers.[85] Their reports highlighted the military readiness and training of the armed forces. They also reflected on the nature of the threats facing Kenya and Kenya's ability to meet them.

The defense adviser could also be involved in Kenyan planning and decision-making, particularly when this concerned relations with Britain. In 1970, in discussions considering the future of the British training team, "the British High Commissioner and his Defence and Air Advisers were brought into discussions unofficially . . . so the proposals are no surprise."[86] In fact, Defense Adviser Tayleur seems to have suggested the proposal for senior British military advisers to remain in Kenya after the rundown of the training team.[87] The defense adviser thus attempted, and here was able, to use his influence to shape Kenyan military policy. Leading Kenyans, including Defence Minister Gichuru and Chief of Defence Staff Major General Joseph Ndolo, were open to working with him to achieve this. The Kenyans wanted close military relations with Britain and were thus prepared to have such informal and private cooperation.

Defense advisers could have an important behind-the-scenes role in Kenyan defense planning and organization. In 1978, President Kenyatta died and was constitutionally replaced by Daniel arap Moi. In the same year, there was a large expansion of the Kenyan armed forces when much new equipment was ordered, and the Kenyans thereafter struggled with absorption and logistics. This also meant a large repayment schedule. In response, the British set up a "Military Assistance Programme, aimed at assisting the Kenyans to absorb new British equipment" and organized by the defense adviser, Colonel W. G. Alderman.[88] Alderman had "close involvement" with this expansion, and the problems of absorbing equipment were "frequently discussed."[89] This was true at both formal and informal levels. Informally, he was asked for advice by individuals in new roles they were unaccustomed to: "a charming Brigadier in the appointment of Chief of Logistics said to me 'It really would be most helpful if you could brief me on the duties of your QMG [Quartermaster General].'" More formally, Alderman was also "invited to draft" the Charters for the Chief of General Staff and the Permanent Secretary in the Ministry of Defence.[90] The defense adviser was brought into military discussions and decision-making at the very top and involved in the fundamental organization of the Kenyan armed forces and in defining its roles. This also shows what Alderman described as "the lack of experience and expertise in the Department of Defence and Service Headquarters."[91] With the slow process of Africanization in the colonial period, there had been limited time to build up such experience. Defense advisers frequently highlighted that the Kenyans had few logistical and staff officers and that those there were had limited training and knowledge of their positions. Yet this also speaks to the level of trust the Kenyan military placed in the defense adviser and their British connections more generally. The defense adviser was here allowed and encouraged to have a significant role in shaping the Kenyan armed forces.

This position was facilitated by Alderman's informal and personal contacts with the Kenyan military. In his report for 1978, he highlighted that "a very close working and social relationship is enjoyed with the Kenya Armed Forces. Despite their fetish over confidentiality at all levels, we have freedom of access to all staff officers in Kenya MOD without appointment. . . . I am an honorary member of the Army Headquarters Officers' Mess and the Kenya Navy Mess in Mombasa and receive invitations to both formal and informal military and social functions."[92] He demonstrates here the social and informal relationships he had with the Kenyan military. Alderman argued that "this relationship stems from our traditional links with the Armed Forces and their confidence that they can seek British advice without the attachment of 'political strings.' . . . It is satisfying to note that after only 15 years of Independence that [sic] British help and advice is sought and respected."[93] Although Kenya had ordered equipment from multiple sources, Britain remained a partner of choice and Alderman believed that being the former colonial power encouraged the Kenyans to seek British assistance and advice. This relationship was built on connections formed with the British military during the colonial period and contacts made while training in Britain or with British instructors in Kenya. These long-term relations were both significant and valuable.

It was very soon after Alderman wrote this, however, that this close relationship between the defense adviser and the Kenyan military began to decline. Future defense advisers would find it more difficult to access information. Alderman left in 1980, replaced by Colonel Prestige, who believed that "the old extremely close relationship between the British Defence and Air Advisers and the Kenyans is slowly waning."[94] The relationship was becoming more formalized, and he complained that "we now (1981) have to make appointments before we visit any one in the Department of Defence; in 1980 we never used to."[95] Individual contact was less frequent and Kenya was increasingly looking to America. In 1980, Kenya offered America use of air and naval facilities in return for substantial military and economic aid.[96] The Americans were thus coming to replace the British as Kenya's predominant military ally.

This decline in personal relations was perhaps due in part to an increase in the number of defense attachés resident in Kenya. Until 1980, there had been the two Britons, an Ethiopian, and a Sudanese attaché, as well as a US liaison officer. In 1980, French and Canadian defense attachés arrived, and Prestige wrote that "the Kenyans are outwardly friendly and courteous in their relations with this small group of overseas military, but they do nothing to make our task any easier. Apart from inviting us all to dinner (much to our astonishment and pleasure) at an [*sic*] hotel, they have arranged for us nothing at all. Indeed they appear to go out of their way to keep us in the dark. We watch pass-out parades."[97] As he makes clear, having a larger official group of representatives did not encourage the Kenyans to be more open toward them, and they all struggled for the access they would have liked. In 1982, there was an attempted coup by the Kenya Air Force, and although this did not succeed, it probably did not encourage Kenyan openness to let outsiders see their military.[98] When, in 1982, the group asked to see the training college, "this request was immediately turned down flat."[99] Prestige and Air Adviser M. J. Blofeld remained members of the officers' messes and therefore did continue to have some access, as well as having "established friendly personal relations with a number of officers from whom we sometimes glean information."[100] Personal and informal relations here helped the British above their French and Canadian counterparts, who were treated more formally and did not have such established relationships to fall back on. Colonel M. J. Doyle, who replaced Prestige, noted in his 1983 report that he had only once been permitted into an army camp and had not been able to see any training, so "cannot comment on the effectiveness of the army."[101] This was very different from the position in earlier years, when the British had had much access to the Kenyan military, and defense advisers had commented extensively on the state and readiness of their forces.

Nonetheless, Doyle continued to highlight how much Britain gained from Kenya and its importance to the British military, despite the increase in American influence and the more distant personal relations. "British Army training has continued here, the British Army Training and Liaison Staff Kenya remain accommodated outside Nairobi, RAF [Royal Air Force] aircraft use Nairobi Airport and RN [Royal Navy] ships visit Mombasa," with the particularly striking feature that the liaison team paid little rent and no bills.[102] Notably, all three branches of the British military received benefits from this relationship: staging facilities for the RAF, mooring facilities for the Royal Navy, and training for the British Army. This gave the whole of the British armed forces an interest in securing relations with Kenya. As contemporary readers of the report commented, this "brings out very clearly just how good value for money we get from Kenya."[103] At a time when the British government was concerned with its own finances, "the money and effort we spend on providing training assistance to the Kenyan armed forces are well-spent given the valuable training facilities we receive in return."[104] The relationship was always a form of exchange, and the substantive benefits Britain received made Kenya worth investing in. Despite the fact that relations were becoming more formalized and less close, Kenya continued to offer key military benefits to Britain into the 1980s.

Conclusion

This chapter began by considering the 2017 "UK's International Defence Engagement Strategy." As has been shown, the policies advocated are not wholly new. While some of the details are different, considering Kenya in the first decades after independence reveals many of the same priorities. These included capacity-building and training relationships, defense sales, and creating "friendly" personal relations. The British defense advisers were at the center of the multiple and overlapping military networks that existed between Britain and Kenya. The high commissioner in 1980 argued that "the harmonious and constructive relationship which exists between the Defence Adviser's office and the Kenya Department of Defence is a valuable element in the overall friendly relations between the High Commission and the Kenya Government and between Britain and Kenya as a whole."[105] Military connections helped sustain the wider diplomatic relationship. Importantly, this was a relationship of exchange, with benefits accruing to both governments. The ability for British troops to train in Kenya made Kenya important to the British military in a way that few other places in Africa were, and also made it worth investing in the relationship. British military training in Kenya has remained significant through the whole period of independence. Jackson in 2006 pointed to its ongoing importance, with three battalion exercises per year and a British Army training unit to support these.[106] Although there has at times been criticism of British training in Kenya, and pauses,[107] both sides have largely continued to see benefits.

Kenya was particularly significant to Britain because of the sustained postcolonial influence that the British were able to pursue. Defense Adviser Alderman argued that, even in 1980, "British interests in Kenya rely on the continuation of friendly relations with a former colony."[108] Kenya's colonial military inheritance was furthered rather than abandoned. British policy-makers at independence did not push Kenya to a formal defense agreement, which had been tried and had failed in Nigeria. However, through informal exchanges and agreements, they were able to secure their military interests over and above those in most former African colonies. Kenya's armed forces continued to value British assistance, use much British equipment, and be based on British models and structures. These connections were strengthened through British personnel stationed in the Kenyan military; through training that encouraged the use of British equipment, thereby promoting defense sales; and through formal and informal personal relations, including those of the defense adviser. For the British, these continued postcolonial connections were unusual in their depth and breadth in the African context, and this made them well worth sustaining. But they had to tread carefully not to make their influence too explicit or their training exercises and personnel too visible, to avoid Kenyan and wider African criticism. The British position changed in the late 1970s, and especially after the expansion of Kenya's military in 1978, with a growing role of the United States in particular but also of Israel, India, France, and West Germany. Alongside this, the defense adviser's access and influence declined. The Kenyans were becoming less willing to simply rely on their old colonial relations, although they still did not reject these.

NOTES

1 MOD and FCO, "UK's International Defence Engagement Strategy," Crown Copyright, MOD, 2017, 1.
2 "UK's International Defence Engagement Strategy," 11.
3 Called "adviser" rather than "attaché" because of being in a Commonwealth country.
4 For excellent comparative data on British assistance to various African countries, see M. J. V. Bell, "Military Assistance to Independent African States," *Adelphi Papers* 5, no. 15, (1964): 3–16.
5 Chester A. Crocker, "External Military Assistance to Sub-Saharan Africa," *Africa Today* 15, no. 2, (1968): 18.
6 Crocker, "External Military Assistance," 17.
7 See David Anderson, *Histories of the Hanged: Britain's Dirty War in Kenya and the End of Empire* (London: Weidenfeld & Nicolson, 2006); Caroline Elkins, *Britain's Gulag: The Brutal End of Empire in Kenya* (London: Jonathan Cape, 2005); Huw Bennett, *Fighting the Mau Mau: The British Army and Counter-*

Insurgency in the Kenya Emergency (Cambridge, UK: Cambridge University Press, 2013).

8 Statement by His Excellency the Governor, "Jomo Kenyatta," May 9, 1960, The National Archives, Kew, UK (hereafter TNA), FCO 141/6769/66.

9 Njagi Arthur Munene, *The Colonial Legacy in Kenya-British Military Relations: 1963–2005* (MA thesis, Kenyatta University, 2013).

10 On this wider point, see Poppy Cullen, *Kenya and Britain after Independence: Beyond Neo-Colonialism* (Basingstoke, UK: Palgrave Macmillan, 2017).

11 See David French, "Duncan Sandys and the Projection of British power after Suez," *Diplomacy & Statecraft* 24, no. 1 (2013): 41–58.

12 For this argument in more depth, see Timothy H. Parsons, *The 1964 Army Mutinies and the Making of Modern East Africa* (Westport, CT: Praeger, 2003).

13 See, for examples, Captain Cameron, 11 Kenya Rifles, January 29, 1964, Kenya National Archives, Nairobi (hereafter KNA), AG/16/343/5; 2nd Lieutenant Tonje, 11 Kenya Rifles, January 29, 1964, KNA AG/16/343/4.

14 On this point, see John Lonsdale, "Jomo Kenyatta, God and the Modern World," in Jan-Georg Deutsch, Peter Probst and Heike Schmidt, eds., *African Modernities: Entangled Meanings in Current Debate* (Oxford, UK: James Currey, 2002), 31–66.

15 Parsons, *1964 Army Mutinies*, 169.

16 Charles Hornsby, *Kenya: A History Since Independence* (London: I. B. Tauris, 2013), 99.

17 Anton Andereggen, *France's Relationship with Subsaharan Africa* (Westport, CT: Praeger, 1994).

18 David French, *Army, Empire and Cold War: The British Army and Military Policy, 1945–1971* (Oxford, UK: Oxford University Press, 2012), 259.

19 Hilda Nissimi, "Illusions of World Power in Kenya: Strategy, Decolonization, and the British Base, 1946–1961," *International History Review* 23, no. 4 (2001): 841.

20 See French, "Duncan Sandys," 47–49.

21 Stanley to Major General Price, August 24, 1964, TNA DO 213/136/29.

22 "Supplementary Directive to Commander British Army Training Team Kenya," December 14, 1964, TNA DEFE 25/121/A66/01.

23 "Planning for Evacuation of British Subjects from Certain Countries in Africa," June 24, 1964, TNA DEFE 6/95/22; Chiefs of Staff Committee, "The Protection of United Kingdom and Friendly Nationals in Kenya," April 12, 1967, TNA DEFE 6/103/31.

24 David Percox, *Britain, Kenya and the Cold War: Imperial Defence, Colonial Security and Decolonisation* (London: I. B. Tauris, 2004).

25 Marco Wyss, "A Post-Imperial Cold War Paradox: The Anglo-Nigerian Defence Agreement 1958–62," *Journal of Imperial and Commonwealth History* 44, no. 6 (2016): 976–1000.

26 Holton to Aspin, February 24, 1964, TNA DO 213/137/5; Olasupo Ojedokun, "The Anglo-Nigerian Entente and Its Demise, 1960–1962," *Journal of Commonwealth Political Studies* 9, no. 3 (1971): 218–219.

27 Wyss, "Anglo-Nigerian Defence Agreement," 976.

28 Memorandum of Intention and Understanding regarding Certain Financial and Defence Matters of Mutual Interest to the British and Kenya Governments, June 3, 1964, TNA DO 213/136/1.

29 G. R. Berridge, *Diplomacy: Theory and Practice*, 5th ed. (Basingstoke, UK: Palgrave Macmillan, 2015), 153.

30 A. N. Prestige, "Defence Adviser's Final Report," October 8, 1982, TNA AIR 8/3265/12.

31 Geoffrey Moorhouse, *The Diplomats: The Foreign Office Today* (London: Cape, 1977), 335. For the individuals in position each year, see *The Diplomatic Service List* (London: FCO, 1965–1984).

32 See E. S. Williams, *Cold War, Hot Seat: A Western Defence Attaché in the Soviet Union* (London: Robert Hale, 2000), 19; Moorhouse, *The Diplomats*, 335–337.

33 Berridge, *Diplomacy*, 152.

34 Moorhouse, *The Diplomats*, 335–336.

35 Directive to the Defence Adviser in Kenya, 1976, TNA FCO 31/2028/16.

36 Ashley Jackson, "British–African Defence and Security Connections," *Defence Studies* 6, no. 3 (2006): 362.

37 Hornsby, *Kenya*, 230.

38 Brian Tayleur, "Report by the Defence Adviser, for the period 1 January–31 March 1971," April 22, 1971, TNA FCO 31/868/5.

39 R. M. Begbie, "Annual Report on Kenya," 22 April 1974, TNA DEFE 71/135/2A.

40 Begbie, "Annual Report on Kenya."

41 Speech to be Delivered by the Prime Minister on the Occasion of the Inauguration of the Kenya Air Force in Nairobi, June 1, 1964, KNA KA/4/9/6.

42 Daniel Branch, *Kenya: Between Hope and Despair, 1963–2011* (New Haven, CT: Yale University Press, 2011), 49–50.

43 De Freitas to Kenyatta, March 25, 1964, TNA DO 213/135/103.

44 Kenyatta to de Freitas, April 7, 1964, TNA DO 213/135/103.

45 De Freitas to Kenyatta, April 30, 1964, TNA DO 213/135/118.

46 Kenyatta to de Freitas, May 4, 1964, TNA DO 213/135/121.

47 Blake Humphrey Whitaker, "The 'New Model' Armies of Africa?: The British Military Advisory and Training Team and the Creation of the Zimbabwe National Army" (PhD diss., Texas A&M University, 2014), 3.

48 "Directive for the Commander of the British Army Training Team Kenya," December 14, 1964, Annex A, TNA DEFE 25/121/A66/01.

49 Dalton to McNeill, November 23, 1968, TNA FCO 46/461/14.

50 Dalton to McNeill, January 31, 1969, TNA FCO 46/461/22.

51 Rampton to Baker, February 20, 1969, TNA FCO 46/461/23.

52 Telegram, Defense Adviser to FCO, March 4, 1969, TNA FCO 46/461/26.

53 Tayleur to Owens, March 4, 1970, TNA FCO 46/541/6.

54 Norris to Smedley, August 11, 1970, TNA FCO 46/542/71.

55 Telegram, Defense Adviser to MODUK, [May 1971], TNA FCO 31/867/18.

56 See Prestige and Blofeld, "Annual Report on Kenya 1980/81," May 22, 1981, TNA AIR 8/2826/16.

57 Begbie, "Annual Report on Kenya," April 22, 1974.

58 Memorandum of Intention and Understanding regarding Certain Financial and Defence Matters of Mutual Interest to the British and Kenya Governments, June 3, 1964, TNA DO 213/136/1.

59 Telegram, Nairobi to Commonwealth Relations Office, June 24, 1965, TNA DO 213/136/45.

60 Tayleur, "Report by the Defence Adviser, for the Period 1 January–31 March 1971," April 22, 1971, TNA FCO 31/868/5.

61 Article quoted in Telegram, FCO to Certain Missions, January 20, 1971, TNA FCO 31/866/16.

62 Telegram, FCO to Certain Missions, January 20, 197.

63 Jackson, "British–African Defence and Security Connections," 369.

64 Tayleur, "Report by the Defence Adviser, for the Period 1 January–31 March 1971," April 22, 1971.

65 Allans to Duggan, November 16, 1971, TNA FCO 31/866/33.

66 Allinson to Le Tocq, November 30, 1971, TNA FCO 31/866/36.

67 Duggan to Biggin, December 15, 1971, TNA FCO 31/866/39.

68 Abraham to Secretary to Minister of State, June 18, 1976, TNA DEFE 13/1252 /2.

69 Frizzy to MOD AT2, December 21, 1978, TNA FCO 31/2585/4.

70 Prestige and Blofeld, "Annual Report on Kenya 1980/81."

71 Tayleur, "Report by the Defence Adviser, for the Period 1 October–31 December 1970," March 3, 1971, TNA FCO 31/868/1.

72 Prestige and Blofeld, "Annual Report on Kenya 1980/81."

73 Waterton to Lieutenant Colonel Horwood, October 27, 1980, TNA FCO 31/2836/16.

74 Colonel Alderman, "Annual Report on Kenya 1978," February 19, 1979, TNA FCO 31/2588.

75 A.N. Prestige, "Kenya 1981/2: Defence Adviser's Report," May 14, 1982, TNA AIR 8/3265/1.

76 Telegram, Commonwealth Office to Nairobi, January 23, 1967, TNA FCO 16/115/41. On the Bamburi Understanding, see Cullen, *Kenya and Britain after Independence*, 156–162.

77 Prestige, "Kenya 1981/2: Defence Adviser's Report."

78 Daniel Branch, "Violence, Decolonisation and the Cold War in Kenya's North-

eastern Province, 1963–1978," *Journal of Eastern African Studies* 8, no. 4 (2014): 1–16. On the *shifta* campaign, see also Hannah Whittaker, *Insurgency and Counterinsurgency in Kenya: A Social History of the Shifta Conflict, c. 1963–1968* (Leiden, Netherlands: Brill, 2015).

79 Telegram, Defense Adviser to MOD, June 1971, TNA FCO 31/867/19; Macpherson to Gubbins, June 22, 1971, TNA FCO 31/867/24.

80 Telegram, Defense Adviser to MOD, July 21, 1971, TNA FCO 31/867/27.

81 Prestige and Blofeld, "Annual Report on Kenya 1980/81."

82 Prestige and Blofeld, "Annual Report on Kenya 1980/81."

83 Prestige and Blofeld, "Annual Report on Kenya 1980/81."

84 Prestige, "Kenya 1981/2: Defence Adviser's Report."

85 See, for example, Tayleur, "Defence Adviser's Quarterly Report," October 1971, TNA FCO 31/868/12.

86 Tayleur to Griffith, July 6, 1970, TNA FCO 46/545/1.

87 Ndolo to Gichuru, "The Future of the British Training Teams," July 1, 1970, TNA FCO 46/545/1; Tayleur, "Report by the Defence Adviser, for the Period 1 October–31 December 1970," March 3, 1971, TNA FCO 31/868/1.

88 Alderman, "Annual Report on Kenya for 1979," February 19, 1980, TNA AIR 8/2825/5.

89 Alderman, "Annual Report on Kenya 1978."

90 Alderman, "Annual Report on Kenya 1978." Both of these charters are included in this report.

91 Alderman, "Annual Report on Kenya for 1979."

92 Alderman, "Annual Report on Kenya 1978."

93 Alderman, "Annual Report on Kenya 1978."

94 Prestige and Blofeld, "Annual Report on Kenya 1980/81."

95 Prestige and Blofeld, "Annual Report on Kenya 1980/81."

96 Hornsby, *Kenya*, 337.

97 Prestige and Blofeld, "Annual Report on Kenya 1980/81."

98 For details of the coup attempt, see Branch, *Kenya*, 154–159.

99 Prestige, "Kenya 1981/2: Defence Adviser's Report."

100 Prestige and Blofeld, "Annual Report on Kenya 1980/81."

101 M. J. Doyle, "Defence Adviser's Annual Report," December 30, 1983, TNA FCO 31/4340/2A.

102 Doyle, "Defence Adviser's Annual Report."

103 Wenban-Smith to Squire, February 3, 1984, TNA FCO 31/4340/3.

104 Wilton to Doble, Wenban-Smith, February 9, 1984, TNA FCO 31/4340/3A.

105 Williams to Lord Carrington, "Defence Adviser's Annual Report on the Kenyan Armed Forces," March 5, 1980, TNA FCO 31/2837/1.

106 Jackson, "British–African Defence and Security Connections," 365.

107 See "Kenya and United Kingdom Resume Joint Military Training," *Daily Nation*, October 11, 2016, https://www.nation.co.ke/news/kenya-uk-resume

-joint-military-training/1056–3413364-cc03ip/index.html; J. Vitor Tossini, "The British Forces in Africa—The Training Unit in Kenya," *UK Defence Journal* (March 30, 2017), https://ukdefencejournal.org.uk/the-british-forces -in-africa-the-training-unit-in-kenya/.

108 Alderman, "Annual Report on Kenya 1979."

8

Nurturing a "Delicate Flower"
British Military Attachés in Cairo and Defense Engagement in Egypt, 1968–1973

Geraint Hughes

Between the Six Day War (June 5–11, 1967) and the Yom Kippur War (October 6–25, 1973) Anglo-Egyptian diplomatic relations evolved from a state of mutual hostility and suspicion toward a rapprochement, as London and Cairo gradually reestablished defense ties severed after the overthrow of the Egyptian monarchy in July 1952. The primary role of the military personnel attached to the British embassy in Cairo during this period initially consisted of intelligence gathering,[1] but by the eve of the Yom Kippur War, the defense attaché's team was at the forefront of a process of defense diplomacy, promoting arms sales to Egypt while facilitating visits by officers from its armed forces to the United Kingdom, supporting their participation in training and professional military-education courses with their British counterparts.

This chapter describes this transition in Anglo-Egyptian relations and the role played by the United Kingdom defense attaché and his subordinates in Cairo. It concludes that there was a genuine spirit of reconciliation on both sides and that the British attaché team was fully committed to the reestablishment of amicable relations with Egypt. However, progress was ultimately hampered by four political and strategic factors that were beyond the attachés' control. The first was Cold War–related, concerning whether Egypt had expelled all of the USSR's "advisers" after their eviction was formally announced in July 1972. If this was not the case, there was a potential security risk for Britain if it supplied the Egyptians with advanced weapons that could be examined by Soviet-bloc military and intelligence personnel. The second involved the inevitability of armed conflict between Israel and its Arab adversaries after June 1967 and the United Kingdom's fears (confirmed after October 6, 1973) that a regional war would have highly adverse consequences, ranging from a superpower confrontation to an Arab oil embargo against the West. The third involved the potentially damaging impact that British defense sales to Egypt could have on Anglo-American relations, given the United States' close alliance ties with Israel. Finally, Anwar al-Sadat (the Egyptian president from October 1970 until his assassination eleven years later) ultimately saw realignment with the United States rather than the United Kingdom as his main foreign-policy priority. Although Sadat favored improved relations with Britain, in overall strategic terms his main interests — notably a peace settlement with Israel and the restoration of territory Egypt lost in June 1967 — could only be delivered through an alliance with the Americans.

The Historical Context: 1882–1968

In the summer and autumn of 1882, a British expeditionary force invaded and occupied Egypt, an autonomous province of the Ottoman Empire, to secure control of the strategically vital Suez Canal. In December 1914, the British formally imposed a protectorate on Egypt, maintaining its substantial military garrison in that country despite the Egyptian declaration of independence eight years later.[2] Britain's hold over the Suez Canal and its continued meddling in national politics provoked widespread indigenous resentment, and between 1951 and 1954, British troops in the Canal Zone fought a low-level guerrilla war instigated and backed by the Egyptian security forces.[3] The July 1952 military coup led to the establishment of a junta eventually directed by Colonel Jamal Abdel Nasser, whose pan-Arab nationalism and determination to undermine Britain's imperial sphere of influence in the Middle East made him an enemy to successive British governments, Conservative and Labour alike.[4]

The bilateral treaty signed by Nasser and Anthony Eden — the then–British foreign secretary and future prime minister—on October 19, 1954, initially appeared to herald a new chapter in Anglo-Egyptian relations, as the UK government agreed to withdraw troops from the Canal Zone by June 1956. However, the nationalization of the Suez Canal the following month enraged Eden, who developed a fixation with overthrowing Nasser that led him to conspire with France and Israel to invade Egypt. The Suez War (October 20–November 6, 1956) was a strategic and diplomatic catastrophe for Britain, isolating it from the international community while abruptly ending Eden's premiership. Nasser became a hero to millions of Arabs, and the establishment of the United Arab Republic with Syria in 1957, followed by the military coup that overthrew the pro-British monarchy in Iraq in July 1958, created alarm in Whitehall. Egypt's alignment with the Soviet Union also meant that Nasser was treated as a Cold War–related threat by both the United Kingdom and the United States.[5]

Prior to December 1971, Britain retained a permanent military presence in the Persian Gulf. Until November 1967, it also had a naval and air base in the crown colony of Aden and was attempting to establish a pro-British successor state out of its protectorates in South Arabia. Furthermore, London had a defense treaty with Oman, and British officers commanded and trained this Sultanate's armed forces.[6] The United Kingdom's military commitments in the Arabian Peninsula, Nasser's regional aspirations, and the future of the pro-British rulers of Kuwait, Bahrain, Qatar, the Trucial States (now the United Arab Emirates [UAE]), and Oman became the causes of an Anglo-Egyptian proxy war. Cairo supported both the insurgency in the Southern Omani province of Dhofar[7] and the nationalist guerrillas that fought the British in South Arabia and Aden from 1962 to 1967.[8] Following Egypt's intervention in Yemen in support of the Republican regime that seized power in San'aa in September 1962, Britain provided weaponry and mercenaries to the Royalist rebels during the ensuing civil war.[9] From the British perspective, the Egyptian threat to the United Kingdom's regional interests did not just involve the Yemeni intervention and proxy warfare. Egyptian cultural missions and teachers working in the Gulf, and Cairo Radio's broadcasts, had a cumulative effect in promoting Nasser's pan-Arabism, while fostering indigenous hostility toward Britain and its allied monarchs.[10]

Anglo-Egyptian hostilities were exacerbated on May 22, 1967, when Nasser ordered the closure of the Straits of Tiran to shipping bound for

Israel, precipitating a crisis that led to the Six Day War. The Labour prime minister Harold Wilson and Foreign Secretary George Brown proposed the creation of a multinational naval task force to break the blockade, but this initiative foundered because of a lack of US and French support; there was also no mood within Wilson's cabinet or the Ministry of Defence (MOD) for a potential confrontation between a Royal Navy task group and Egyptian forces.[11] After the war, Cairo Radio broadcasts declared that the Israeli Air Force's (IAF) preemptive strikes against Egypt on June 5 were assisted by American and British warplanes, and the "Big Lie" (as it was dubbed in Whitehall) contributed to both an Arab oil embargo in both the United States and the United Kingdom and anti-Western rioting across the region. Britain also blamed Egypt's postwar black-propaganda campaign for an uprising by the local police in Aden on June 20, 1967, during which twenty British soldiers were killed by the mutineers.[12]

Of further concern to Whitehall was the increase in Soviet aid to Egypt that followed the Six Day War. The Egyptian armed forces had suffered a devastating defeat, and its frontline with the Israeli Defense Force (IDF) was now the Suez Canal itself. Moscow responded with increased arms shipments to its regional allies, with Egypt as a primary recipient. The Soviet Union also sent 4,000 military advisers to retrain the Egyptian armed forces, and in the summer of 1969 it deployed a task force of 10,000 troops to Egypt, which included autonomous air-force and air-defense (PVO) units.[13] The Soviet Mediterranean Squadron was also given access to Alexandria (a former Royal Navy base) and an anchorage at Mersah Matruh, enhancing both its sustainability in and its potential wartime threat to NATO's Southern Flank.[14] The UK government, the Joint Intelligence Committee (JIC), and the British Chiefs of Staff (COS) saw the USSR's reinforced position in Egypt both as a military risk—the COS concluded that Soviet aircrew were flying reconnaissance missions by Tu-16 bombers over NATO naval exercises in the Eastern Mediterranean, even though the planes had Egyptian Air Force (EAF) insignia—and a wider political one.[15] The JIC's assessment was that the USSR's main intentions were to reinforce alliance ties with Cairo and to bolster its influence in the Arab world by backing Egypt against Israel. However, during the "War of Attrition" along the Canal (March 1969–August 1970), Soviet-piloted MiG-21 fighters became engaged in dogfights with the IAF, raising the worrying prospect that an Egyptian-Israeli confrontation could lead to direct military intervention by Moscow and a major East-West crisis.[16]

By the end of 1967, Egypt appeared fully dependent on military aid from the Soviet Union. Memories of the occupation era and the Suez crisis—not to mention the clandestine proxy war that had seen Egyptian-trained insurgents kill British soldiers in South Arabia, and British-backed Royalists kill Egyptian troops in Yemen—fueled animosity between London and Cairo.[17] For any contemporary observer of Anglo-Egyptian relations, the prospects for any meaningful improvement would have appeared bleak to nonexistent.

Nasser's Final Months: December 1968–September 1970

On December 12, 1967, the British embassy in Cairo was reopened after a two-year suspension of diplomatic relations, and Brown nominated a former ambassador to Egypt, Sir Harold Beeley, to take charge of this post. Beeley had earned Nasser's trust during his service in Cairo from 1961 to 1964, and he was also renowned within the Foreign and Commonwealth Office (FCO) for his anti-Israeli opinions.[18] The UK's role in securing UN Security Council Resolution 242 (SCR242)—calling for a "just settlement of the [Palestinian] refugee problem" and a return of Arab territory lost in the Six Day War—was also welcomed by the Egyptian president.[19] The end of Britain's colonial rule in South Arabia (November 1967), the Wilson government's declaration that it would withdraw British forces from the Persian Gulf in January 1968, and the Libyan revolution of September 1, 1969, (followed subsequently by a demand from Muammar Gaddafi's regime for the closure of British bases in Libya) also gradually removed one significant Egyptian grievance against the United Kingdom, namely, Britain's residual imperial presence in the Arab world.[20]

At this time, there was also a gradual deterioration in Anglo-Israeli ties, arising not only from SCR242 but also from a bilateral quarrel over arms sales. Even before the Six Day War, there was a consensus within the FCO that military relations between Britain and Israel were undermining the more extensive and lucrative economic interests that the United Kingdom had in the Arab world.[21] Following the "East of Suez" withdrawals, Britain's only prospects of preserving any influence over its former Persian Gulf protectorates involved the supply of military equipment and advisers to the latter. The British armed forces assigned loan-service personnel to their counterparts of the newly independent UAE after December 1971 (the Emirati army being a direct offshoot of the British-commanded Trucial Oman Scouts), and also to the Sultan's Armed Forces in Oman, which was fighting the Popular Front insurgency in Dhofar.[22] From the late 1950s to 1970, Britain had provided 660 Centurion tanks to the IDF, but despite Wilson's pro-Israeli sympathies, the Labour government responded to FCO and MOD concerns over the United Kingdom's economic and strategic interests in the Middle East by refusing in November 1969 to sell Israel the Chieftain, a more advanced main battle tank. This decision was regarded by the Israelis as a British sellout, influenced by the threat of economic blackmail by the Arab states.[23]

With the advantage of hindsight, the reorientation of Egyptian foreign policy from pan-Arab nationalism and alignment with the USSR could be seen during the aftermath of the Six Day War. Following the Khartoum Summit in August 1967, Cairo became increasingly dependent on Saudi aid, subsequently supplemented by subsidies from Kuwait and Libya, and by 1969 all three states were providing Nasser with an annual stipend of £104.4 million (approximately 261 million US dollars). The three donors all opposed the Soviet presence in Egypt, and the Saudis and Kuwaitis implicitly made it clear that, in exchange for financial assistance, Nasser should abandon his sponsorship of revolutionary movements in the Persian Gulf.[24] From the British perspective, a rapprochement with Cairo and its realignment from the USSR would also constitute a major foreign-policy success. Egypt was the most populous of the Arab states and was perceived by its peers as a regional leader. Furthermore, as the "East of Suez" withdrawals accelerated, and while Oman was trying to recover Dhofar from the Popular Front's control, the United Kingdom needed stability within its former dependencies as Bahrain, Qatar, and the UAE made tentative steps toward independence.[25] The cessation of Egyptian-inspired propaganda and subversion against pro-British rulers in the Gulf would therefore be a favorable development for the United Kingdom.

However, Anglo-Egyptian relations were strained throughout the remainder of Nasser's presidency. Beeley attributed this diplomatic impasse to the military confrontation along the Suez Canal and the West's relationship with Israel, but his successor, Sir Richard Beaumont, and Michael Stewart (Brown's successor as foreign secretary after March 1968) concluded that there remained fundamental policy differences between London and Cairo, not just on Middle Eastern matters but also (to cite one example) over the United States' intervention in the Vietnam War. After the Egyptian president's philippic against Britain delivered at the congress of the ruling Arab Socialist Union (ASU) on July 23, 1969, Beaumont argued that "Anglo-Egyptian relations will never prosper while President Nasser and his cronies remain in power," citing as one significant reason the ingrained Anglophobia of the president and his inner circle.[26]

The Cairo embassy's staff included a British Army colonel appointed as the defense attaché, with a Royal Navy commander and (from 1970) a Royal Air Force (RAF) wing commander serving respectively as the subordinate naval and air attachés. Beeley was unhappy with their presence, and in June 1969, the JIC debated a request by him to curtail their activities. The ambassador complained that their intelligence-gathering efforts were attracting the attention of the Egyptian security police (*Mukhabarat*), and he recommended the removal of the naval attaché, arguing that the latter's reports should be "weighed against the potential [diplomatic] embarrassment" that the attaché caused by his intelligence-gathering activities. The MOD (and its Defence Intelligence Staff) was aghast, stressing the value of the attachés' visual and photographic reporting, particularly on the Soviet military presence in Egypt,[27] and the information on the Cairo embassy's staff in the annual *Diplomatic Service List* during this period suggests that the MOD was successfully able to persuade the JIC to disregard Beeley's complaints.[28] A Royal Navy intelligence report dated autumn 1970 hints at another service the attaché team provided: the United States had no diplomatic representation in Cairo at this time, and therefore the military staff at the British embassy consisted of NATO's principal eyes and ears on the ground.[29]

At this time, the United Kingdom's attachés in Cairo were focused almost exclusively on intelligence work, first on assessing Egypt's capacity to resume hostilities against Israel, and second on the Soviet military presence on the ground. Diplomatic representation was a secondary concern, defense sales a "minimal third" (in the words of the naval attaché, Commander R. A. S. Irving), and "advising-training a non-existent fourth" because of Soviet influence over the Egyptian armed forces. The Cairo attachés were constrained by Mukhabarat surveillance and also security regulations that placed most of Egypt out of bounds to foreign diplomatic personnel.

Nonetheless, Irving noted in one of his reports that during his tour he had "learned more about Soviet military hardware than he ever knew about British material" and that despite the restrictions placed on him and other attachés, he was able to take photographs of Soviet air-defense systems deployed to Egypt, including an SA-3 surface-to-air missile (SAM) battery positioned conveniently close to his villa in Alexandria in March 1970. Irving's limited contacts with his hosts also revealed the tensions that existed between them and Soviet personnel; he quoted an Egyptian Navy Captain's bitter statement that "[we] are having to shake hands with the devil, and Cairo is full of them." The Royal Navy's representative in Egypt was therefore not only in a position to report on the technical capabilities of Soviet military equipment but also gained the justified impression that the alliance between Egypt and the USSR had fragile foundations.[30]

Sadat and the Expulsion of the Soviets: October 1970–July 1972

Nasser died on September 28, 1970, and was succeeded by Sadat, who was regarded both within and beyond Egypt as a transitional figure.[31] The new president was ridiculed by his countrymen for pompously declaring 1971 to be "the year of decision" with Israel and was almost ousted in a coup plotted by Ali Sabri (the secretary-general of the ASU) eight months after assuming power. In June 1970, the Conservatives won the British general election, and four months later the new foreign secretary, Sir Alec Douglas-Home, enraged the Israeli government with a speech delivered to Tory activists in Harrogate in which he argued that another Middle Eastern war was inevitable if Israel did not comply with SCR242 and return to its Arab neighbors the territory the IDF seized in June 1967.[32] In September 1971, Douglas-Home (who had earlier represented Britain at Nasser's funeral) paid a successful visit to Egypt. The foreign secretary was at first glance an unlikely emissary of goodwill, as not only had he been one of the more hawkish of Eden's ministers during the Suez crisis, but during his brief premiership (October 1963–October 1964) he had also backed covert action against the Egyptians in Yemen. Nonetheless, the United Kingdom's pro-Egyptian stance in Middle Eastern peacemaking and Sadat's desire for better relations with the West provided the basis for reconciliation between

London and Cairo.³³ Sadat's intentions in this regard were also substantiated by the purge of pro-Soviet ASU officials (notably Interior Minister Shawari Gom'aa) following Sabri's aborted coup.³⁴

Beaumont had served as the United Kingdom's ambassador to Baghdad until June 1967, when he was forced to evacuate his embassy after Iraq cut off diplomatic relations with the United Kingdom following the Six Day War. Having experienced the collapse of Britain's ties with one Arab state, he fostered a revival of them with another during his service in Cairo, although in one dispatch in February 1971 he described the burgeoning relationship between the United Kingdom and Egypt as "a delicate flower."³⁵ Beaumont also had a far greater appreciation of his service attachés' work than his predecessor, and his military subordinates became fully involved in redeveloping bilateral ties. On July 14, 1971, Irving's successor, Commander John Marriott, received an unexpected invitation to meet the chief of staff of the Egyptian armed forces, Major General Sa'ad Shazli. During the course of their discussion, Shazli told Marriott that not only did he want to ease security restrictions imposed on foreign attachés, but that Egypt was also interested in purchasing arms from the United Kingdom.³⁶ Two months later, Rear Admiral Ashraf Mohammed Rifaat, the Egyptian chief of naval operations, accepted an invitation to both the Royal Navy's Staff College in Greenwich and its annual equipment exhibition. Rifaat's delegation included Major General Mustafa Kamel (the Egyptian armed forces' head of technical intelligence); not only was this the first visit by a senior Egyptian military delegation for nearly twenty years, but it appeared to substantiate Shazli's remarks to Marriott about Egypt's renewed interest in buying British weaponry. Its navy was in particular need of modernization, as the fleet consisted largely of not only increasingly obsolete Soviet vessels and weaponry but also British-built ships of Second World War vintage.³⁷

Nonetheless, progress in defense diplomacy was uneven. The defense attaché, Colonel Tony Lewis, and the RAF representatives (Wing Commander W. E. Hamilton and, after the end of Hamilton's tour in November 1971, Wing Commander David Barnicoat) established some tangible links with the Egyptian Army and the EAF. In February 1972, Lewis reported on the visit of the chief of military medical services, General Rifai Kamel, to Britain, where he was hosted by the Royal Army Medical Corps; Kamel subsequently expressed an interest in enrolling Egyptian military doctors in

British courses. Major General Mahrus Abu Hussein (the Egyptian Army's director of signals) attended the British Army's Defence Signals Course in September 1971, and the following month an Egyptian delegation witnessed a Royal Artillery firepower demonstration on Salisbury Plain. EAF medics were invited to meet their counterparts at RAF Akrotiri in Cyprus, and in turn the commander of British Forces in the Near East, Air Marshal Sir Derek Hodgkinson, visited Egypt from February 24 to 28, 1972. However, despite Rifaat's tour of Greenwich and the Egyptian Navy's evident need for modernization, Marriott made little progress with his sister service, attributing this to the navy's insularity and its animosity toward the rest of the Egyptian military. Britain's naval attaché also blamed a "cult of security" and a lack of initiative within Egypt's armed forces, which meant that any potentially contentious problems (such as a request by a foreign attaché for access to ships or senior officers) were automatically rejected. For his part, Lewis expressed frustration with the inefficiency of his hosts' Military Attachés Liaison Branch, stating that opportunities to enroll Egyptian officers in defense courses in the United Kingdom were lost because of the incompetence and inertia of its uniformed bureaucrats.[38]

The defense attaché's team continued to conduct intelligence work, which in turn could conceivably have contributed to any lingering mistrust from the Egyptians. Lewis noted that he and his two subordinates were searching for newer Soviet-supplied weaponry, not least the SA-6 SAM with its tracked and mobile launcher system. Egypt offered an opportunity for the Soviet Union to field-test its weaponry even after the formal end of the War of Attrition in August 1970, although Marriott reported that the local climate (notably the temperature and humidity) had an adverse effect on Soviet weapons systems, such as the Styx surface-to-surface missiles that were the main armament on the Egyptian Navy's patrol boats. In a similar vein, Barnicoat noted in his 1972 report that sand-silting damaged radar sets supplied to the Air Defence Force.[39] In addition to these technical problems, the defense attaché's team also reported on the deterioration of Egyptian-Soviet relations, which culminated with Sadat's decision to expel the USSR's advisers and its autonomous military contingents on July 18, 1972.

There were indications of tensions between Moscow and Cairo beforehand. During a meeting with the foreign secretary in London in December 1970, Mohammed Heikal (the editor of the newspaper *Al-Ahram* and a for-

mer confidante of Nasser's) pointedly stated that Egypt "was not Czechoslovakia"; the suppression of the Prague Spring was recent history, so this
statement was possibly an implicit assertion of Egyptian sovereignty on
Heikal's part. Sadat also grew to resent the arrogance of the Soviet ambassador, Vladimir Vinogradov, whom he compared in his memoirs to the British
high commissioners of the occupation era.[40] The COS and the British attachés in Cairo estimated that there were 20,000 Soviet personnel in Egypt,
consisting not only of the autonomous air and PVO contingents but also
of around 6,000 advisers assigned to the Egyptian Army, 1,100 to the EAF,
and 1,000 to the navy. British military-intelligence assessments concluded
that the Soviet presence served as a valuable deterrent against an Israeli onslaught (specifically with reference to the PVO units) but that it was also
essential in restoring the combat effectiveness of the Egyptian armed forces
after their mauling by the IDF in June 1967.[41]

Prior to July 1972, the three attachés and other FCO sources continu-
ally reported growing Egyptian resentment over their Soviet "allies," who
were generally perceived to treat their host nation and its military with contempt. Soviet personnel refused to socialize with their hosts or admit them
to their own messes, and Egyptian officers were also convinced that the
USSR's "advisers" abused their powers by arranging for any of their number deemed to be anti-Soviet to be cashiered. Senior Egyptian commanders
such as General Mohammed Ahmed Sadeq (the war minister) and Air Vice-
Marshal Abd al Latif al-Baghdadi (the chief of the EAF) openly loathed
the Soviets, and this attitude percolated down the ranks.[42] After the expulsions, both Marriott and Barnicoat were briefed by the Egyptian director of
military intelligence, Major General Mehrez Abdul Rahman, who stressed
that "all repeat all Soviet military personnel would be leaving Egypt," although some technical staff would be retained to perform essential maintenance tasks where their expertise was irreplaceable. Rahman complained
that "[during] the past year the Russians were getting more from the Egyptians than the Egyptians were getting from the Russians," with the latter acquiring an "unacceptable degree of control" over his country. Although the
Soviet Mediterranean Squadron would still have port access to Alexandria
and Mersa Matruh, their shore facilities would be closed, and the Egyptians
would take control of the national air-defense network. Egypt was, in Rahman's words, "essentially a Western-oriented country" and would never be

a "Soviet satellite." By year's end, Beaumont concluded that the Egyptians had been true to their word, stating that his attachés estimated that there were only around 100 Soviet technicians left in the country.[43]

One curious source of information for Lewis's, Marriott's, and Barnicoat's reports was the chief of the Soviet attaché mission in Egypt. Rear Admiral Nikolai Ivliev's Second World War service reportedly included liaison with the Royal Navy's Arctic convoys, but in peacetime he was declared persona non grata as the Soviet Union's naval attaché in both London and Paris. The staff at the UK's Cairo embassy suspected correctly that Ivliev was a GRU (Soviet military intelligence) officer—he was in fact the GRU's *Rezident* (head of station) in Egypt—but nonetheless the Royal Navy and RAF attachés were impressed with his apparent candor and good humor. In conversations with his British counterparts, Ivliev flatly contradicted *TASS* reports that the USSR's withdrawal was a mutually agreed-upon process, admitting that his compatriots were being thrown out of Egypt against Moscow's will. Following a discussion with Ivliev in November 1972, Marriott noted that he "seemed very fair" in his comments on the Egyptian Navy and was "not at all bitter or unduly scathing." Ivliev asserted that the Egyptians had reacted poorly to training methods that were intended to prepare them for the rigors of major combat operations against Israel and that they blamed the Soviets for any of their own shortcomings in equipment maintenance or on their exercises. Furthermore, he claimed that his subordinates had requested the reassignment or removal of Egyptian officers only if they were deemed professionally incompetent, rather than for being anti-Soviet. Ivliev may have been indulging in special pleading, and it pays to be wary of any apparently affable military or diplomatic representatives of an adversarial power. Yet as it turned out, Ivliev's comments on the scale of the Egyptian-Soviet breach—and his conclusions that this could not be restored—were accurate.[44]

This eviction of the USSR's advisers and combat units removed a potential wartime threat to NATO's Mediterranean flank. It also led British Prime Minister Edward Heath to request advice from Whitehall as to how the United Kingdom could reinforce Sadat's breach with Moscow, particularly by facilitating arms sales to Egypt. Yet as the subsequent section shows, the Cairo embassy and its military attachés faced significant and ultimately insurmountable constraints that prevented them from making any significant progress in establishing defense ties with the Egyptians.[45]

The Arms Sales Conundrum: 1972–1973

Beginning in the summer of 1972, Sadat was preparing to resume hostilities with Israel, planning a surprise assault to seize the Eastern bank of the Suez Canal, then subsequently relying on a defensive screen of Soviet-supplied SAM and antitank defenses to enable the Egyptian Army to hold its ground against qualitatively superior Israeli ground and air forces. Sadat concluded that the imposition of heavy losses on the IDF—and international diplomatic pressure for a ceasefire—would enable Egypt to compel Israel to return the Sinai as part of a peace settlement. Following a meeting with the Supreme Council of the Armed Forces on October 24, 1972, the president fired General Sadeq after the latter protested that the armed forces were unprepared for war. Sadat subsequently planned a two-front attack on Israel with the Syrians and was successfully able to conceal his preparations for war not only from IDF intelligence but also from the two superpowers. The Egyptian assault across the Sinai Canal at 1400 local time on October 6, 1973—and the concurrent Syrian offensive in the Golan Heights—therefore took the Israelis and the international community completely by surprise.[46]

Until November 1967, Britain would not sell the Egyptians any equipment that could be used either to support its operations in Yemen or to assist anti-British guerrillas in South Arabia,[47] and even after the withdrawal from Aden, Whitehall's interdepartmental Release of Military Information Policy Committee ruled that, because of Soviet influence in Egypt, Cairo could not be provided with any classified information or any equipment that could compromise sensitive intelligence on the British armed forces' military capabilities. Furthermore, after the Six Day War, UK government policy banned the sale of any weaponry to the "front-line" states (either Israel or its immediate Arab neighbors) that would upset the military balance between them and potentially encourage one side to resume hostilities. Another Middle Eastern conflict would not only be a body blow to the British economy—with the anticipated cutoff of regional oil supplies—but could also irreparably damage Anglo-American relations, particularly if the United States concluded that war had been provoked by the sale of British military equipment to Egypt or any of Israel's other Arab adversaries. This posed an insurmountable dilemma for the British, as one factor behind Sadat's breach with Moscow was the Soviet Union's refusal to supply weapons systems (such as long-range bombers) that would enable Egypt to directly attack Israel.[48]

In early January 1972, Barnicoat reported that the EAF expressed an interest in purchasing fifteen Jaguar ground-attack jets. While Beaumont concluded that this could be an Egyptian ploy to compel the Soviets to supply long-range aircraft, he also suggested that it possibly represented "the first major opportunity the West has had to reverse the tide of Egyptian dependence" on the USSR. Prior to the expulsion of the Soviet advisers, Cairo sounded out London on the acquisition of antitank missiles and antisubmarine-warfare (ASW) technology. During the summer of 1972, these Egyptian requests were confirmed, with a particular interest not only with Jaguar but also both the short-range Rapier SAM system and the Sea King ASW helicopter.[49]

From a British perspective, the provision of these weapons posed the following complications. First, Jaguar and Rapier were being introduced into service with the RAF and the British Army to upgrade their respective ground-attack and air-defense capabilities, and they could not be supplied in sufficient quantity to the Egyptians until the requirements of Britain's own armed forces had been satisfied. Second, Jaguar was a joint Anglo-French project, while the British firm Westland had a license from a parent American manufacturer to build Sea King; the Mark 44 torpedo fitted to this helicopter was also US-designed. The UK government therefore did not possess unilateral authority to approve their sale to Egypt. Third, the COS was alarmed by the potential exposure of sensitive British technology, particularly as the Jaguar's avionics and the Sea King's sonar were judged to be far more advanced than that of their Soviet equivalents. The latter was particularly prized by the Royal Navy as its surface fleet's best defense against the USSR's submarine threat in wartime. In this respect, the JIC concluded that, even after the withdrawal of Soviet advisers and combat units, the KGB, GRU, and Eastern-bloc services could conceivably have recruited agents within the Egyptian military and security forces, who in turn could leak information on the technical specifications of Western-supplied equipment. From the MOD's and the intelligence community's perspectives, there was a clear preference for either refusing to sell these weapons to Egypt or to at least provide "sanitized" versions that were less combat-effective but also did not contain any sensitive technical components.[50]

Finally, potential arms sales to Egypt were opposed by the British Jewish community and also pro-Israeli MPs on both sides of the House of Commons and were particularly contentious domestically because of acts of Palestinian terrorism, such as the massacre of eleven Israeli athletes by Black September at the Munich Olympics (September 6, 1972). Furthermore, if the EAF acquired Jaguar, it would gain the capability to strike targets not just beyond the Canal into the Israeli-occupied Sinai Peninsula but in Israel's cities too.[51]

Some FCO officials, as well as the MOD Defence Sales Department and the Cairo embassy staff, regarded the COS and JIC's security concerns as overplayed. Not only were the Egyptians undertaking to remove all Soviet advisers from their country, but Sadeq guaranteed to protect all British-supplied equipment from Eastern-bloc espionage; supporters of arms sales deemed this a significant promise given the Mukhabarat's traditionally comprehensive approach to internal security.[52] British officials were in this respect unaware that Sadat's expulsion of the USSR's military personnel drastically curtailed KGB activities in Cairo and that Egypt had also dismissed the East German *Stasi* advisers assigned to its Interior Ministry, although both these developments could only have been observable in retrospect.[53] Beaumont and Lewis also fretted over Whitehall's slow response to Egyptian defense-sales requests, concluding either that Cairo would be encouraged to turn back to the Soviet bloc for aid or that French and Italian competitors would steal emerging business opportunities from British firms. When Sadeq was replaced with General Ismail Ali on October 24, 1972, both the attachés in Cairo and MOD Defence Sales were alarmed. During a visit by Reginald Anderson, the MOD's assistant undersecretary (defense sales), to Cairo in late May 1972, the war minister claimed that he was struggling against a pro-Soviet clique in his efforts to align Egypt with the West. His dismissal by Sadat five months later raised British concerns that the United Kingdom had missed an important opportunity because of its apparently sluggish response to Egyptian arms requests.[54]

The British faced an insurmountable challenge. The Egyptian military demanded equipment that would enhance its combat capabilities against the IDF, and Britain's efforts to promote less contentious sales (such as the British Aircraft Corporation's Strikemaster trainer jet) were rejected by Cairo. These deliberations over arms transfers were discussed by the cabinet's Defence and Overseas Policy Committee on September 13, 1972, and although the Heath government ruled out the sale of Jaguar, it approved Sea King and a "sanitized" model of Rapier similar to that sold to Iran, overriding the COS's security concerns.[55] In late June 1973, the United Kingdom agreed to sell thirty Sea Kings to Saudi Arabia, which was purchasing the helicopters on Cairo's behalf, and the total earnings for British defense sales to Egypt for the 1973–1974 fiscal year were projected at £150 million (compared to £15 million the previous year). However, shortly after the outbreak of the Yom Kippur War, the Heath government imposed an arms embargo on all the combatants, and the proposed arms contracts with the Egyptians ended up in abeyance.[56]

Beginning in early 1972, the defense attaché and his two subordinates enthusiastically promoted military sales to Egypt. Anderson praised the service representatives in the Cairo embassy for their support for his visit in late May, and Lewis, Marriott, and Barnicoat developed a shared interest with the MOD's Defence Sales Department in promoting closer military ties with the Egyptians. The defense attaché also expressed frustration that the efforts of the Cairo team to develop contacts between UK defense industries and the Egyptian armed forces appeared to be unappreciated by the MOD, and he was also keen to explore options to sell a sanitized variant of Jaguar to the EAF before Heath's cabinet vetoed this decision.[57] The extent of the attachés' assistance to businesses such as British Aircraft Corporation, Plessey, and Marconi were such that FCO officials fretted that they might inadvertently encourage Egyptian expectations over equipment that the United Kingdom would be unable to sell on political grounds. Lewis and his two subordinates had to strike a delicate balance between supporting the British defense industry's contacts with Egypt and ensuring that they did not indicate that Britain was prepared to support the sale of any weapons systems that would inevitably complicate Anglo-American or Anglo-Israeli relations.[58]

In their reports in January 1973, both Lewis and Barnicoat in particular noted that their specific priorities were now dominated by promoting defense sales (including visits by representatives of industry and of the British Army and RAF to provide weapons demonstrations) and also arrangements for Egyptian personnel to study in British military courses. Although Marriott continued to find the establishment of closer ties with the Egyptian Navy a challenge, the other two UK attachés (along with other foreign representatives) were invited to the Egyptian Military and Air Academies. Barnicoat concluded that he had established an amicable relationship with Baghdadi's successor, the future president Hosni Mubarak, and Lewis noted that "the gathering of intelligence, though of undiminished importance, now takes second place" to what had become routine liaison work.[59]

Nevertheless, the three UK service representatives in Cairo continued to assess the likelihood of war between Egypt and Israel. From their own observations, they concluded that the Egyptian armed forces were too feeble to resume hostilities, particularly after Sadat's decision to evict the Soviets. Lewis came close to anticipating future developments when he reported in January 1973 that if Egypt went to war, "her least damaging solution would be to cross the [Suez] Canal to a limited depth of about 12 kilometres" and to rely on its SAM and antiarmor weapons systems to hold out against the IDF until the superpowers imposed a ceasefire. In their defense, Lewis and his two subordinates were possibly overstretched by their roles in managing growing bilateral defense ties while also reporting on Egyptian military capabilities. Indeed, some of their conclusions (notably on the rigidity of officer cadet training in the Military Academy, and the imbalance in professional skills and tactical initiative between the EAF and IAF) were confirmed by the course of the Yom Kippur War. In addition, the Egyptian armed forces were highly successful in preserving operational security not just from foreign diplomats but also from the US and Israeli intelligence communities. The presumption that Egypt could not fight without extensive Soviet assistance was in fact a common one across Whitehall.[60]

Conclusion

In March 1976, Sadat denounced the Treaty of Friendship with the Soviet Union, breaking the alliance Nasser had established with Moscow in the mid-1950s and signaling Egypt's turn toward the United States. Three years later, the Egyptian president signed a peace treaty with Israel that led not only to the return of the Sinai Peninsula but to the removal of the main constraint affecting UK arms sales to Egypt. However, it was the Americans rather than the British who were the primary beneficiaries of these developments. From the early 1980s, the US and Egyptian Armed Forces regularly conducted bilateral training with the Bright Star exercises, and the United

States became Egypt's main source of foreign aid.[61] Despite the hopes of Lewis and his fellow attachés, British firms did not reap any significant benefits from Egyptian military modernization, as Cairo subsequently sought American arms and equipment when upgrading its armed forces.[62]

During the late 1960s and early 1970s, Egyptian-British relations nonetheless changed fundamentally, due to Cairo's growing dissatisfaction with the Soviet Union and also the end of the United Kingdom's military presence "East of Suez." The demise of Nasser's brand of nationalism was also significant: not only did Egypt cease subverting pro-Western regimes in the Arab world, but radical movements such as the Dhofari Popular Front, the Arab Nationalist Movement, and the Palestinian *fedayeen* were more inspired by the "Tricontinentalist" ethos associated with the Cuban and Vietnamese revolutions than traditional pan-Arabist ideologies.[63] However, despite the best efforts of successive British ambassadors to Cairo and their attachés, there were significant limitations on the development of Anglo-Egyptian military relations. Although after July 1972 the Heath government hoped that the United Kingdom could gain tangible commercial benefits while encouraging Egypt's estrangement from the Soviet Union with increased defense sales, the arms the Egyptians wanted to purchase (notably Jaguar) were politically impossible for the British to supply. There was also a consistent tension between Egypt's aim of acquiring weapons systems that would enable it to resume hostilities with Israel—which the United Kingdom was determined to avoid, not just because of the economic impact of another Arab-Israeli war but also of the likely response from Richard Nixon's administration—and Britain's attempts to supply relatively low-grade equipment to mollify Cairo. While some FCO and MOD officials chafed at the restrictions on defense sales, the consensus in Whitehall was that Britain could ill afford to indirectly provoke a regional conflict that would have grave domestic implications (not least because of a likely cutoff in oil supplies) and undermine the "special relationship" with the United States.[64]

Nonetheless, the reporting from the Cairo attachés during this period offer fascinating insights into the Egyptian armed forces. One common theme was that despite the legacy of confrontation between the United Kingdom and Egypt, the latter's officer corps appeared to retain a residual respect for British military expertise, deriving in part from the participation of officers in training programs and courses provided by Britain's armed forces up until the mid-1950s. Marriott reported in January 1972 that Egyptian naval officers trained by their Royal Navy counterparts prior to 1955 had fond memories of the latter (particularly when compared with experiences with their Soviet equivalents subsequently), and Barnicoat noted the following year that the RAF's AP129 *Manual of Flying* was still used by directing staff at the EAF's Air Academy and that the cadets' instruction was still mainly delivered in English.[65] As Marriott suggested, some Egyptian expressions of Anglophilia could have been intended to flatter. Yet the conclusions of these dispatches are supported by more recent scholarship arguing that Arab armed forces receiving Soviet assistance did not incorporate the USSR's doctrine and training wholesale but adopted it alongside theoretical and practical inheritances from the former imperial powers (in Egypt's case, this involved the British).[66] The attachés' contacts with Egyptian officers and Soviet advisers—notably the GRU Rezident Ivliev—also emphasized one of the main factors in the collapse of alliance ties between Cairo and Moscow. The USSR's military presence in Egypt from the late 1960s to the early 1970s became as unacceptable to indigenous opinion as that of the British during the occupation (1882–1954), only this time it was Soviet service personnel who became loathed for their arrogance and ill-concealed disdain toward their hosts.[67]

In January 1973, Lewis wrote that some constraints on Anglo-Egyptian defense ties came from the British side and were not just related to security concerns. He noted that "[recent] past history and the abysmal qualities of [Egypt's] forces do not encourage serving officers either in the Ministry or the Services to look favourably on closer military co-operation." This reflected not only institutional memories of the rout the IDF inflicted on the Egyptians in June 1967 and the latter's mediocre performance in the subsequent War of Attrition but also potentially an implicit antipathy in British military circles deriving from legacy of the Nasser era, including Egypt's support for the South Arabian insurgents during the 1960s.[68] Lewis and his colleagues genuinely championed Egypt's case for acquiring sophisticated arms from the United Kingdom after the eviction of the Soviet advisory mission, so much so that it could be argued that they had experienced the not-uncommon traits of "going native" and of becoming advocates for their host government's case.[69] However, when Sadat, Sadeq, and other senior Egyptian officials requested Jaguar and other controversial weapons systems, they may have sought to exploit Britain's eagerness to develop bilateral defense ties by demanding the impossible as leverage for British concessions, using the threat of renewed ties with Moscow as an additional means of imposing pressure on the United Kingdom to concede to lesser requests. If so, the Heath government's decision to offer Sea King despite the COS's concerns over potential security breaches may well have represented the successful application of this bargaining tactic. Finally, the attachés were wrong to assume that Egypt could not wage war with Israel without Soviet support and that the July 1972 expulsions made a renewed Arab-Israeli conflict less likely. Yet they were not alone in drawing this erroneous conclusion.

Nonetheless, even with the advantage of scholarly hindsight, it is impressive to see how a small team of attachés adjusted to changed circumstances during a short period of time, transitioning from an intelligence-gathering role conducted under the hostile gaze of the Mukhabarat to the provision of support for defense sales, the exchange of visits, and the assistance given to Egyptian officers participating in British military courses. The United Kingdom's military representatives in Cairo during this period were acting in accordance with British policy toward the Arab world in the aftermath of the "East of Suez" withdrawals, using defense diplomacy to maintain residual influence after the end of the United Kingdom's formal military presence in the region. Furthermore, as Beaumont noted in March 1972, it was also "remarkable how much, in the virtual absence of any overt information from Egyptian official sources, can be gathered by the good use of eyes and ears by officers who are new to the country or even the region." A comparison between their reporting and more recent scholarship demonstrates how much insight on the Egyptian armed forces they were able to gain, despite operating in an authoritarian and (until late 1971) a generally unwelcome environment.[70]

NOTES

The analysis, opinions and conclusions expressed or implied in this chapter are those of the author and do not necessarily represent the views of the Joint Services Command and Staff College, the Defence Academy, the MOD, or any other UK government agency.

1   Michael Herman observes that military attachés "belong to both the diplomatic and intelligence worlds, as indeed is recognized in the special procedures for

their accreditation." See his *Intelligence Power in Peace and War* (Cambridge, UK: Cambridge University Press, 1996), 120.

2 M. S. Anderson, *The Eastern Question 1774–1923: A Study in International Relations* (Basingstoke, UK: Macmillan, 1991), 240–250, 385–387; Keith Jeffery, *The British Army and the Crisis of Empire, 1918–1922* (Manchester, UK: Manchester University Press, 1986), 110–121; Michael Doran, "Egypt: Pan-Arabism in Historical Context," in *Diplomacy in the Middle East: The International Relations of Regional and Outside Powers*, ed. L. Carl Brown (London: I. B. Tauris, 2001), 98–101.

3 David French, *The British Way in Counter-Insurgency 1945–1967* (Oxford, UK: Oxford University Press, 2011), 68, 114, 135–136, 189–190; William Roger Louis, "Prelude to Suez: Churchill and Egypt," in *Ends of British Imperialism: The Scramble for Empire, Suez and Decolonisation* (London: I. B. Tauris, 2006), 609–613.

4 Robert McNamara, *Britain, Nasser and the Balance of Power in the Middle East 1952–1967* (London: Frank Cass, 2003); Michael Doran, *Ike's Gamble: America's Rise to Dominance in the Middle East* (New York: Free Press, 2016).

5 Keith Kyle, *Suez: Britain's End of Empire in the Middle East*, 2nd ed. (London: I. B. Tauris, 2003); McNamara, *Britain, Nasser*, 64–92. Syria split from the UAR in late September 1961, although Egypt retained the official name of "the United Arab Republic" for a further decade. For clarity's sake, the author refers to "Egypt" and "the Egyptians" throughout this chapter.

6 Saki Dockrill, *Britain's Retreat from East of Suez: The Choice between Europe and the World?* (London: Palgrave Macmillan, 2002); Geraint Hughes, "Demythologising Dhofar: British Policy, Military Strategy, and Counter-Insurgency in Oman, 1963–1976," *Journal of Military History* 79, no. 2 (2015): 423–456.

7 J. E. Peterson, *Oman's Insurgencies: The Sultan's Struggle for Supremacy* (London: Saqi, 2007), 196–197.

8 Jonathan Walker, *Aden Insurgency: The Savage War in South Arabia 1962–1967* (Staplehurst, UK: Spellmount, 2005); Admiral Lord Louis Mountbatten (Chief of the Defence Staff) to Peter Thorneycroft (Defence Secretary), July 3, 1964, DEFE13/570, The National Archives, Kew, (hereafter TNA).

9 Clive Jones, *Britain and the Yemen Civil War, 1962–1965: Ministers, Mercenaries and Mandarins: Foreign Policy and the Limits of Covert Action* (Brighton, UK: Sussex Academic Press, 2004); Spencer Mawby, *British Policy in Aden and the Protectorates, 1955–1967: Last Outpost of a Middle East Empire* (Abingdon, UK: Routledge, 2005).

10 James Onley, *Britain and the Gulf Shaikhdoms, 1820–1971: The Politics of Protection* (Georgetown University School of Foreign Service in Qatar, Occasional Paper No. 4, 2009), 17–18.

11 Simon C. Smith, *Ending Empire in the Middle East: Britain, the United States and Post-war Decolonisation* (Abingdon, UK: Routledge, 2012); Michael B.

Oren, *Six Days of War: June 1967 and the Making of the Modern Middle East* (London: Penguin, 2003), 101–116.

12 Walker, *Aden Insurgency*, 231, 239–256; Humphrey Trevelyan (High Commissioner, Aden) to Foreign Office, June 11, 1967, FCO8/252, TNA.

13 Dima P. Adamsky, "'Zero Hour for the Bears': Inquiring into the Soviet Decision to Intervene in the Egyptian-Israeli War of Attrition, 1969–1970," *Cold War History* 6, no. 1 (2006): 113–136; Isabella Ginor, "'Under the Yellow Arab Helmet Gleamed Blue Russian Eyes': Operation *Kavkaz* and the War of Attrition, 1969–1970," *Cold War History* 3, no. 1 (2002): 127–156.

14 DIS Report NI4(N)119, *The Soviet Naval Presence in the Mediterranean*, January 1, 1967, FCO28/455, TNA; "The Soviet Naval Presence in the Mediterranean," *Naval Intelligence Report*, no. 16 (Spring 1968), DEFE63/33, TNA.

15 Minutes of the Chiefs of Staff meeting COS29th/68, March 21, 1968; and COS31st/68, June 5, 1968, DEFE4/228, TNA; "Soviet Use of Egyptian Ports," *Naval Intelligence Report*, no. 21 (Summer 1969), DEFE63/38, TNA; "Soviet Penetration of the Middle East," *Naval Intelligence Report*, no. 28 (Spring 1971), DEFE63/45, TNA.

16 JIC(68)34(Final), *Soviet Intentions in the Mediterranean*, May 20, 1968; and JIC(68)19(Final), *Soviet Policy in the Middle East and North Africa*, June 4, 1968, PREM13/2959, TNA; Ginor, "*Kavkaz*," 143–147.

17 Near Eastern Department (FCO) memorandum, "Visit of UAR Foreign Minister, 24 September 1968. Steering Brief," September 19, 1968, FCO39/275, TNA.

18 "Obituary: Sir Harold Beeley," *Guardian*, July 31, 2001. In his valedictory dispatch, Beeley went as far as to accuse Israel of deliberately provoking discord between Britain and Egypt. See Beeley to Michael Stewart (Foreign Secretary), February 25, 1969, FCO39/552, TNA. In October 1968, the Foreign and Commonwealth Relations Offices were amalgamated; for convenience's sake, the author will refer to the "FCO" throughout this chapter rather than to its predecessors.

19 Frank Brenchley, *Britain, the Six Day War, and its Aftermath* (London: Penguin, 2005), 69–71; Arieh J. Kochavi, "George Brown and British Policy in the Middle East Following the 1967 War," *Middle East Journal* 70, no. 1 (2016): 91–110.

20 William Roger Louis, "Public Enemy Number One: Britain and the United Nations in the Aftermath of Suez," in *British Imperialism*, 689–724.

21 Memorandum by C. McLean (Eastern Department, Foreign Office), September 29, 1965, FO371/180917, TNA.

22 COS1428/833, *Directive to the Senior British Loan Service Officer in the Abu Dhabi Defence Force*, October 16, 1973, DEFE4/279, TNA. Hughes, "Demythologising Dhofar," 425–426.

23 Saul Bronfeld, "The 'Chieftain Tank Affair': *Realpolitik*, Perfidy and the Gen-

esis of the Merkava," *Contemporary British History* 29, no. 3 (2015): 380–400; Simon C. Smith, "Centurions and Chieftains: Tank Sales and British Policy towards Israel in the Aftermath of the Six Day War," *Contemporary British History* 28, no. 2 (2014): 219–239.

24   Sir Richard Beaumont (HM Ambassador Cairo) to Stewart, *United Arab Republic: Annual Review for 1969*, January 23, 1970, FO407/415, TNA; JIC(A) (69)43(Final), *Prospects for the UAR: 1970–1971*, February 13, 1970, CAB186/3(TNA).

25   D. E. Adamson (assistant director sales, MOD), *Brief for Defence Sales Team Visit to Cairo—19/23 May 1972*, FCO39/1250, TNA.

26   Beeley to Stewart, February 25, 1969; Stewart to Beaumont, May 7, 1969; and Beaumont to Stewart, August 5, 1969, FCO39/552, TNA; Beaumont to Stewart, January 23, 1970, FO407/415, TNA.

27   JIC(A)(69)22nd meeting, June 5, 1969; and JIC(A)(69)25th meeting, June 26, 1969, CAB185/1, TNA.

28   *The Diplomatic Service List 1969* (London: HMSO, 1969) lists Defence Attaché Colonel Frederick De Butts and Naval Attaché Commander R. A. S. Irving as being assigned to the Cairo Embassy. According to the 1970 edition, they were joined by Wing Commander W. E. Hamilton as the air attaché.

29   "No Passing to Forigner [*sic*] (An attaché's year)," *Naval Intelligence Report*, no. 26 (Autumn 1970): DEFE63/43, TNA.

30   "The Egyptian Is Not a Nautical Animal," *Naval Intelligence Report*, no. 18 (Autumn 1968): DEFE63/35, TNA; "No Passing to Forigner"; DEFE63/43, TNA.

31   Beaumont to Douglas-Home, December 2, 1970; J. F. Walker (Northern Africa Department—NAD) to Sir Philip Adams (Assistant Under-Secretary, NAD), October 22, 1970; FCO39/737, TNA.

32   Conversation between Edward Heath and Golda Meir (prime minister of Israel) in 10 Downing Street, November 4, 1970, PREM15/105, TNA; Memorandum by M. A. Holding (NAD), February 15, 1971, FCO39/961, TNA.

33   FCO to Cairo, No. 980, September 29, 1970, FCO39/736, TNA; Richard J. Aldrich and Rory Cormac, *The Black Door: Spies, Secret Intelligence and British Prime Ministers* (London: William Collins, 2017), 250–251; Geraint Hughes, "Britain, the Transatlantic Alliance, and the Arab-Israeli War of 1973," *Journal of Cold War Studies* 10, no. 2 (2008): 10–16.

34   Christopher Andrew and Vasili Mitrokhin, *The KGB in Europe and the West: The Mitrokhin Archive II* (London: Penguin 2006), 153–155; Markus Wolf (with Anne McElvoy), *Memoirs of a Spymaster: The Man Who Waged a Secret War against the West* (London: Pimlico, 1998), 257–258.

35   "Obituary: Sir Richard Beaumont," *Daily Telegraph*, January 28, 2009; Beaumont to Douglas-Home, January 25, 1971, FCO39/961, TNA.

36   M. I. Goulding (NAD) to Holding, July 14, 1971; Memorandum by Cdr.

J. P. Marriott (RN), July 14, 1971; Marriott, September 6, 1971, FCO39/1001, TNA.

37 Cdre. G. R. Villar (Defence Intelligence Staff), N/7497/73, *The Egyptian Navy*, May 1973, DEFE63/26, TNA; Cairo to FCO, No. 1195, September 17, 1971; A. James Craig (head of Near East and North Africa Department — NENAD), *Naval Sales to Egypt*, October 4, 1971; Marriott, *Visit by Senior Egyptian Officers to the Royal Navy Equipment Exhibition and the Royal Naval College, Greenwich, 21st to 25th September 1972*, October 5, 1971, FCO39/1001, TNA.

38 Col. A. D. Lewis to Beaumont, *Annual Report 1971*, February 9, 1972; Annex A, *Report by the Naval Attaché, Cairo*, February 9, 1972; Annex B, *Annual Report for 1971 by the Air Attaché*, February 9, 1972, FCO39/1262, TNA.

39 Minute by Marriott, September 6, 1972, FCO39/1001, TNA; Lewis to Beaumont, February 9, 1972, FCO39/1262, TNA. Wing Cdr. D. Barnicoat (RAF), *Annual Report for 1972 by the Air Attaché*, January 9, 1973, FCO93/65, TNA.

40 Meeting between Douglas-Home and Heikal, December 8, 1970, FCO39/765, TNA; Anwar al-Sadat, *In Search of Identity* (London: Collins 1978), 231.

41 Lewis to Beaumont, February 9, 1972, FCO39/1262, TNA; COS29/72, *Sale of Jaguar Aircraft to Egypt*, March 3, 1972, DEFE5/192, TNA.

42 Lewis to Beaumont; Annex A; Annex B, February 9, 1972, FCO39/1262, TNA; R. A. Keally (Kuwait City) to Goulding (Cairo), July 20, 1972, FCO39/1265, TNA.

43 Note by Craig, July 18, 1972, FCO39/1264, Cairo to FCO, No. 1101, July 27, 1972; Cairo to FCO, No. 1670, December 2, 1972, FCO39/1265, TNA.

44 Annex A, February 9, 1972, FCO39/1262, TNA; D. A. Gladstone (Cairo) to Craig, November 21, 1972; Marriott, *Call on Admiral Ivliev*, November 19, 1972, FCO39/1265, TNA. Ivliev's GRU status is confirmed in Isabella Ginor and Gideon Remez, *The Soviet-Israeli War, 1967–1973: The USSR's Intervention in the Egyptian-Israeli Conflict* (Oxford, UK: Oxford University Press, 2017), 148, 287, 298. During one conversation between Ivliev and Barnicoat (shortly after Sadat announced the Soviet contingent's expulsion) the former "laughed and nodded" at the RAF attaché's joke that he would no longer have to resolve any disciplinary incidents involving his off-duty compatriots. Cairo to MOD, July 21, 1972, FCO39/1264, TNA.

45 Tom Bridges (Private Secretary to PM) to J. A. N. Graham (FCO), July 26, 1972; DP Note 222/729 (Revised Final), *Sale of Defence Equipment to Egypt*, August 15, 1972, DEFE11/733, TNA.

46 Abraham Rabinovich, *The Yom Kippur War: The Epic Encounter that Shook the Middle East* (New York: Schocken, 2004), 25–26; Kenneth Pollack, *Arabs at War: Military Effectiveness 1948–1991* (Lincoln: University of Nebraska Press, 2002), 98–108; Ahron Bregman, *Israel's Wars: A History Since 1947* (Abingdon, UK: Routledge, 2004), 108–123. Uri Bar-Joseph analyzes the rea-

sons behind the IDF's intelligence failures in *The Watchman Fell Asleep: The Surprise of the Yom Kippur War and Its Sources* (Albany: State University of New York Press, 2005).

47 Memorandum by E. W. Cooke (FCO), January 25, 1967; D. J. Porter (MOD) to M. E. Cripps (Ministry of Technology), April 20, 1967; and R. S. Price (FCO, Defence Supply Department) to Cripps, January 16, 1968, FCO39/290, TNA.

48 DP Note 222/72, DEFE11/733, TNA. Air Marshal Sir Denis Smallwood (Vice Chief of the Air Staff) to Adams, February 3, 1971, FCO39/1001, TNA.

49 Cairo to MOD, January 3, 1972; and Cairo to FCO, no. 26, January 5, 1972, FO141/1512, TNA; P. Nixon (NENAD), *Discussion with the United States on Defence Sales to Egypt*, January 29, 1974, FCO93/400, TNA.

50 Memorandum from Defence Intelligence Staff, *The Sale of the Rapier Air Defence System to Egypt and Israel—JIC(A)(72)28*, August 11, 1972; Admiral Sir Michael Pollock (First Sea Lord) to Lord Carrington, August 16, 1972; and DP Note 222/72, DEFE11/733, TNA; Antony Parsons (Assistant Under-Secretary, NENAD) to Sir Stewart Crawford (Chairman JIC), August 7, 1972; and Crawford to Parsons, August 8, 1972, FCO39/1253, TNA.

51 R. J. Andrew (MOD) to Antony Acland (FCO), August 21, 1972; and Burke Trend (Cabinet Secretary) to Heath, September 12, 1972, PREM15/1483, TNA; Craig to Alan Urwick (Counsellor, Cairo), September 15, 1972, FCO39/1255, TNA; DOP(72)14, *Sale of Military Equipment to Egypt and Libya*, March 10, 1972, CAB148/122, TNA.

52 Lewis to Rear Admiral H. L. N. Goodhart (MOD), March 11, 1972, FCO39/1249, TNA; Cairo to FCO, no. 779, May 23, 1972, FCO39/1251, TNA; Parsons to Douglas-Home, July 24, 1972, FCO39/1253, TNA; Beaumont to Parsons, August 29, 1972, FCO39/1255, TNA.

53 Percy Cradock (JIC Assessments Staff) to Parsons, August 15, 1972, FCO39/1254, TNA; Andrews and Mitrokhin, *KGB in Europe and the West*, 158. Wolf, *Spymaster*, 258.

54 Adamson to Lewis, October 27, 1972; Barnicoat to Adamson, October 24, 1972; Lewis to Adamson, October 31, 1972, FCO39/1256, TNA.

55 DOP(72)14, CAB148/122, TNA; DOP(72)15th meeting, September 13, 1972, CAB148/121, TNA; DOP(73)15th meeting, June 21, 1973; DOP(73)16th meeting, June 28, 1973, CAB148/129, TNA.

56 N. C. R. Williams (NENAD) to D. Wigan (Tripoli), June 27, 1973, FCO93/59, TNA; Note for Lord Balniel (Minister of State FCO), October 17, 1973; H. L. Suffield (AUS [Sales] MOD) to Carrington, October 24, 1973, DEFE13/942, TNA. Using contemporary figures, £15 million in 1973 is worth around £157.5 million (US$204 million) in 2019, while £150 million is equivalent to £1.6 billion (US$2 billion).

57 Lewis to Goodhart, FCO39/1249, TNA; R. S. Anderson (AUS Sales), *Report on Visit of Defence Sales Team to Egypt, 19th to 23rd May 1972*, May 25, 1972,

FCO39/1251, TNA; D. Adamson (Deputy AUS Sales) to Marriott, June 23, 1972; and Adamson to Barnicoat, June 23, 1972, FCO39/1252, TNA.

58 Cairo to FCO, no. 304, March 13, 1973, FCO93/59, TNA; Craig to M. S. Faber (Cairo), September 7, 1973, FCO93/63, TNA.

59 Lewis to Beaumont, *Annual Report 1972*, January 9, 1973; Barnicoat, *Annual Report for 1972 by the Air Attaché*, January 9, 1973, FCO93/65, TNA.

60 Lewis, *Annual Report 1972*; Marriott, *Report of the Naval Attaché, Cairo—1972*, January 9, 1973; Barnicoat, *Annual Report for 1972*, FCO93/65, TNA; Pollack, *Arabs at War*, 126–131; Hughes, "Arab-Israeli War," 17–18.

61 Raymond Garthoff, *Détente and Confrontation; American-Soviet Relations from Nixon to Reagan*, 2nd ed. (Washington, DC: Brookings, 1994), 604, 642–643.William B. Quandt, "America and the Middle East: A Fifty-Year Overview," in Brown, *Diplomacy in the Middle East*, 67; "The Reality behind Bright Star," *The Times*, November 26, 1981.

62 By 1979, the Egyptian armed forces' equipment was mainly of Soviet-bloc origin, although the EAF had eighty-five US F-4s and F-5s on order, plus fourteen French Mirage 5 fighters, fifty-four Gazelle (French), and fifty UK-built Lynx helicopters. The Egyptians had five Sea Kings, but their source of manufacture (the US or Britain) is not specified; see *The Military Balance 1979–1980* (London: International Institute of Strategic Studies [IISS] 1979), 38–39. By 2000, the Egyptian military had acquired a greater proportion of American arms (notably the M-1 Abrams main battle tank and the F-16 fighter jet) but had very few British-made weapons systems (see *The Military Balance 1999–2000* [Oxford, UK: Oxford University Press/IISS 1999], 130–131).

63 Abdel Razzaq Takriti, *Monsoon Revolution: Republicans, Sultans and Empires in Oman, 1965–1976* (Oxford, UK: Oxford University Press, 2013), 84–116; Yezid Sayigh, *Armed Struggle and the Search for State: The Palestinian National Movement 1949–1993* (Oxford, UK: Clarendon, 1997), 217–242.

64 Donald Tebbit (Washington, DC) to Sir Denis Greenhill (Permanent Under-Secretary FCO), August 31, 1972, FCO93/400, TNA; Parsons to Douglas-Home, May 2, 1973, PREM15/1764, TNA; FCO to Washington, DC, no. 1269, June 15, 1973, PREM15/1981, TNA.

65 "No Passing to Forigner,"; DEFE63/43, TNA; Annex A, February 9, 1972, FCO39/1262, TNA; Sir Philip Adams (HM Ambassador Cairo) to Douglas-Home, *The Egyptian Armed Forces in 1972*, March 12, 1973, FCO93/58, TNA; Barnicoat, *Annual Report for 1972*, FCO93/65, TNA.

66 Michael Eisenstadt and Kenneth Pollack, "Armies of Snow and Armies of Sand: The Impact of Soviet Military Doctrine on Arab Militaries," *Middle East Journal* 55, no. 4 (2001): 549–578.

67 Lewis to Beaumont; and Annex A, FCO39/1262, TNA; Cairo to FCO, no. 1045, July 19, 1972, FCO39/1264, TNA.

68 Memorandum by Holding, March 30, 1973; and Lewis, *Annual Report 1972*, FCO93/65, TNA.

69 This tendency can also be seen in two dispatches from UK diplomatic missions in the Middle East after the Yom Kippur War. See Sydney Giffard (Tel Aviv) to David Gore-Booth (NENAD), February 13, 1974; and Gladstone to Gore-Booth, February 27, 1974, FCO93/528, TNA.

70 Hughes, "Arab-Israeli War," 13; Beaumont to Douglas-Home, *The Egyptian Armed Forces in 1971*, March 3, 1972, FCO39/1262, TNA.

9

The Use of British Seconded and Contracted Military Personnel to Advance Britain's Interests
A Case Study from the United Arab Emirates from 1965 to 2010

Athol Yates

Introduction

This chapter is a case study that examines the comparative contributions of British seconded officers[1] and contract officers[2] to advancing British defense and national interests in the United Arab Emirates (UAE) and its precursor, the Trucial States. The UAE is a federation formed in 1971 when seven Trucial State Emirates—Abu Dhabi, Ajman, Dubai, Fujairah, Ras al Khaimah, Sharjah, and Umm al Quwain—came together.

Each emirate is in effect a city-state with the name of the emirate coming from its largest settlement. Each emirate is headed by a ruler who is an absolute monarch. The UAE is headed by a president who is elected by the seven rulers. The president has always been the ruler of Abu Dhabi, which is the most powerful, wealthiest, and physically largest emirate. Abu Dhabi's rulers in the period relevant to this case study have been Sheikh Shakhbut bin Sultan Al Nahyan (r. 1928–1966), his brother Sheikh Zayed bin Sultan Al Nahyan (r. 1966–2004, and UAE president 1971–2004), and Sheikh Zayed's son, Sheikh Khalifa bin Zayed bin Sultan Al Nahyan (r. 2004–present, and UAE president 2004–present).

For over a century and a half before the formation of the UAE, the Trucial States had been protected states of Britain. The arrangements were spelled out in a series of treaties between the British and the rulers and meant that Britain was responsible for each emirates' external defense and foreign affairs, with each ruler having internal sovereignty over his emirate. This responsibility arose out of Britain's maritime dominance in the Arabian Gulf in the early 1800s, which was driven both by commercial factors and by a need to protect the western flank of the British Empire's most important asset—India. Up until the early 1900s, Britain's interests in the Trucial States and lower Gulf area was limited to the maritime domain. This changed in the 1930s with the establishment of an air station at Sharjah, which was a refueling and stopover point on the air route from Britain to India and beyond; however, even then, Britain had little interest outside of securing its air facilities. At this time, the emirates were as they had been for centuries—a subsistence economy based around fishing, pearl diving, simple agriculture, animal husbandry, and trading. The population of around 80,000 was almost entirely illiterate, and the area had no paved roads, electricity, piped water, modern schools, or health services.

In the 1950s, oil exploration got underway in earnest in the Trucial States, and this period saw Britain starting to take greater interest in their security and development.[3] This was because it wanted to facilitate oil development, to counter anticolonial propaganda that Britain had neglected the native populations under its influence, and to eliminate slave trafficking, which was damaging the image of the empire. This required Britain to become involved in the internal affairs of the emirates. One manifestation of this was the 1951 formation of the Trucial Oman Levies, a British-officered, Arab-manned force tasked with improving security in the mostly lawless interior.

The discovery of oil, first in Abu Dhabi (1958) and then in Dubai (1966) and Sharjah (1971–1972), elevated the importance of the Trucial States to Britain because of its dependence on reasonably priced oil, as well as the desire to benefit commercially from the rulers' growing wealth. The oil wealth allowed rulers to rapidly accelerate the development of their emirates, which included the formation of militaries under their control.[4] In January 1968, Britain unilaterally announced it was going to annul its treaties of protection by 1971 and withdraw its military forces. This it did on December 1, 1971, and the following day the UAE came into existence.

This history explains the long-standing British connection to the emirates and why the UAE has valued its relationship with Britain to the present day, and vice versa. This does not mean that this relationship has been unconditional, for it has occasionally been strained. An appropriate characterization of the relationship from the UAE perspective is encapsulated in the statement from the UAE president that Britain is valued as it is the "least unreliable of our friends."[5]

As a consequence of Britain's long involvement in the region, Britain has long been a source of seconded and contract officers for the UAE. These officers were initially needed to form and lead military forces in the emirates, as the emiratis have very little military experience. Over the decades, British officers along with other nationalities have been continuously engaged to overcome shortages of expertise and experience, as well as to facilitate the introduction of new equipment, modernize forces, and prepare emirati forces for operations. Up until the early 1990s, the overwhelming majority of Western personnel who had served in emirati militaries were British. After this, US personnel, along with those from South Africa, Australia, and several other Western countries, began to be engaged in larger numbers. However, British officers remained the majority until around 2010, when their numbers were sharply reduced, reflecting both tensions between the UAE and the United Kingdom and a strategic decision by the UAE leadership to increasingly align with the United States.

This chapter uses the UAE to examine the contribution of British seconded and military personnel to advance British interests. The UAE was chosen for two reasons. First, there is a long history of British seconded and contract officers being engaged by emirati militaries. This means there is a large volume of primary sources that provide the details about not only the personnel themselves but also the thinking of the British at the time. This chapter draws mainly from archival material and interviews of past seconded and contract military officers.[6]

Second, the UAE is typical of countries that have had a long experience with British provision of loan-service personnel, as well as with training teams, training in Britain, and government-backed defense sales, all of which are referred to today as international defense-engagement (IDE) activities. This means that this chapter's findings are generally representative of a large number of countries in which Britain had been the source of both seconded and contract officers. In the post–World War II period, Britain carried out IDE activities in the southern Mediterranean, Near Eastern, and Middle Eastern regions, among others, and where the threat to British interests was primarily indirect; for example, internal insecurity leading to regional insecurity that would threaten the flow of oil. Using British forces directly was not a sustainable way of addressing these kinds of indirect threats, but IDE was viewed as such.[7] This contrasts with Eastern Europe, where the Soviet Union and its allies posed a direct threat. British forces were deployed directly in these areas as there was no need or opportunity to utilize IDE activities.

In the Gulf region, in the decades after World War II, the lead agency for facilitating and sometimes providing IDE activities was the Foreign and Commonwealth Office (FCO).[8] The FCO sometimes itself provided IDE activities in the Trucial States; for example, it established, paid for, and administered the Trucial Oman Levies. In 1951, the FCO engaged a British contract officer to build the force and worked with the War Office to provide weapons, equipment, and so forth.[9] Even when command of the Trucial Oman Levies passed to serving British Army officers in 1953, the FCO still controlled the force until it was disbanded in 1971.[10]

The FCO considered IDE activities effective in advancing British national interests, and this motivated it to push the Ministry of Defence (MOD) to prioritize provision of these types of activities. This can be seen in the following extract from the head of the FCO's Middle East Department, referring to the UAE defense attaché's 1973 annual report on UAE military forces. The FCO officer wrote that the report

draws attention to the relevance of military training . . . as a means of indirect influence, and suggests that thought should be given now to providing adequately for an increased training commitment, particularly for the Middle East. This view coincides with our thinking and the subject has been under active consideration in Whitehall for some time: our purpose is to have foreign training accepted into the Service policy framework instead of being regarded as a peripheral activity as at present. We hope that the Ministry of Defence will shortly come out with a policy paper making the first step in this direction.[11]

The provision of IDE activities became more formalized as MOD policy in 1981, when it was included in the 1981 Defence Review (*The United*

Table 9.1. Four Categories of Engagement Activities as Defined in the 2017 "International Defence Engagement Strategy"

Defense Diplomacy	Defense Support to UK Prosperity	Building Capability	Enabling Capability
• Defense attachés	• Support to UK defense exports	• UK-based training & education	• UN peacekeeping
• Seconded officers	• Developing new technologies.	• Overseas training & education delivered by short-term training	• Specialist capabilities, such as provision of intelligence,
• Liaison & exchange	• Collaboration with allies & partners	officers teams & permanent overseas training hubs	reconnaissance, air lift, maritime patrol, medical support, or
• International visits	• Economic development for potential trading partners.	• Defense exercises	cyber defense
• Staff talks	• Stabilization & institutional-capacity building		• UK investment in joint projects
• Ministerial visits	• Supporting the security of trade routes & key natural resources		• Direct gifting of equipment
• British defense staffs			• Support to humanitarian assistance & disaster-relief operations

Kingdom Defence Programme: The Way Forward, known as the *Nott Review*). At that time, it was termed "foreign military assistance"[12] and it would be renamed "defence diplomacy" in the 1998 Strategic Defence Review.

Since the release of the 2013 *International Defence Engagement Strategy*, IDE has been using the term formally. The updated 2017 IDE Strategy provides a list of IDE activities, and these are grouped into four categories, as seen in Table 9.1. The Defence Diplomacy category includes seconded officers. Contract officers are not mentioned in the IDE Strategy.

Military Forces of the Emirates

Historically, the rulers of each of the emirates competed fiercely against each other to maximize population, resources, and economic activity, all of which were important to generating wealth and prestige. This competition also created a strong sense of sovereignty and a robust desire to protect this sovereignty. As a result, each emirate formed a military if it had the money. The first to do so was Abu Dhabi in 1965, followed by Ras al Khaimah in 1968, and Dubai in 1970.

In 1971, the UAE was created, and under its constitution, the federal government had exclusive responsibility for foreign affairs, defense, federal armed forces, and protection of the UAE's security against internal or external threats.[13] Despite this mandate, not only did those emirates with militaries not transfer them to federal control immediately after the 1971 federation, but two more emirates formed ruler-controlled militaries after 1971 — Sharjah and Umm Al Quwain. This can be explained by a combination of constitutional vagueness, unwillingness on the part of some emirates to give up what they saw as sovereign powers, and concern over the disharmony caused by pushing for greater federal control.

Thus, in the early 1970s, there were five ruler-controlled forces in the UAE. Of these, by far the largest and most technologically advanced was the Abu Dhabi Defence Force (ADDF). By 1976, this force had over 15,000 men and fielded a well-equipped and modern land, sea, and air force.[14] The second largest, which was the Dubai Defence Force, had around 2,600 men with only a land and limited air force in 1976. The other forces were all small and consisted solely of land forces.

Table 9.2. Militaries of the Trucial States and UAE

Emirati-Controlled Militaries		British-Controlled Militaries
Ruler-Controlled Militaries	Federally Controlled Militaries	
• Abu Dhabi Defence Force (ADDF, 1965–1976)	• Union Defence Force (UDF, 1971–1974)/ Federal Armed Force (1974–1976)	• Trucial Oman Levies (TOL, 1951–1956)/ Trucial Oman Scouts (TOS, 1956–1971)
• Dubai Defence Force (DDF, 1971–1976)/ Central Military Command (1976–1998)	• UAE Armed Force (1976–present)	
• Sharjah National Guard (SNG, 1972–1976, 1984–1990)		
• Ras Al Khaimah Mobile Force (1969–1976, [RAKMF]/Badr Brigade 1978–1979)		
• Umm Al Quwain National Guard (UAQNG, 1975–2006)		

Note: For details on the forces, see Athol Yates, *The Evolution of the Armed Forces of the United Arab Emirates* (Abingdon, UK: Helion, 2020).

In addition to these five ruler-controlled forces, there was one federally controlled military. When Britain annulled its treaties of protection in 1971, it gifted the equipment and facilities of its force, the Trucial Oman Scouts, to the UAE federal government. When this occurred, all TOS members were discharged and invited to join a new force—the federally controlled Union Defence Force (UDF). The vast majority of TOS members agreed to continue to serve, including all of its serving British Army personnel, who now became seconded officers within the UDF. Thus, on the first day of the federation, the UAE federal government had a fully operational, 1,500-man motorized infantry force. Within a few years, this became the Federal Armed Force, which by 1976 had grown to a regular infantry brigade of 4,600 men.

In 1976, the five ruler-controlled forces and the one federally controlled force were merged to form the UAE Armed Forces. The 1976 unification did not completely bring an end to locally controlled forces; there were periods when one or more emirates maintained semi-independent forces up until the mid-2000s. The UAE Armed Forces today numbers around 50,000 and is probably the best Arab military force in the world, boasting small but technically advanced land, naval, and air and air-defense forces, plus a Presidential Guard division. The forces that have existed in the emirates since 1951 are summarized in Table 9.2.

Seconded and Contract Officers in the Emirates

SECONDED OFFICERS

Seconded officers are serving British Commissioned Officers and Other Ranks who are loaned out to a foreign government. They are treated as members of their host military force and are required to obey orders from the host force's superior officers, under whose command they are placed, providing that the orders are consistent with their home country's military regulations[15] and are lawful.

The first British seconded officers to an emirati military were appointed in 1965. Two officers—Major (later Colonel) E. B. (Tug) Wilson and Captain C. (Charles) Wontner—were provided to serve as the force's commanding officer and deputy commanding officer, respectively. British seconded personnel subsequently served in the DDF starting in 1970, the UDF starting in 1971, and the UAE Armed Forces starting in 1976. The Ras Al Khaimah Mobile (RAKMF), Sharjah National Guard (SNG), and Umm Al Quwain National Guard (UAQNG) never had seconded officers.[16]

Seconded officers over the last five decades have ranged in rank from junior noncommissioned officers (NCO) to brigadiers. Seconded officers have been provided from all three UK military services, but the vast majority have come from the British Army. No British female seconded officer has been identified as ever having served in an emirati force. The bulk of seconded officers over the last five decades have been officers rather than other ranks, although at various times, such as in 1978, the relative numbers were reversed.[17]

The legal arrangements governing the seconding of British officers to the emirates have taken two main forms—exchanges of letters and memorandums of understanding (MoUs), and defense-cooperation agreements. An exchange of letters is where one party sends a letter offering the provision of seconded personnel under specified conditions, and the other party sends an acceptance letter agreeing to the terms. These are in effect ad hoc arrangements. British loan-service personnel were provided to the ADDF between 1965 and 1968 using an exchange of letters. MoUs have been used continuously since 1968 to the present day. During the Trucial States period, MoUs were signed with individual emirates, which reflected their individual sovereignty. Thus, MoUs were signed with Abu Dhabi and Dubai. Unusually, despite the UAE becoming a federation in 1971, individual MoUs remained in operation with both emirates, and an additional one was struck to cover the Union Defence Force (UDF)/Federal Armed Force (FAF). Despite the unification of the various militaries in 1976, a separate MoU with Dubai remained in effect alongside one covering the UAE Armed Forces. This reflected the semi-independent nature of Dubai's component of the UAE Armed Forces. All the MoUs were consolidated into one in 1991, and this one appears to have remained in force at least until 2010.[18]

The posting cycle for a seconded officer over the last six decades has generally been two years, which includes midcycle leave and multi-weekend-of-service leave. A seconded officer can request a further extension that can occur if their home unit and the UK Ministry of Defence agrees.

Within each group of seconded officers, the most senior is appointed as the senior seconded officer.[19] He (for there were no identified female seconded officers to the emirates) has normal military disciplinary and reporting powers over his group members as per the British chain of command.

CONTRACT OFFICERS

Contract officers are those engaged under an employment contract with a local military. The officer is either directly contracted or engaged via an intermediary organization, such as a manpower provider. In this chapter, the term is used to mean contracted former military professionals rather than nonmilitary professionals such as doctors or those providing defense-industry services contracted through private companies.

The first British contract officer in an emirati force was engaged in 1967 by the ADDF.[20] Contract officers have served in all seven emirati forces to the present. They served as commanding officers for all the pre-1976 forces. Up

Table 9.3. Seconded and Contract Officers' Work Roles with Examples

Work Roles (Definition and Subcategories)	Positions Held by Britons
Executive command involves exercising the power of command to lead a military element. It includes: • Leadership in operations • Force generation leadership*	• First Infantry Regiment Commanding Officer (during 1973 Oman deployment)[a] • Patrol Boat Captain (on patrol in Abu Dhabi's territorial waters)[b] • ADDF Commanding Officer[a,b] • DDF Commanding Officer[a] • Armored Squadron Commander[a,b] • Emiri Guard Officer Commander[b] • Force Workshop Officer Commander[a,b] • Force Education Officer[a,b]
Staff officer work involves assisting commanders in the planning of their orders and coordinating the efforts of military elements to achieve the intent of the commander and other more senior staff officers.	• Chief of Staff[a,b] • SO2 (Intelligence)[a,b] • SO1 (Personnel)[a,b] • SO3 (Training)[a,b]
Specialist tasks involve undertaking a specialist function, which is often but not necessarily technical.	• Hunter Pilot[b] • Desert Intelligence Officer[a,b] • Armorer[a,b] • Hygienist
Advising involves providing advice ranging from informal opinions to comprehensive written reports, mentoring, and coaching. It includes: • Private advising • Military advising	• Infantry Battalion Advisor[a,b] • Reconnaissance Battalion Advisor[b] • Emissary of the Ruler[b] • Aide-de-camp to the Ruler[b] • Military Advisor on border security strategy
Training and education involves a structured teaching activity within a training system to transfer skills and knowledge. It includes: • Individual training/education, instructing • Collective training facilitation • Training system development and management	• Weapons Instructor[a,b] • Small Unit Tactics Instructor[a,b] • Drill Instructor[a,b] • PT Instructor[a,b] • Staff College Instructor[a,b] • Combat Training Center Observer[b] • Doctrine Writer[a,b]

*Force generation is the process to generate trained and ready forces that can be used operationally.

[a]Seconded officer

[b]Contract officer

until the 1990s, most contract officers wore emirati military uniforms with ranks. After this, there were periods when groups of contract officers again wore uniforms, but very few do today. During the periods when contract officers wore ranks, their ranks ranged from lieutenant to major general.

Contract officers serve under a local chain of command and can be tasked by their immediate superior. There has never been a separate chain of command for contract officers, although at certain times there has been a centralized support and coordination group for groups of contract officers.

WORK ROLES

The work of seconded and contract officers in emirati militaries spans a huge range of tasks, which can be grouped into five main roles: executive command, staff work, specialist tasks, advising, and training/education.[21] Table 9.3 provides definitions of each of the roles with examples of positions for each, noting which ones were seconded and/or contract officers. This classification may create the impression that officers are engaged for one specific role, but this was not the case, as individuals invariably undertook multiple work roles, and these could change over time.

As can be seen from the table, both seconded and contract officers held positions in all four work roles. In addition, many posts were filled at various times by both types of officers, which suggests that they were interchangeable. However, a better characterization of the two groups is that they were complementary by design, based on the expatriate requirements of the force. This complementarity could be in terms of age, skills, skills currency, and the currency of MOD security clearances.

THE NUMBERS

The number of British seconded and contract officers in emirati militaries from 1965 to 2010 is shown in Figure 9.1.[22] As can be seen, both types of officers served simultaneously, with contract officers always outnumbering seconded officers. The graph shows three distinct periods—from 1965 to 1980, when the numbers rose, then fell; from 1980 to the early 1990s, when numbers were low and constant; and from the early 1990s to 2010, when there was continual growth in the numbers of contract officers, though the

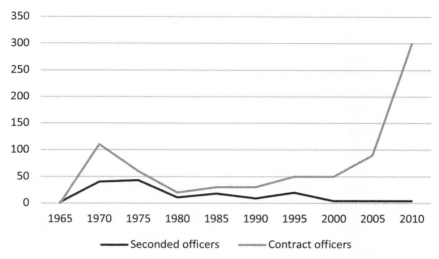

Figure 9.1. Estimated Numbers of British Seconded and Contract Officers in Emirati Militaries, 1965–2010. The numbers are based on the author's research undertaken in writing the book *Invisible Expatriates: Western Military Professionals and the Development of the UAE Armed Force.*

numbers of seconded officers initially increased in in the mid-1990s, and then fell and remained low until 2010. An interesting observation discussed in the article "Western Expatriates in the UAE Armed Forces, 1964–2015" identifies that the number of British officers at any one time corresponds to the degree of the rulers' enthusiasm to build or modernize their forces.[23]

The first period from 1965 to 1980 coincides with the formation of the five ruler-controlled militaries, plus the conversion of around fifty British Army officers of the TOS to seconded personnel in the UDF. These British officers, along with other expatriate personnel, were engaged by the rulers to establish, lead, and train their forces. In the federally controlled UDF and every ruler-controlled military except for the very small Umm Al Quwain force, British personnel served as the forces' founding commander. In the larger forces of the ADDF, DDF, and UDF, they also served in executive-command positions at all levels and across services, as well as in the other three work roles. From the mid-1970s, the number of British personnel declined, as their positions were filled by newly trained emiratis or experienced personnel from other Arab countries or Pakistan. This decline primarily relates to a deliberate effort by the UAE president/ruler of Abu Dhabi to reduce the British presence for political reasons.[24]

The second period, from 1980 to the early 1990s, coincided with a consolidation phase in the UAE Armed Forces. During this decade, the forces were relatively stable in size, and little new equipment was introduced. Consequently, the need for foreign officers was limited.

The third period starts in the early 1990s and has continued to the present day. It covers a period of ongoing military modernization and large-scale weapons-acquisition programs, which has seen the UAE become a regional military power. The phase starts with the end of the Gulf War in 1991, when the vast gulf in capabilities between Western forces and what was thought to be the premier Arab force—Iraq—became apparent. The modernization of the UAE military has been driven by ongoing insecurity in the region—notably rising tensions with Iran in the 2000s—increasing regional insecurity following the 2003 invasion of Iraq, the Arab Spring at the end of the 2000s, and the regional interventions of the 2010s. Although the 1990s saw an increase in the number of seconded officers as Britain sought to leverage its military capability to build UAE forces, the number fell to just a handful from the early 2000s onward because of a lack of available manpower in the British forces, given its own shortage of personnel and its operational commitments. The number of British contract officers in the UAE rose steadily in the 1990s, and in 2003 it increased dramatically following the creation of the Military Contract Officers (MCO) Program. This program involved the engagement of large numbers of mostly British former commissioned officers and noncommissioned officers (NCOs). Initially the MCO Program had the modest goal of improving recruit and NCO training, but this rapidly expanded as the benefits of the program were recognized. At its peak in 2009, the program had over 300 contract officers providing a wide range of individual training, collective training, advice, and operational assistance across fifty-six different areas of the UAE Armed Forces.[25]

Advancing Interests

At its core, IDE seeks to advance two types of British interests—defense interests and national interests. Defense interests are advanced through enhancing the partner nation's military capability, which in turn increases that country's stability and regional security and builds additional forces capable of fulfilling peacekeeping roles. National interests are advanced through the access and influence gained by seconded officers, which allows British political, economic, and commercial interests to be realized.

IDE activities advance both sets of interests because British military-based engagement allows bilateral relations to be established, deepened, or rebuilt with both the host country's military and its government. Through these relationships, Britain is able to influence the host country's decision-making.

Below is a discussion of the contribution that both British seconded officers and contract officers have made to these two types of interests.

DEFENSE INTERESTS

Using definitions from the 2017 IDE Strategy, defense interests primarily correspond to the "building capability" category of engagement activities, although they also spill over into the other three categories (see Table 9.1). Examples of capability-building activities in the IDE Strategy include preparing partner "forces to deploy on peacekeeping missions or improving the capacity of partners to deal with internal security challenges ... [and] ... counter terrorism, counter-improvised explosive devices (C-IED), migration and the leadership and management of Defence," as well as providing UK-based training and education and exercising with British forces.[26]

As can be seen in the previous section on work roles, both seconded and contract officers in the emirates held posts in the areas that are the fundamental building blocks of capability (e.g., command, management, collective training, major platforms, and support) as well as working to combine these multiple inputs within an operational military force.

To illustrate their contribution, examples are given below of British officers working in each of the activities listed in the IDE Strategy. In terms of peacekeeping-mission preparations, the seconded officer, Brigadier J. A. (Hamish) McGregor, who served in the UAE Armed Forces from 1991 to 1993, assisted the UAE military to deploy with the United Nations Operation in Somalia. Col. McGregor advised deploying battalion commanders on stabilization tactics and training preparation. This included advice on area control, installation protection, patrolling, and demining.[27] Regarding internal security, the contract officer, Captain Robin Hitchcock (1967–1970), who served in the ADDF, introduced antiriot, search, and detention procedures for the infantry squadron and battalion he commanded at that time, who acted as the first responders for internal security.[28] With respect to counterterrorism, in the early 1990s a combination of seconded UK special forces personnel and British contract officers, who were all former Special Air Service and Special Boat Service operators, established a special-operations force with teams specializing in maritime and land counterterrorism operations.[29] For C-IED preparation, members of the MCO Program developed a training program for emirati units that were deploying to Afghanistan in the 2000s. Improving the control of irregular migration was facilitated by MCO Program members working in the UAE Navy through improved maritime-situation awareness and response. Examples of British officers providing leadership and management of defense were seconded officer Lieutenant Colonel A. B. (Tony) Wallerstein, who was commander of the Dubai Defence Force 1972–1974, and the contract officer Lieutenant Colonel D. (David) Neild, who was commander of the Ras Al Khaimah Mobile Force 1969–1972.

Both contracted and seconded officers also played a role in the last two activities mentioned in the IDE Strategy—providing UK-based training and education and exercising with British forces. For example, under the leadership of the contract officer Major General Andy Pillar, who ran the MCO Program from 2004 to 2011, the MCO Program on behalf of the UAE Armed Forces established formal links with all UK officer-training schools and colleges, which included setting up an affiliation with Royal Military Academy (RMA) Sandhurst. MCO personnel introduced and ran a process for selecting and preparing candidates for overseas officer training, particularly for RMA Sandhurst.[30] The MCO personnel were also instrumental in establishing exercises with foreign forces, including British ones. In the case of the UAE Navy, contract officers provided low-risk pathways to allow emirati personnel to exercise with UK and other foreign forces. This started with contract officers organizing an invitation from visiting UK naval vessels and inviting UAE naval personnel as observers to UK exercises. Over time, this expanded into small-scale activities that minimized the risk of embarrassment for either side, and finally larger scale naval exercises.[31]

In summary, with regard to advancing British defense interests through building emirati military capability, both seconded and contract officers have each made significant contributions. For the former, this has occurred through British government–directed military assistance. For the latter, this arose without any British government direction.

NATIONAL INTERESTS

National interests primarily correspond to two categories of engagement activities as defined in the 2017 IDE Strategy (see Table 9.1). These are: (1) develop understanding, which "means the UK ensures that the UK understands other nations' defence perspectives and equally that they understand UK intent and capability," and (2) develop access and influence that "seeks to build and maintain the relationships which allow the UK to influence partners . . . in support of UK values and interests."[32]

Category 1: Developing Understanding. Developing understanding in the context of British nationals engaged in foreign militaries refers primarily to the collection of information on the host military and its political leadership; specifically their intents, capabilities, and plans. These are, in effect, intelligence inputs. The links between seconded personnel, provision of information, and an intelligence product has long been recognized by the British military leadership, as seen in the following extract from a 1979 Chiefs of Staff Committee's document:

A knowledge of the capability and intentions of a nation's armed forces . . . is an important contributory factor in efforts to promote stability and to protect UK interests by being able to anticipate events. In those countries where the UK has a substantial interest, it is considered to be important that the UK should be capable of making an independent intelligence assessment. Defence representation including LSP [loan-service personnel] and visiting military personnel can make an important contribution to this.[33]

Evidence from British National Archive documents and interviews indicate that seconded and contract officers in the emirates commonly provided information in two ways—through discussions with British officials and by supplying documents to emirati militaries. The scale of information flow is difficult to assess, but it appears to have been considerable due to the extremely high quality of defense-attaché reports on the state of emirati forces in the 1970s, a time when there were large numbers of British personnel working in the UAE military.[34]

Some of the information provided would have been explicitly authorized by the emirati leadership for political or personal reasons. In other cases, permission was implied,[35] or the information was provided without permission.

There is no direct evidence of who actually provided unauthorized information to the British government. However, it is logical that it would mostly have been seconded officers, as they filled senior executive and staff officer posts and therefore were the only British officers to have regular access to high-level, consolidated information of the sort needed to make the comprehensive defense-attaché reports of the 1970s. In addition, no junior seconded or contract officer who was interviewed by the author stated that British officials had asked them to provide intelligence. This is probably because junior officers did not have access to useful information, since they lacked awareness outside their areas of responsibility. The assertion that the providers were seconded officers also rests on the logic that they could have been instructed directly by their superior British officers. On the other hand, British officials could not demand that contract officers provide information, nor would contract officers voluntarily do so, for it not only would jeopardize their employment and be unethical but also carried the risk of imprisonment.[36]

There were several significant constraints on the provision of information by seconded officers. First, they needed to have access to it, and as soon as they lost their senior-executive and staff-officer posts, access to such information ended. This may explain why the quality of the defense attaché's reports declined in the 1980s, which was a time when there were no seconded officers in senior positions in the UAE Armed Forces, excluding Dubai's force. Second, seconded officers had to want to provide such information. Examples can be found in which they did not want to do so or did so reluctantly. One example can be seen in the following letter from the commander of the ADDF to the British political representative in Abu Dhabi in 1966, discussing information-sharing with the British-controlled TOS:

While I am perfectly willing to discuss policy matters which affect the two Forces, such as training, internal security, patrolling, plans for operations, etc, I do not see the necessity of discussing internal ADDF matters, unless it affects TOS in any way. I am afraid I cannot agree to send Commander TOS a copy of a document [the ruler's report] which is personal between myself and the Ruler of Abu Dhabi. In point of fact, I am not quite happy about the ethics of sending you and the PRPG [political resident Persian Gulf] a copy. I do so entirely without the sanction of His Highness and it seems to me in some ways rather underhand. Naturally, I keep you informed of developments and I realise PRPG much be kept fully "in the picture" but I do not wish to be involved in a breach of confidence or good faith.[37]

The nonprovision of information by seconded officers has been observed in other countries, which points to it not being unique to the emirates. An example from neighboring Oman illustrates that seconded officers can withhold absolutely critical information from a British perspective. The case involved the British seconded officer, Air Vice Marshal Eric Bennett, who served as commander of the Sultan of Oman's air force from 1975 to 1990. At the beginning of the Iraq-Iran War in late 1980, Iraqi transport-aircraft-bearing helicopters passed through UAE airspace and arrived in Oman, with Iraq's intention being to launch an attack on Iran from there.[38] The plan was canceled and the aircraft returned to Iraq. Had the attack occurred, it would have brought Oman and possibly the UAE into the war and thus also dragged British military personnel into the conflict, as large numbers of seconded personnel then staffed Oman's military. The Iraqi operation could only have been carried out with the full knowledge of AVM Bennet. As the operation was occurring, he did not provide information to the British embassy in Oman, which resulted in him being heavily criticized. The assistant undersecretary of state at the Foreign Office stated that it was "clearly unsatisfactory that Bennett would have acted as if his first allegiance were not to ourselves as a serving British officer."[39]

In summary, authorized information important for Britain's understanding of the intents, capabilities, and plans of the emirati military and political leadership has been provided by both seconded and contract officers. In the case of the unauthorized provision of information, it is far more likely that seconded rather than contract officers were the source of such information. The provision of useful confidential information is normally only available from those holding senior executive and staff posts, and only when there is a willingness to do so. Contract officers are much more unlikely to pass on such information, and sometimes even seconded officers are not willing to do so for professional or personal reasons.

Category 2: Obtaining Access and Influence. The purpose of IDE as a mechanism to advance British interests by providing access and influence has long been explicitly recognized by both Britain's political leadership and by seconded personnel. This can be seen in a 1982 letter from the minister of defense to the prime minister regarding the then-review of foreign military assistance and training. He wrote that "successive governments have recognised that providing help of this kind is valuable in the context of our bilateral relations with many countries, and can promote British interests and influence."[40]

The political role is also recognized by seconded personnel, as illustrated in a 1983 letter from the commander of the Kuwait Liaison Team to the MOD. It states that the mission of the team provides

little or no military advantage to the UK. . . . Our real purpose in being here therefore must be to help the Ambassador and his staff to further the political and economic interests of Britain in this part of the World. We do this firstly by encouraging the organisation, training, tactics and logistics along suitably modified British lines with the object of keeping the Kuwait Forces "thinking British"; secondly, by encouraging the military training links between Britain and Kuwait and by building up the Kuwaiti training system; thirdly, by trying to influence defence sales in Britain's favour and by providing some cover for after service of British equipment.[41]

An officer's ability to obtain access and influence was directly related to the position he held. Of greatest value were executive-command posts, according to British officials. For example, in 1973, a Chiefs of Staff Committee meeting reported the assistant chief of the Defence Staff (Policy) as saying, "our political and defence objectives in the Gulf would be better served by continuing to deploy British loan service personnel in executive positions in the local forces within the UAE rather than by a training/liaison team arrangement. . . . The latter arrangement would not provide the same degree of political influence as the former."[42] This view was also held by the Foreign Office, as seen at the same 1973 meeting when the deputy undersecretary of state stated that "the FCO feared that, with a/training/liaison team solution, we should find it very difficult to exert effective influence in the ADDF. . . . Moreover, the retention of executive posts was also important in the context of orders for military equipment."[43]

Staff-officer-grade personnel were also influential, according to a senior contract officer who served as an adviser in the UAE Armed Forces Infantry, 2005 to 2010. This, he claimed, was because "UAE officers were able to plagarise work directly."[44]

In addition to training posts being less influential, so too were specialist and technical work. This was noted in a review by the commander of the Kuwait Liaison Team in 1983 on the future of his team. He lamented that British seconded personnel working on aircraft and armored vehicles had become "White Pakistanis," a phrase that captures a Gulf states' cultural paradigm of Western expatriates being hired to provide specialist manual labor that nationals did not want to do. He noted that British provision of specialist and technical support undermined the British interest in both building up local military capability and increasing defense sales. He is quoted as stating that his team's work resulted in the Kuwaitis not needing to "trouble themselves . . . in details of planning, management or training other than by putting in the occasional appearance on the workshop floor [which does not allow us] to influence the Kuwaitis towards greater self-sufficiency nor does it present us with much opportunity to influence defence sales."[45]

Numbers were also noted by British officials as being important to obtaining access and influence. This was recognized in a 1973 Chiefs of Staff Committee meeting minutes that discussed a decline in the numbers of seconded officers in the ADDF. The chief of the General Staff noted "that there was only a small number of loan service personnel in the ADDF—23 out of a total of 568 officers and this would be reduced to 11 in one year's time, three of whom would be advisers, and he could not see that such a small proportion of the total number of officers could really be very influential."[46]

While sufficient numbers of British officers holding command or senior-staff-grade posts might have been essential to obtaining access and exerting influence, this does not mean that such access and influence were automatic.

For seconded officers, an important constraint on their access and influence was that the rulers collectively distrusted them. The rulers knew that the loyalty of these officers was to the British Crown and not to the host country's leadership. This was explicitly spelled out to the rulers when they requested the secondment of British officers,[47] and the senior seconded officer was instructed that he was to seek the advice of the British political representative if the "orders issued by the Abu Dhabi authorities to British loan service personnel may be contrary to the interests of Her Majesty's Government or may involve you in a conflict of loyalties."[48]

Another constraint on British seconded officers' ability to influence is that they can be seen as unreliable at times when the emirates needed them most, which is during conflict. This concern arises because of the terms of their engagement as specified in the relevant MoUs. A clause states that "seconded personnel will not take part in any hostilities or other operations of a warlike nature undertaken by the UAE Armed Forces nor any operation of those Forces concerned with the preservation of peace, with internal security or with the enforcement of law and order unless properly authorised by the UK authorities."[49] This clause exists to prevent serving UK personnel from being involved in activity that would be politically damaging to the British government, for example, if there was fighting between two countries that both had British seconded officers. There was potential for this situation to occur in the UAE from the 1960s to 1980s because of border disputes with all three of its neighbors. The clause was seen as encroaching on emirati sovereignty[50] and probably contributed to the more rapid removal of seconded officers from executive-command and staff posts as compared with contract officers.

A final constraint on the ability of Britain to wield influence via seconded officers is that the officers could not always be guaranteed to follow instructions to do so. Evidence indicates that in cases where there was a tension between British interests and the interests of the local force, secondees would make judgments on the relative merits of the instruction and do what they thought was right. This judgment was likely to have been influenced by considerations such as military efficiency and effectiveness; fair treatment of the emirates by Britain; professional integrity that demanded they provide advice that was in the best interest of their superior; impact on and value to the emirates; and loyalty to the ruler, particularly when he was personally known to the seconded officer.

An illustration of how these judgments played out in the mind of a seconded officer is documented in the eight-volume archive of Colonel E. B. Wilson, commanding officer ADDF from late 1965 to May 1969. He was engaged by Sheikh Shakhbut bin Sultan Al Nahyan, ruler of Abu Dhabi, to establish an Abu Dhabi military. When the sheikh's family and Britain organized to replace the ruler with his brother in August 1966, Colonel Wilson instructed his force not to come to the aid of Sheikh Shakhbut but to instead remain in barracks. Part of his motivation to do so appears to have been personal, for on the day after the ruler's deposition, he wrote to an MOD (UK) official stating "that the hand of tyranny has been removed.... I cannot tell you how I feel this morning having worked for a year under extreme provocation and frustration [of Sheikh Shakhbut] who made everybody's lives such a misery."[51]

The new ruler, Sheikh Zayed bin Sultan Al Nahyan, retained Colonel Wilson as commander ADDF, and Colonel Wilson supported the sheikh strongly, as reflected in a letter he sent to his British Army superior, commander of Land Forces Gulf, in 1967. He wrote: "I am determined that this Ruler and his people will have my utmost help and support without being disloyal to Her Majesty the Queen and the Government of Great Britain."[52]

Colonel Wilson's support extended to advocating the purchase of Italian rather than British combat aircraft to the ruler, a recommendation that was not supported by the British government. Following Britain's January 1968 announcement to withdraw its protection of the Trucial States by 1971, Sheikh Zayed ordered that an air force be established with both tactical transport and ground-strike/air-defense capabilities. British national interests were best served, according to the Foreign Office, if the ruler had bought British aircraft and if these aircraft had such limited capabilities that they "would not be likely to generate friction with neighbouring States."[53] Specifically, Britain was concerned that if it provided advanced aircraft, this would undermine moves toward a federation of the Trucial States and Qatar, contribute to a regional arms race, and attract international opprobrium toward Britain for fueling such a race.[54] Colonel Wilson organized a comparison between the British offering, the Strikemaster, and the Italian Aeromacchi[55] that showed that the Aeromacchi was superior. Sheikh Zayed consequently stated he would not buy the British aircraft. Colonel Wilson was blamed for Sheikh Zayed's decision[56] and he recognized that this was against British interests and would probably result in his being kicked out of the Army.[57] This was apparently a reasonable assessment, for the *Telegraph*'s obituary of Colonel Wilson noted that, at the time of the aircraft purchase, Colonel Wilson met the just-retired UK chief of the Defence Staff, Lord Mountbatten, who told him that Wilson's resistance to the UK's preferred aircraft "would cost him his job."[58] However, Wilson was not subsequently sacked.

Colonel Wilson not only resisted what he considered direct British influence but also implemented organizational structures to constrain British influence. Two examples illustrate this: First, he advocated the continued use of an independent agent (Charles Kendall and Partners) rather than a Crown agent for purchasing military items in Britain. Writing to the ruler of Abu Dhabi before his end of service in May 1969, he observed that using Kendall would give "absolute independence from British Government interference [and to change this would have meant] the equipping of the Force will then be entirely in the hands of the British Government."[59] He warned the ruler about the arguments that the British would use to persuade him to use Crown agents and the consequences of doing so, as seen in the following extract from a letter to the ruler:

They will tell you that they [Crown agents] have direct access to Government Stores; that they have experts in every field and that their charges are nominal. This, I am afraid, is not true in practice. ADDF will become an index number, there will be interminable delays when ordering stores, especially if the equipment in question doesn't happen to fit in with the policy of the British Government. There will be no priorities and the whole momentum of build-up [of the ADDF] will be lost.[60]

The second organizational arrangement established by Colonel Wilson to constrain British influence was to limit the number of seconded officers in the ADDF, to prevent them from holding certain positions, and to ensure that their presence did not lead to British interests dominating in the force. This is reflected in the following extract from a letter from Colonel Wilson to the ruler in preparation for the takeover in mid-1969 of a new seconded officer as the commander of the ADDF and around thirty additional seconded officers:

I have said from the very outset this is the national force of Abu Dhabi and not a British sponsored Army, and I have always worked to fulfil the policy expressed by Your Highness; at no time have I allowed British interference. When these Officers arrive, if the position is not carefully watched, control could be lost and development may be slowed or directed to suit the political aims of an outside government. This is obviously unacceptable to Your Highness and the Government of Abu Dhabi.

In creating the order of battle (establishment of Officers), I have been very careful to ensure that the balance between British Seconded Officers and the Contract Officers (whom I call Abu Dhabi Regular Officers) is very carefully preserved. The Sea and Air Wings have been specially designed so that there are no Seconded Officers in them. The reason for this is, that should the British Government change its mind on secondment policy, your Force would be able to continue under the command of Abu Dhabi Regular Officers and your aircraft and naval craft would remain fully operational.

It is vital that the position of the Contract Officers is not undermined or that they are reduced in number. . . . These Officers are professional soldiers with a knowledge of the Arab. They are your Officers, owing allegiance to nobody but yourself and your country. They have all been fully briefed by me and I trust each and every one of them will serve you loyally.[61]

Like seconded officers, contract officers held command or senior-staff-grade posts and were engaged in large numbers that theoretically gave them great access and influence. Through their personal relationships with senior emiratis, they could have opened doors for British interests, as well as advanced Britain's agenda directly by advocating for Britain or, at the very least, explaining British motivations using their home-country knowledge.

There is some evidence to suggest that British officials thought along these lines. This can be seen in a 1973 letter from the chief of defense staff to the secretary of state that discussed the transfer of command of the ADDF from a seconded to a British contract officer. He wrote that when the transfer occurs, we can "expect to retain some influence within the ADDF."[62] Another example is contained in a 1969 memo from the British political agent in Dubai, which reflects on the appointment of the contract officer, Lieutenant Colonel David Neild, to form Ras Al Khaimah's military. The political agent wrote, "Neild is a man who could serve Sheikh Saqr [the ruler of Ras Al Khaimah] without losing sight of HMG's interests."[63] This message was received by Lieutenant Colonel Neild as noted in his memoir, in which he writes that a senior British official in Dubai "made it very clear that my loyalty should always remain first to the British Government and second to Sheikh Saqr."[64]

Although British officials may have expected contract officers to support British interests, this appears to have been a questionable assumption, as seen in Lieutenant Colonel Neild's response to the British official's approach. He outright rejected this and told the official that his loyalty was to the ruler of Ras Al Khaimah and to him alone.[65] This attitude was a common response of contract officers interviewed by the author. It also stands to reason that this would be the case, for to do otherwise would jeopardize the relationship the contract officer had with their emirati superior and their employment, as well as breach their own ethical standards. Thus, it appears that contract officers were not "directable" in terms of taking instructions from British officials, nor would they advance British interests above local ones through any sense of loyalty to Britain. It could be argued that contract officers might advance British interests if these interests aligned with the best interests of their host force and political leadership, but equally they might not even do this, because they did not want to be seen as acting as agents of their nation.

In summary, obtaining access and influence was perceived to be primarily dependent on holding executive and staff-officer-grade posts. In the case of seconded officers, even when they held these posts, their influence was constrained both because they were not trusted by the ruler and because it could not be guaranteed that they would automatically follow instructions from their British superior when those instructions were against the interests of the ruler. For contract officers, there appears to have been no willingness to advance British interests in terms of access and influence.

Conclusion

The future presence of British seconded personnel in the UAE Armed Forces is likely to consist of only a handful of midlevel officers providing specialist tasks and possibly undertaking advising and training/education. Their small numbers and lack of responsibility for command and staff work at senior ranks mean that they are destined to make only a small contribution to the two objectives of IDE—advancing British defense and national interests. This points to the need for a more realistic assessment of the effectiveness of seconded officers as a mechanism for advancing British defense and national interests.

In contrast, the number of British contract officers is likely to remain many times that of seconded officers; they are likely to continue to hold positions in all work categories; and a few will hold command and senior-staff-grade posts. (As of 2018, there are no British contract officers holding command and senior-staff-grade posts, but US and Australian contract officers do. This is likely to change with improved UAE-UK relations.)

Contract officers have never been considered part of Britain's IDE strategy, but given their much greater presence compared to seconded officers in the UAE and some other states, it may be time to reconsider this exclusion. Contract officers are achieving one of the goals of seconded officers, which is advancing British defense interests through their work in building their employing country's military capability. While the idea of incorporating contract officers into Britain's IDE strategy may seem radical, it is just an extension of IDE's "full-spectrum" approach, which already includes other nongovernment defense-related groups, notably defense manufacturers and defense service providers.

So how could contract officers be incorporated into IDE policy? The answer is to recognize that contract officers, like other nongovernment groups in the IDE strategy, have different interests that are sometimes in conformance and sometimes in conflict with British state interests. They cannot be directed, which means they cannot readily be used to advance national interests by developing British understanding of the military of the contract officers' employing country, nor by obtaining access and interest for Britain.

Recognizing this, IDE strategy should focus on helping contract officers to do what they are engaged for; that is, to advance the military capability of their employing country, assuming it has a positive relationship with Britain. Support for these officers must always be transparent to ensure host countries do not view contract officers as representatives of the British government who serve at its direction.

British government support to contract officers should be in three areas: facilitation of contract officer's recruitment, skills maintenance, and ability to reach back into the British military.

When countries want to hire former British military personnel, typically this is done via the networks of those already hired or through public advertisements. A better approach would be a process similar to that which operated in the 1960s, when the MOD facilitated recruitment by distributing information on employment opportunities and making available a candidate's personnel records to the recruiter so that a better assessment could be made. This is particularly important when large numbers of personnel need to be hired quickly, which is when there appears to be an increased level of unsuitable candidates being hired.[66]

The second area—skills maintenance—addresses an ongoing challenge for former military personnel. Separated personnel lose skill currency, despite efforts to stay abreast of developments, through personal research and discussions with still-serving members. It is in the United Kingdom's interests to ensure that British contract officers are current with the latest British training, tactics, equipment, and so forth. This would ensure that this information can be passed on to the contract officer's host military, which encourages the host country to align with Britain's doctrine, methods, and so on, with all the attendant benefits that this brings. To enable contract officers to maintain their skills currency, the British government should allow contract officers to access British military and security professional-development opportunities, such as training programs, skills certification, refresher courses, conversion courses, and lessons-learned workshops, as well as appropriate MOD intranet material such as information bulletins, training material, and doctrine updates. Just as seconded officers benefit from pre-secondment training, so too would contract officers. As such, the British government should allow contract officers to attend Arabic language courses at the MOD's Defence Centre for Languages and Culture.

Finally, contract officers need to have a formal and reliable mechanism to reach back into the MOD and British Armed Forces to help them to assist their host country. Contract officers have traditionally done this through their own personal networks for more informal requests, and through the local defense attaché if requests need to be more formal. The success of the latter route depends on the attitude and capacity of the defense attaché and the relevant British military area. Formalizing communication via policy- and process-articulation, plus points of contact within the MOD, would ensure a more transparent, consistent, and supportive approach to facilitating host-country requests. Importantly, it would also speed up response times for organizing visits and accessing resources, which can at times be rather slow.

Collectively, these changes would bring an additional resource to advancing Britain's IDE strategy, albeit one that is not under government control.

NOTES

1 This chapter uses the term *seconded officers* to also include loan-service officers. Although there is a difference in these two, such as the person's immediate pay-master and the taxation arrangements, this is irrelevant in this chapter's context, so both groups are merged. In addition, this chapter also uses *seconded officers* to refer to the small number of officers who were technically attached from another military, but again, this distinction is irrelevant.

2 The term *officer* is used to mean both Commissioned Officers and Other Ranks personnel.

3 Ash Rossiter, "Britain and the Development of Professional Security Forces in the Gulf Arab States, 1921–71: Local Forces and Informal Empire" (PhD diss., University of Exeter, 2014).

4 This was true across the Gulf. Ash Rossiter, "'Screening the Food from the Flies': Britain, Kuwait, and the Dilemma of Protection, 1961–1971," *Diplomacy & Statecraft* 28, no. 1 (2017): 85–109.

5 Rt. Hon. Julian Amery, MP, to Rt. Hon. Sir Geoffrey Howe, Secretary of State, FCO, NB 087/2, in FCO 8/6177, the National Archives, Kew, UK (henceforth TNA), 1986.

6 The archival material covers a number of holdings, notably TNA and the eight-volume personnel archive of Col. E. B. Wilson, the first seconded officer in the Abu Dhabi Defence Force, 1965–1969. The archival material covers the period up to 1990, which is the latest year material was released, whereas interviews span the period from the 1960s to the present. The interviews are from personnel who served with the various emirati militaries and British officials to 2010. The sources used in this chapter were collected through the author's work in producing the books *The Evolution of the UAE Armed Forces* and *Invisible Expatriates: Western Military Professionals and the Development of the UAE Armed Forces*. Details on the data's provenance can be found in the introduction section of both books.

7 This is reflected in the 1981 Nott Review when IDE was introduced as a mission of the British Armed Forces. The Nott Review stated IDE was focused in areas outside of NATO where it was needed because of "growing Soviet military reach and readiness" and because "Britain's own needs, outlook and interests give her a special role and a special duty in efforts of this kind." Within the NATO region, IDE was not needed, as military power was projected directly by Britain and its allies. 79 1981 UK Secretary of State for Defence, "The United Kingdom Defence Programme: The Way Forward" (Her Majesty's Stationery Office, 1981), 11.

8 The use of FCO in this chapter includes its antecedent departments such as the Colonial Office and Commonwealth Office.

9 Athol Yates, *The Evolution of the Armed Forces of the United Arab Emirates* (Abingdon, UK: Helion & Co., 2020).

10 This is explicitly stated in the Chiefs of Staff Committee's 1967 directive issued to the last regional British military regional commander who was responsible for the Trucial Oman Scouts. The directive stated that the TOS is "controlled by the Political Resident Persian Gulf [the local British diplomatic representative] and their employment is subject to his authority, exercised where appropriate through the Political Agent, Dubai and Abu Dhabi." Maj. Gen. J. H. Gibbon, secretary, Chiefs of Staff Committee, "Directive for the Commander, British Forces Gulf," in CAB 163/116, TNA, 1967.

11 P. H. R. Wright, Middle East Department, FCO, *Annual Report by the Defence Attaché*, in FCO 8/2371, TNA, 1974.

12 A 1979 Chiefs of Staff paper defined military assistance as covering "a wide range of activities including the provision of military advice, loan service personnel, training teams, training in the UK, and government-backed defence sales." MOD (UK) Chiefs of Staff Committee, "Defence Options Available to the United Kingdom in Contributing to the Stability in the Gulf and Former CENTO Areas," in AIR 8/3682, TNA, 1979, Annex A.

13 Article 120 of the constitution.

14 Ash Rossiter, "Strength in Unity: The Road to the Integrated UAE Armed Forces," *Liwa: Journal of the National Archives* 7, no. 13 (2015): 41–54.

15 In the case of the United Kingdom, the orders need to be consistent with United Kingdom Regulations, which are those statutes, orders, rules, regulations, warrants, or instructions relating to a UK forces.

16 While the rulers of these militaries expressed interest in obtaining British seconded officers when they were forming their forces, once Britain's reluctance on supplying secondees for smaller militaries was known, the respective ruler did not make a formal request.

17 At this time, there were seventeen seconded officers, of which seven were officers and then other ranks. Chiefs of Staff Committee, "Defence Options Available."

18 This MoU is titled "Military Personnel Loan Agreement" and was signed January 18, 1991. UK Ministry of Defence, Freedom of Information Request Ref: FOI2016/12402, 2017.

19 Officially his title has been "Senior Loan Service Officer," regardless of whether he is a seconded or loan-service officer.

20 The first is unknown but is believed to be one of the following: Colin Barnes, R. J. F. (Bob) Brown, Guy Wallace, Hart or Ian Donaldson.

21 The list and an explanation of the content analysis method used to develop the categories are detailed in Yates, *Invisible Expatriates: Western Military Professionals and the Development of the UAE Armed Force* (Abingdon, UK: Helion, 2020).

22 This is the author's estimates, for there are no continuous series of figures on either seconded or contract officers from either UK or emirati sources. Official figures on seconded officers are occasionally released from the UK government, with another source being archival information. Figures on contract of-

ficers are far scanter, and sources are primarily archival information from the 1960s and 1970s, when numbers were occasionally recorded in official British correspondence, and from the author's research.

23 Athol Yates, "Western Expatriates in the UAE Armed Forces, 1964–2015," *Journal of Arabian Studies* 6, no. 2 (2016): 182–200.

24 Yates, "Western Expatriates."

25 Brig. A. Pillar, Senior Military Contract Officer 2002–11, UAE Armed Forces, "Review of MCO Contribution to UAE Armed Forces" (Yates Collection, n.d.).

26 UK Ministry of Defence & Foreign and Commonwealth Office, "International Defence Engagement Strategy" (2017), 14.

27 Brig. J. H. A. (Hamish) McGregor, CBE MC, Loan Service Officer, UAE Armed Forces (1991–93), interview, UK, May 30, 2016.

28 Capt. R. Hitchcock, OC A Squadron and founding OC 2nd Infantry Regiment, ADDF (1967–70), interview, Cambridge, UK, August 20, 2015.

29 The team also included US contract officers. Subject 121, "Contract officer, Former US Army officer, Working in Special Forces, UAE Armed Forces, 1990s," interview in Abu Dhabi, February 5, 2015.

30 Brig. A. Pillar, Senior Military Contract Officer 2002–11, UAE Armed Forces, email, May 12, 2016.

31 Subject 699, "Expatriate Serving in a Training Institute from the Late 2000s to Mid-2010s," interview, 2017.

32 UK Ministry of Defence & Foreign and Commonwealth Office, "International Defence Engagement Strategy," 2.

33 Chiefs of Staff Committee, "Defence Options Available."

34 For example, the 1977 annual report was twenty-four pages and contained detailed organizational charts of the militaries, the order of battle, and the location of all units. Col. T. N. Bromage, Defence Attaché, *Annual Report on the UAE Armed Forces for 1977*, in FCO 8/3105, TNA, 1978.

35 A likely example of this was noted by an official in the British embassy in the UAE, in describing how it obtained in 1973 a copy of Pakistan's agreement with Abu Dhabi over the provision of seconded Pakistani officers. The official wrote that the agreement "was sent under cover of a letter from Shaikh Faisal [undersecretary of the Ministry of Defence (Abu Dhabi)] to the Ministry of Finance with a copy to HQ ADDF, perhaps with the intention that it should reach us [via British personnel in HQ ADDF]." Ibbot to Hunt, "TelNo. 107 of 5 April," in FCO 8/2136, TNA, 1973.

36 This did not mean that contract officers did not provide such information, for at least one person was identified in the 1990s as having done so, with the result being deportation. However, it is likely to have been far less common.

37 Colonel Wilson's Archives, vol. 3 (Abu Dhabi: unknown, n.d.), Lt. Col. E. B. Tug to A. T. Lamb, political agent, Abu Dhabi, "G. 1004, " December 1, 1966, 24.

38   The UAE did allow Iraqi Ilyushins transporting helicopters to fly through Abu
     Dhabi on their way to Oman, but Iraq decided against a strike and withdrew its
     forces. Iran did not respond to this development. D. A. Roberts, UK Ambas-
     sador, Abu Dhabi to FCO, "Iraq/Iran," in PREM 15/1843, TNA, 1980.

39   P. H. Moberly to Mr. Gillmore (UK MOD), "British Service Commanders in
     Oman," in FCO 8/3701, 1980.

40   UK Minister of Defence to Prime Minister, "Military Assistance and Training
     Charges," in FCO 8/4360, TNA, 1982.

41   Col. J. C. M. Ansell, Commander, Kuwait Liaison Team to DMAO MOD,
     "The Role and Strength of the KLT and the Provision of Calibration Techni-
     cians," in AIR 8/3682, TNA, 1983.

42   The speaker was Rear Admiral Morton. Air Commodore BGT Stanbridge, sec-
     retary, Chiefs of Staff Committee, "Directive to the Senior British Loan Service
     Officer in the ADDF," in DEFE 4/279, TNA, 1973.

43   The speaker was Sir Stewart Crawford, "Directive to the Senior British Loan
     Service Officer in the ADDF."

44   Lt. Col. N. D. S. (Nigel) Smith, UAE Armed Forces Infantry Advisor, 2005–10,
     email, October 8, 2018.

45   Ansell, "The Role and Strength of the KLT."

46   Stanbridge, "Directive to the Senior British Loan Service Officer in the ADDF."

47   For example, in 1968 a British official requested that it be made "clear to the
     Ruler that the Senior British Loan Officer [who at that time was Commander
     ADDF] is not responsible to him." UK Foreign Office, "Confidential Note to
     'Agreement Between the Government of the United Kingdom of Great Britain
     and Northern Ireland and the Government of Abu Dhabi Concerning the Pro-
     vision of British Loan Personnel,'" in FCO 8/882, TNA, 1968.

48   MOD (UK) Chiefs of Staff Committee, "Directive to Senior British Loan Ser-
     vice Officer in the Abu Dhabi Defence Force," in DEFE 5/197, TNA, 1973.

49   UK Government and UAE Government, "Memorandum of Understanding
     between the Government of the United Kingdom of Great Britain and North-
     ern Ireland and the Government of the United Arab Emirates Concerning the
     Provision of Personnel of the United Kingdom Armed Forces on Secondment
     to the Armed Forces of the United Arab Emirates (draft)," in FCO 8/4406,
     TNA, 1982.

50   Lt. Col. G. W. A. MOD Napier, to Mr Skilback, Foreign Office, "UK Military
     Personnel of the UAE," in FCO 8/2135, TNA, Annex A to DPS(C), 153.

51   Colonel Wilson's Archives, vol. 3, Lt. Col. E. B. Wilson to Brig. F. D. King,
     Military Advisor (Overseas Equipment), MOD (UK), "G.1004, " August 7,
     1966, 79.

52   Lt. Col. E. B. Wilson to Brig. F. D. King, 1: Col. E. B. Wilson, Commander
     ADDF to Brig. I. R. R. Hollyer, Commander, Land Forces Persian Gulf, "G.
     1004," May 14, 1967, 205.

53 J. P. Sheen, Ministry of Technology, "AP/32/036," in WO 32/20760, TNA, 1968.

54 This was noted by Sir Stewart Crawford, political resident in Bahrain, who wrote, "Abu Dhabi plan to acquire prestige aircraft . . . [would] deal a mortal blow to the Union Force Idea. . . . Besides alarming Dubai and Qatar (the latter might well feel obliged to try to emulate Zaid), it would I imagine have wider repercussions in Arabia and the Gulf—and also bring blame on to our heads for not stopping Zaid." S. Crawford, "Telegram No 685 of 30 November," in FCO 8/1237, TNA, 1968.

55 C. B. Benjamin, Ministry of Technology, "Aircraft for Abu Dhabi," in "Telegram No 685 of 30 November," attachment "Received from Mr. R. J. W. Brown on 3rd December 1968. "

56 C. J. Treadwell, political agent, Abu Dhabi, "Telegram No 500 to Bahrain from Abu Dhabi," in FCO 8/1237, TNA, 1968.

57 C. B. Benjamin, "Aircraft for Abu Dhabi."

58 "Colonel Edward 'Tug' Wilson," *Telegraph*, February 3, 2009.

59 Colonel Wilson's Archives, vol. 1, Col. E. B. Wilson, Commander ADDF to His Highness Shaikh Zaid Bin Sultan Al Nahayan, "Future of ADDF, " February 2, 1969, 144–147.

60 "Future of ADDF," February 2, 1969.

61 "Future of ADDF," February 2, 1969.

62 Chief of Defence Staff, to Secretary of State, "British Military Personnel in the UAE, Document Considered at Chiefs of Staff Meeting Held on 3 April 1973, Draft Submission," in DEFE 4/276, TNA, 1973.

63 J. L. Bullard, political agent, Dubai to Bahrain Political Residency, "Dubai telegram no 84 to Bahrain," in FCO 8/1245, TNA, 1969.

64 David Neild, *A Soldier in Arabia* (Surbiton, UK: Medina, 2016), 106. This perception may well have continued to recent times, as noted by a senior contract officer in the 2000s: "The contract officer was viewed as someone who could provide a valuable link and trusted influence," October 8, 2018, email from Smith.

65 Neild, *A Soldier in Arabia*, 106.

66 This was a common observation across the decades. For example, one of the first seconded officers in the ADDF regarding the 1968 expansion stated, "I believe the selection of contract officers at that time should have been put on a far more professional footing . . . the trouble being the Force was suddenly obliged to expand massively overnight and I think proper selection procedures were largely ignored." Subject 124, "Seconded British Army Officer to the ADDF Armoured Squadron, late 1960s," email, October 15, 2018.

10

The Nature, Character, and Viability of Modern UK Defense-Engagement Policy

Col. O. C. C. Brown and Group Captain P. D. Kennett

In 1956, Britain played her part in the Suez Canal Crisis, a strategic blunder that accelerated the end of Britain as an imperial power. Thereafter, Harold MacMillan's government disengaged from areas of the world in which Britain had been persistently engaged for years. In 2015, Britain codified persistent engagement overseas as a tool of policy, with the aim of reenergizing long-term engagement with a number of regions and countries. Although still a relatively new concept to the United Kingdom's strategic policy-making elite, it is already clear that the constituent activities are complex and the results largely unmeasurable.

This chapter will initially define persistent engagement, then consider the utility of persistent engagement overseas as a tool of strategy in the current era through two lenses. First, the study will consider "strategy in theory" to establish whether contemporary theories of international relations provide a rationale for persistent engagement. Second, it will consider persistent engagement as a tool of "strategy in practice" to establish whether it has real-world utility. To do so, the chapter will analyze whether the United Kingdom can feasibly realize the objectives of its International Defence Engagement Strategy (IDES), which are to develop understanding, to prevent conflict, to build capability and capacity, to promote prosperity, and to gain access and influence.[1] Finally, the concepts surrounding defense engagement will be situated within the context of the United

Kingdom's Brexit (withdrawal from the EU) dilemma and an analysis provided of the utility of the concept in the post-Brexit strategic condition. The chapter will argue that the nature of international relations in the modern world is such that persistent engagement has utility as a tool of "strategy in theory" for the United Kingdom. Furthermore, it will be argued that persistent engagement can be used effectively as a tool of "strategy in practice," but that to achieve utility the United Kingdom will need to apply considerable effort. These efforts must ensure linkage between cross-governmental policy and persistent engagement activities so as to achieve the degree that synergy of effect requires to achieve outcomes. The chapter will also argue that British political culture presents pitfalls that may reduce the utility of these tools.

The manifestation of persistent engagement in British security strategy is defense engagement (DE), which was first espoused as a British military activity in the National Security Strategy of 2010 as a means of tackling risks before they escalate.[2] The 2015 Strategic Defence and Security Review formalized the concept. IDES defined DE as "the use of our people and assets to prevent conflict, build stability and gain influence"[3] and is the "non-combat use of military power."[4] Much of the conceptual work to define the scope of DE is still to be completed, and it is likely to broaden to include security-force assistance. Persistent engagement encompasses military engagement across the mosaic of conflict, including security-force assistance during combat operations. The methods through which persistent engagement is delivered generally sit at the tactical level and perhaps the operational level, but they are not strategic in nature. DE comprises defense diplomacy, defense support to UK prosperity, and capacity-building.[5] As with most military activities, persistent engagement will be most effective if integrated across all the five military domains and with activity from across all governmental levers of power.

Strategy in Theory

First, it is worth considering the question, Do contemporary theories of international relations support the utility of persistent engagement? The contemporary environment is characterized by social inequality, rapid change, a profusion of information and data, and interconnected states, organizations, and individuals. Globally, there has been a steady rise in the number of conflicts, with 2016 experiencing the most conflicts since the 1990s.[6] These conflicts have given rise to an unprecedented 65.6 million displaced people, including 22.5 million refugees.[7] Forty-seven conflicts were intrastate conflicts, of which 38 percent were internationalized in 2016.[8] Furthermore, new domains (cyber and space) offer new opportunities and create new threats. In this operating environment, many argue that soft power has become increasingly important,[9] as "the second face of power."[10] Joseph Nye defines soft power as "the ability to attract, and attraction leads to acquiescence."[11] If strategy is the art of creating power, doing so through acquiescence must be the apogee. Generating soft power is difficult and nuanced and is defined not by the instrument of state power employed but by the ways it is used. It "involves building long-term relationships that create an enabling environment for government policies."[12] In theory, persistent engagement is a valuable tool in the creation of trust, understanding, and interconnectedness that enables soft power. Forward presence reassures, defense diplomacy generates long-term relationships built on trust, and military capacity-building creates mutual understanding.

For many states, the effective generation of power relies on coalitions of those with common goals. Creating and husbanding a coalition's power is a collective effort that requires states to act in concert. Kira Peterson characterizes this type of power as *concerted power*—a group's ability to change or establish a political order in which maintaining the will of the group is critical.[13] She argues that the generation of power is more likely to be horizontal than hierarchical and that interdependence may well be a factor. Understanding collective dynamics and persistent monitoring of the relationships between partners will be important in optimizing a group's concerted power. Personal interaction, as the basis on which trust hinges, plays a significant part in this. Persistent engagement presents an effective mechanism for the gearing of this type of relationship, offering the opportunity to develop mutual understanding and to foster trust.

Another factor of the modern environment is the difficulty in formulating coherent strategy in an era characterized by constant change and unforeseen normative events.[14] In this environment, most commentators agree that effective strategies are iterative.[15] They are a process rather than a plan and require a deep understanding of the operating environment to inform an accurate diagnosis and ensure that activities remain coherent amid environmental friction and the actions of both adversaries. Developing understanding is one of the fundamental aims of UK DE,[16] in which regional specialists are valued for their ability to better inform decisions and to generate deep insights that allow a more accurate forecast of reactions.[17] Combined with persistent presence, constant intelligence feeds, and the maintenance of relationships in the countries and regions of interests, they provide the opportunity to develop significantly deeper understanding.

Therefore, in theory, persistent engagement seems to have considerable utility in support of strategic policy aims. It is now important to consider whether the reality of the operational environment is such that the benefits of these tactical activities can be realized as "strategy in practice." The IDES objectives are fivefold: to develop understanding, to prevent conflict, to promote prosperity, to build capability and capacity in other security forces, and to gain access and influence. These support the United Kingdom's national-security objectives of protecting its people, promoting prosperity, and projecting global influence.

Strategy in Practice

It is necessary to first give a note of caution. The way IDES seeks to align the ends, ways, and means of strategy is fraught with danger. IDES seems to present DE as an end in itself rather than a method of delivering conflict prevention. Capacity-building is presented as an objective of DE, rather than as a method of contributing to stability. The strategic choice here is to generate stability and, in doing so, to reduce threats to UK security and prosperity. The method of doing so is DE. This is more than semantics; it's illustrative of muddled policy-making, and the danger is that it imbues DE with a logic of its own and allows tactical activity to subsume the aims of strategy. Practitioners must guard against activity by default and ensure progress to "ends" by design. Having identified this caveat, it is now possible to examine the IDES objectives in turn.

Understanding

The first objective is to develop understanding. Hans J. Morgenthau identifies that "the middle ground of subtle distinctions, complex choices and precarious manipulations" is that which foreign policy occupies. The nuanced understanding required to operate effectively in this strategic space was illustrated earlier. Indeed, the link between the failure to develop a deep understanding of the operating environment and the inability to achieve strategic aims is well founded. The Winograd Report[18] on the Israeli and Lebanese conflict in 2006 and the Chilcot Report both make this point explicitly.[19] Persistent engagement can make a substantial contribution to understanding operating environments,[20] through both broader familiarity and more intelligence feeds from a wider variety of sources. Persistent engagement affords the opportunity to develop expertise and to develop a knowledge base deep enough to generate insight and the ability to forecast. The development of regional specialists is on the military agenda through a number of initiatives such as enlivened defense-attaché networks and the alignment of British Army brigades with regions.

This realignment of resources represents a step in the right direction, but what counts is whether this deep expertise and the increased inflow of intelligence can effectively inform operational design and strategic choices. The growing tri-service coherence that the Ministry of Defence (MOD) is bringing to DE is progress, but this will need to be matched by a commensurate coherence cross-government. The new cross-government "fusion doctrine" is a further attempt to engender a "comprehensive approach," or "full spectrum effect," and an acknowledgment that previous approaches have not yet been effective. Structures continue to predicate against cross-governmental intelligence coherence; for instance, defense intelligence is not considered as part of the British intelligence trinity with the Secret Intelligence Service (MI6), Government Communications Headquarters (GCHQ), and the Security Service, and the MOD operates a separate secret communications system. Whether deeper understanding generated through persistent engagement will enable better strategy has yet to be tested, but in order to do so, it must be synthesized with wider intelligence assessments, then reach point of need.

Conflict Prevention

The second IDES objective, "conflict prevention," is very broad, in that it encompasses preemptive activity to stop conflict occurring, peace enforcement to separate belligerent parties, and peacekeeping, which aims to maintain peace.[21] There is a strong ethical and economic case for preemptive activity to stop the outbreak of conflict, but the success of efforts to prevent conflict remains contested. The successes in the 1980s and early 1990s, in Namibia and El Salvador, were based on early warning, preventative deployment, and disarmament—all areas in which military engagement was key.[22] However, there are many examples where, despite military engagement, preemptive activity failed, such as the Democratic Republic of the Congo (DRC) and Sudan; in these cases, engagement came too late to succeed. There are likely to be more failures than successes, and when prevention does work, the circumstances are specific.[23] Thus it would be intensely naïve to consider that preemptive deployment activity is reliably achievable. Even when successful, it is by no means risk-free: financial costs can be significant, and political exposure can be high. This fiscal element brings into question the current political appetite to invest early enough with the resources necessary to make a difference.

When conflict becomes inevitable, there may be strategic advantage in committing military forces to restore peace, particularly where there are wider potential benefits to be realized in the country or region. In these circumstances, military personnel, able to work in high-risk environments, offer the opportunity to provide persistence during the conflict, as in the case of Oman in the late 1960s and 1970s. Britain was engaged before the communist insurgency in Dhofar became destabilizing. Their cultural and environmental understanding greatly assisted a positive outcome while partnering with the Sultan's forces. The campaign achieved a degree of regional stability, ensured British regional access, and protected national interests. This clear-sighted strategic choice to invest military resources has had enduring dividends. Most recently, this includes the Duqm dockyard joint venture between Babcock International and the Oman Drydock Company. This provides the United Kingdom with a joint logistics support base in the region and a training facility connected to other Gulf countries by the Gulf Rail Project.[24]

On a larger scale, persistent engagement combined with other levers of power can be a means of deterrence. Military assets can be positioned to generate presence and indicate posture, the ultimate example of this being NATO's presence in Western Europe during the Cold War. Modern examples include the impact of American military trainers in Georgia and the British "Enhanced Forward Presence" in Estonia. In all these cases, the strategic decision to forward-base military assets may in itself deliver the strategic effect required, regardless of the tactical activity of those involved in the resultant tactical activity. Equally clear is the fact that deterrence strategy will be effective when threats are understood. Developing this nuanced understanding relies on the knowledge and insight generated through regional experts, and here persistent engagement is a considerable asset. However, our ability to measure the deterrent effect of persistent engagement is exceptionally difficult, and in many cases can only be achieved retrospectively.

Capacity-Building

One of the tactical activities used to prevent conflict is capacity-building in support of good governance and stability; this is the third objective of DE. This is well established both in cross-governmental doctrine and in practice, the aims being to build "strong, enduring security institutions that can offer a country's population a sense of stability."[25] The policy objectives achieved through the use of this activity vary, and the benefits will be accrued by both parties. Georgia provides an example. Their commitment of forces to Afghanistan was enabled by a US "train and assist" program in Georgia. This modernized Georgian forces while US presence deterred further Russian interference, to the point that some claim the United States is the anchor of Georgian independence.[26] Alternatively, the activity might support British national interests by the preparation of foreign forces for operations in a region of interest. The British Peace Support Team East Africa trains Kenyans and Ugandans for operations in Somalia. The strategic effects in this case are threefold: stabilization in Somalia, protection of UK interests in Kenya from the threat posed by Al Shabaab, and maintenance of influence and access in Kenya. The preparation and partnering of proxy forces has contributed to perceived success in recent conflicts, such as counter-Daesh operations in 2017. These examples illustrate where the building blocks provided by military activities can contribute to strategic effect.

However, capacity-building can be highly politicized and also carry considerable risk in relation to the desired outcomes and strategic end-state. The performance of partnered forces can become a reputational issue for Britain and contribute to reduced national credibility. Afghan forces were to provide the British an exit strategy from Afghanistan in 2014, but their inability to counter the Taliban threat without Western military support resulted in a resurgent Taliban. For similar reasons, the Department for International Development (DfID) rarely supports police capacity-building, as these internal security forces can become tools of oppression.[27] Robert Johnson points out that capacity-building can distort societal ecosystems through the clash of "the collision of clan politics, western ideas of bureaucracy and cultural norms."[28] The Stabilisation Unit also has concerns that efforts "to rapidly generate security forces invariably create instability,"[29] unless they are accompanied by development across the security sector. So the picture is mixed; results can be achieved but are not guaranteed, and unintended consequences are inevitable. Through this optic, these persistent-engagement activities reveal a similar nature to any tactical activity in conventional operations. They have utility only when they are used as coherent actions in effective operational design that genuinely serve the strategic requirement.

A further dilemma for strategists is that conflict prevention requires long-term commitment. Success requires significant time and resources, so national strategic patience is essential. Where presence in conflict areas aligns with broader British national interests and levels of violence are suppressed, retaining presence is less politically difficult. The British involvement in Cyprus is a pertinent example. However, where levels of violence are high and national interests nebulous, political will is more difficult to maintain. The US commitment to the UN mission in Somalia, which ended in 1995, is an example of this; political will was overmatched by the level of violence. In Western democracies, maintaining this political will is often problematic. Of the fifteen current UN peacekeeping missions, eight have exceeded fifteen years; the longest-serving British government since 1830 has served just nearly eleven years; the ongoing campaign in Afghanistan has spanned four governments, each of which has shown declining political will. Culture may, therefore, be at odds with strategy in this area, with a lack of strategic patience denying persistent engagement its inherent utility.

Promote Prosperity

The fourth objective of DE is promoting prosperity. IDES requires Defence to work with diplomatic and economic partners to further Britain's success as a trading nation. Examples are many. Prime Minister Major signed a UK/United Arab Emirates (UAE) Defence Cooperation Agreement in 1996, which remains key in the bilateral relationship; UAE investment in the United Kingdom is about £40 billion (US$52.56 billion) a year,[30] and 120,000 Britons work in UAE.[31] Duqm Dockyard joint venture is another significant undertaking, and though its worth to Babcock and the United Kingdom is difficult to gauge, the size of the project is clear from investment in the facilities: US$1.7 billion since 2008.[32] These and other investments enabled by military activity have made the Gulf a nexus of prosperity and security accounting for 50 percent of UK defense sales.[33] The indirect benefits of DE are broader; for instance, the United Kingdom buys 25 percent of Kenyan cut-flower exports[34] and has invested in transport infrastructure to support military training around the Nanyuki area. This has proved to be of direct benefit to UK-owned exporters of roses,[35] but its worth, and that of a multitude of similar DE activities, is not quantified.

Given that security enables economic development and increases stability, persistent engagement also offers opportunities in emerging markets. Work to stabilize fragile states offers immediate economic opportunity; the DfID spent £13.4 billion (US$17.6 billion) in Official Development Aid in 2016.[36] The DfID is a commissioning organization and most of its contractors are British, so the investment in development benefits British companies.[37] Furthermore, engagement to stabilize fragile states brings opportunity and reduces threats; the population in sub-Saharan Africa is growing at a very substantial rate and is anticipated to reach 2.5 billion by 2050.[38] Malthusian theory[39] suggests that population increases tend to outstrip subsistence, which leads to fragility and migration, but a significant rise in working-age adults, with careful management, can provide economic opportunity.[40] International activity to generate security, develop mature civil institutions, and catalyze economic development will offset Malthusian concerns. British stabilization and development activity in fragile states therefore offers opportunity to gain access to these markets. Security is the key enabler, and capability-building an integral part of delivering that security, but it must be conducted in a measured manner and coincide with rising maturity in state institutions and accountability.

A further element in the prosperity debate is the cost of conflict. Much work has been conducted to quantify the economic benefits of peacekeeping, and advocates place value in spend-to-save. Malcolm Chalmers estimates that every £1 spent in preventing conflict saves £4.1,[41] and Hannes Mueller[42] goes further, quantifying negative GDP growth in protracted conflicts of up to 40 percent. Persistent-engagement activities that contribute to the prevention of the onset of conflict, or reducing its severity, can therefore contribute to prosperity. Again, though, attribution of cause and effect and quantifying the benefit in each case is almost always extremely difficult—this does make the military contribution very hard to attribute value to. Perhaps the only way to gauge the utility is to consider the counterfactual: If the military contribution to conflict prevention was not present, would success be achievable? In the examples included in this paper, benefits would not have been realized.

Generating understanding, capacity-building, defense diplomacy, defense sales, and military efforts to stabilize areas affected by conflict-assist states, are all activities that contribute to interoperability, interdependence, and trust. As part of a wider country and regional strategy, these can generate the ability to influence other nations and organizations in order to deliver favorable strategic outcomes. Britain's experiences with Oman and Estonia are very tangible examples of this. Access may be an objective achieved through influence in pursuit of an outcome. Influence is, in essence, soft power, which Elliot Cohen argues must be backed by hard power,[43] and is relevant in relation to the amount of soft power available to competitors. In military terms, hard power is the product of capability, proven experience, and a willingness to commit. Britain's military has been reduced in size and capability considerably over time, from over 5 percent of GDP in the 1970s to 2 percent in 2017; the campaigns in Iraq and Afghanistan have raised questions about Britain's strategic competence; and many in the British establishment question the utility of the military instrument. Furthermore, scale has a currency of its own. Britain is assisting Nigeria in its operations to counter Boko Haram—this low-level persistent engagement generates influence. However, in the same time frame, China has launched a satellite for Nigeria,[44] which directly contributes to the maintenance of Nigerian critical national infrastructure, which in turn may well give China a more effective lever of influence should it be needed. Persistent engagement can generate influence and access in support of strategic outcomes, but declining hard power in relation to competitors ultimately reduces soft power.

So how does persistent engagement measure up as a tool of strategy? In the current operating environment, and as a tool of strategy in theory, persistent engagement would seem to be well suited. Persistent engagement enables an effective diagnosis and can also provide a sense-and-warn function that allows deliberate strategy to shift to emergent strategy as situations change. Furthermore, it places a premium on collective power and personal relationships that are very relevant in the interconnected world. In practice, the tactical activities that constitute persistent engagement have utility as tactical tools, though there are challenges. Many modern commentators argue that Britain lacks the structures and institutional intellectual capital to craft effective strategy. So although the tactical activities of persistent engagement can generate operational effect, cohering them to generate coherent action will be very difficult. Or as Sun Tzu puts it in *The Art of War*: "In the absence of effective strategy, tactical activity is merely a prelude to defeat." Having identified an effective strategic approach, coherence must be maintained in its delivery through constant reevaluation and the requirement to prioritize and rebalance ways and means. The United Kingdom can currently be considered weak in this regard here; our ability to leverage cross-government effect and create synergy to achieve unity of effort is not yet well developed. Furthermore, persistent engagement requires strategic patience and early investment to accrue strategic and operational level benefits; British political culture may not allow either of these strategic requirements, which could negate the utility of persistent engagement. Political choices have reduced British hard-power effectiveness in relation to competitors, which devalues the tools. Lastly, the inability to measure the causal effects of persistent engagement makes hard choices about its employment very difficult, and thus these activities are easy to disinvest in. One of the most critical aspects of this self-awareness regarding UK DE is the need to evaluate to what extent it can be thought of as a realistic conflict-prevention strategy. "When conflict breaks out . . . lives are lost, people are displaced, women and girls experience increased levels of violence, trade links are cut, and organised crime groups or terrorists can spread. It is far more cost-effective to invest in 'upstream prevention' . . . than to pay the costs of responding to violent conflict."[45] Malcolm Chalmers's observation points to the evident truth that prevention is preferable to cure when considering the effects of conflict. Beyond the human cost, the financial implications are equally stark. In 2015, the cost of UN peacekeeping was $8.27 billion, which equates to only 1.1 percent of the estimated $742 billion of economic losses caused by armed conflict.[46] It is within this context, and against the reality of an uncertain global-security environment, that the secretary of state for defense and the foreign secretary offered a joint statement that defined defense engagement as "the use of our people and assets to prevent conflict, build stability and gain influence."[47]

Accepting the logic of pursuing conflict prevention and the role articulated by ministers for DE within this endeavor, there are two critical elements that require analysis to arrive at some evaluation of the true utility of DE. The first requirement is to conduct a critical examination of the United Kingdom's strategic ambition for conflict prevention, and specifically the role that DE plays as a tactical tool to achieve this goal. The second is the requirement to understand possible design principles for future DE that seek to optimize its value for conflict prevention in the twenty-first-century world of constant competition. It is agreed that "conflict prevention is like 'venture capital': small investments can yield a big return, but will fail more often than they succeed."[48] Therefore, it is virtually impossible to prevent all instances of armed conflict, and applying DE alone as a means of preventing conflict is destined to fail. A more effective approach would be to consider and use DE as a tool within a cross-government approach, under the emerging Fusion doctrine that seeks to develop resilience in priority regions and countries where UK interests are most at stake.[49] The objective of doing so can be to limit the effect of conflict on the United Kingdom rather than attempting, Canute-like, to stem the inexorable tide of global armed conflict.

Review of UK Ambition for Conflict Prevention

The strategic framework of ends, ways, and means will be employed as the lens through which to consider the United Kingdom ambition to achieve conflict prevention. Analysis of ends illuminates an unbounded ambition to prevent conflict linked to the "Global Britain" narrative "in which we play our full part in promoting peace and prosperity around the world [and] protect our national interests, our national security and the security of our allies."[50] The value of such a declaratory policy, which reassures our partners and allies particularly in the context of political turbulence caused by Brexit, should not be underestimated. In this regard, DE serves as a powerful symbol of the United Kingdom's commitment to remaining a networked, global player.[51] However, the very fact that the ambition is so expansive creates significant challenges for this strategy in both scale and scope.

The scale of ambition appears to reflect a broader agenda of democratic peace theory and an aspiration to prevent conflict by developing states in the United Kingdom's image. This approach raises concerns, as it presents the risk of mission creep from conflict prevention to state building by stealth. A further issue of scale links to the relevance of conflict prevention in an era of constant competition below the threshold of armed conflict where "revisionist powers and rogue regimes are using corruption, predatory economic practices, propaganda, political subversion, proxies, and the threat or use of military force to change facts on the ground."[52] In terms of scope, the 2015 National Security Strategy notes fifty-eight countries on which the United Kingdom intends to have some form of effect.[53] Of these countries, eleven are recognized by the Fragile States Index as having a worsening trend of stability over a ten-year period (2007–2017).[54] The evident implication of such unbounded ends is that "we replace discriminating strategy with indiscriminate globalism, and over-reach becomes inevitable."[55]

Without strategic adjustment, the current UK ambition therefore risks failure on two counts. First, it is too grandiose to be fulfilled, as the ability to identify suitable ways and sufficient means to pursue the ends sought is almost impossible—seeking to do "everything everywhere equates to nothing anywhere."[56] And second, overreach creates vulnerability, as the United Kingdom exposes the limitations of its national power, which can be exploited by competing powers that might seek to distract us from areas where they seek to further their interests at our expense.

DE offers a great number of advantages as a way of pursuing conflict prevention, including signaling commitment to cooperative relations, promoting military transparency, and perceptions of common interest.[57] An obvious attraction lies in the use of capacity-building to grow partner forces that are trained to deter potential aggressors and prevent conflict as a method of overcoming the challenge of generating mass in the context of the current taut fiscal climate. This approach also limits the United Kingdom's exposure to the human cost of conflict. A striking contemporary example of the success of DE is Sierra Leone, where UK engagement efforts from 2000 focused on building effective civil-military relationships and growing the ability of the Sierra Leone Armed Forces. The outcome of that preventative DE effort saw the military being identified as a lead institution in the coordination and management of the successful fight against Ebola in 2014.[58]

Notwithstanding this success and the many others that DE has underpinned, there are limits and risks that must be considered when evaluating the utility of DE in the context of conflict prevention. The greatest limitation is its reliance on state monopoly of violence. Where this condition does not exist, such as in Libya, the effectiveness of DE is neutralized, as pursuing a military relationship and capacity-building with a minority actor that does not dominate the security environment will not establish the conditions for stability to improve.[59] This prevention issue will likely remain a significant limiting factor on the value of DE, as the trend of state failure shows little sign of abating in the near future.[60]

Beyond the issue of limitation, a number of risks emanate from flawed understanding, as Antonio Giustozzi notes: "The folly of our age could be identified as an unmatched ambition to change the world, without bothering to study it in detail and understand it first."[61] First, incorrect diagnosis of the primary drivers for conflict may lead to misplaced emphasis on DE as a tool to remedy acute symptoms of conflict in the physical-security domain. Doing so overlooks the chronic, underlying causes of conflict, which are invariably based in the complexities of human security: social, political, and economic grievance.[62] To stand any chance of success in preventing conflict, it is therefore essential that the United Kingdom approach be framed by the cross-government Fusion doctrine of applying all instruments of national power in a coordinated manner.

Second, DE may lead to a security dilemma that unsettles regional security. Hostility and suspicion may grow between the United Kingdom's partner state and its neighbors on account of a perceived threat from expanded capability or the expectation of direct UK military support to the partner in the event of conflict. The post–Cold War policy of NATO expansion in Russia's near-abroad illuminates this issue and can be seen as an underlying factor in the Russian strategic calculus that led to offensive military operations in Ukraine, because "no Russian leader would tolerate a military alliance that was Moscow's mortal enemy until recently moving into Ukraine. Nor would any Russian leader stand idly by while the West helped install a government there that was determined to integrate Ukraine into the West."[63] This issue illustrates a noteworthy point—the contradiction of using the hard power of the military in a soft guise carries the risk of misinterpretation because "the central purpose of the military profession is to prepare for and engage in war-fighting."[64] Nye would disagree with this proposition, as he believes military cooperation can enhance soft power.[65] His point has validity, but to be effective in the manner he suggests, DE must be supported by unambiguous strategic communication directed purposely to counter the onset or heightening of a security dilemma.

Third, direct support for government or locally raised forces within a fragile state will likely polarize the security environment and force the population to make a stark decision whether to align with forces supported by the United Kingdom or support an adversary organization. In cases where the supported partner force employs illegitimate methods, such as extorting money from the local community, the likely outcome of UK engagement is to reinforce and, perhaps, worsen divisions in society and reinforce structural violence. So, far from preventing conflict, UK engagement may well contravene the "do no harm" principle by increasing the level of instability and likelihood of armed conflict.[66]

Fourth, there is a tendency within the conduct of capacity-building to design and develop military capabilities in the image of Western forces. The evident risk of doing so is that they are ill suited to the societal and economic context in which they will operate, as occurred in Afghanistan with attempts by Western nations to assert systems that the Afghans were not equipped or willing to accept.[67] The issue of "control" is inextricably linked to capacity-building. Two challenges emerge from this: the potential for reputational risk as a result of actions conducted by the partner force; and the reality that the partner force can and will likely act in a manner that does not conform to the United Kingdom's preferred design, by pursuing their own agendas, becoming lawless, and potentially launching a coup d'état.[68]

Finally, consideration of means points to the linked factors of competing activity and limited resources that constrain the effectiveness of DE as a tool for the United Kingdom. In 2017, 264 land-based capacity-building deployments were conducted across sixty-five countries. This demand consumed 1,648 personnel, which, absent the context of other demands, appears entirely manageable. However, the composite effect of multiple commitments, including contingent readiness across Defence, risks overstretch and suboptimal DE outcomes as troops shuttle constantly from one crisis or commitment to another, with little time for the sort of activities—such as language and cultural training—that enable success in these disparate missions.[69] A move to permanence, building on the network of loan service, defense sections, and embedded training teams, would alleviate this issue and afford greater agility in response to partner-force needs, developing crises, and emerging competition.

This analysis indicates that the United Kingdom's approach should not be hostage to the ideal of global-conflict prevention; rather, a more nuanced approach that focuses strictly on anticipating, identifying, and neutralizing threats to UK-specific interests should be pursued.[70] Though it is acknowledged that the United Kingdom cannot step away from international obligations or the international community's expectations of it as a UN P5 member, it should temper its strategic ambition and be more ruthless in its prioritization and judicious application of its capable but limited resources. Using threat as an organizing principle, the United Kingdom should look to limit the effects of conflict and competition upon its interests rather than trying to prevent them. The proposed mechanism for doing so is for the United Kingdom to focus on developing resilience in countries and regions of greatest significance, and in its relationships with them, in order to protect its interests and to generate and sustain the ability to withstand shocks that affect them. A more apposite definition of UK ambition might therefore chime with Boutros Boutros-Ghali's view: "action to prevent disputes from arising between parties, to prevent existing disputes from escalating into conflicts and to limit the spread of the latter when they occur."[71] Therefore, within the context of a full-spectrum approach, DE will continue to play an important role as a way of generating resilience among our key partners. Accordingly, the future challenge and focus of the rest of this chapter is a consideration of the DE design principles that should be applied to address the ways-and-means issues identified above, and to optimize its applicability for the twenty-first-century environment of constant competition.

DE Design Principles for Constant Competition

The first and preeminent design principle is the requirement to operationalize understanding. There are two vital factors that must be addressed to set the conditions for success. First, the United Kingdom must understand its own national intent and the nature of interests at stake so that it is able to prioritize its upstream engagement activity appropriately.[72] Second, the United Kingdom must develop a comprehensive understanding of relevant conflict environments to identify accurately the requirements for and consequences of UK actions within them. This approach must embrace all conflict drivers, not purely the physical-security domain, and it must be a dynamic process of constantly reviewing assumptions and avoiding decisions being taken without comprehension of their implications. The goal must be to develop precise indicators and warnings that illuminate both the likelihood of conflict and increasing competitive activity by adversaries. The United Kingdom must reach out beyond government-department-based analysis to produce the requisite understanding and introduce the diversity of thought needed to support a Chilcot-compliant approach to the challenges in strategic defense-engagement policymaking.[73] The understanding network should therefore include nongovernmental organizations, multinational corporations, regional partners, and academia to form a synthesized and not solely Western view of the situation. As technology develops, artificial intelligence and machine learning must also be exploited to analyze big data and take advantage of its pattern-analysis potential.

The second design principle is burden sharing. This should be exploited to limit the United Kingdom's exposure and the cost of DE and intervention; and as an important method of avoiding the likely polarization caused by inserting Western forces into a conflict environment. Notwithstanding that using another force, either international or regional, may compromise the United Kingdom's ability to counter competitor states, burden sharing with the UN, regional partners, and allies should also be considered.

Increased collaboration with the UN would both share the burden for the United Kingdom and, importantly, support the "Global Britain" agenda through the requirement for the United Kingdom to play a leading role in the UN, as a P5 member, in developing resilience and stability in conflict-stricken regions. This approach offers the opportunity to replicate the success of the UN deployment to Macedonia (UNPREDEP, 1992–1999), in which a force was interposed between ethnic Macedonians and Albanians to prevent the spread of violence and instability from both Bosnia-Herzegovina and later from Kosovo.[74] The evident wider benefit of leveraging UN engagement in this manner is that it would allow the United Kingdom to focus resources on areas of the greatest importance to national interest and where competitive pressure from adversaries is most keenly felt. In addition, this approach is arguably far more effective than increasing the numbers of UK personnel on peacekeeping operations, which places significant strain on the United Kingdom for little strategic effect. The United Kingdom should also look to use regional force capabilities, exploiting their understanding of local dynamics and culture. By working closely with organizations such as the Economic Community of West African States and the African Union, the United Kingdom might avoid the risk of destabilizing the balances of power and influence that may be caused by direct engagement. This approach also offers a mechanism of supporting failed states, whereby local forces may be best placed to support the recovery of state security infrastructure in a manner that will be sensitive to regional dynamics. Replicating the US Global Peace Operations Initiative (GPOI), which is designed to enhance international capacity to effectively conduct UN and regional peace support operations,[75] offers a mechanism by which the United Kingdom could operationalize its relationships with regional forces.

In addition, there is scope for greater burden sharing among close allies—especially within NATO, the five-eyes community, and, Brexit dependant, within the European Union (EU). There will be circumstances in which competing economic interests may militate against this approach; however, there will also be a great number of instances such as in Nigeria, where interests align between the United Kingdom and France in their efforts to address security challenges.[76] Similar opportunities with other allies should be explored.

The third design principle is to expand the use of private security companies (PSCs) as a method of alleviating pressure on UK military resources for the conduct of capacity-building. A connected and positive outcome is the opportunity to support UK prosperity by pursuing contracts through UK PSCs, funded initially by Overseas Development Aid, leveraging the United Kingdom's 0.7 percent spending of gross national income on development.[77] There are risks with this approach from an efficacy perspective, as shown by the experience of train-and-equip programs in Afghanistan, where a 2008 US Government Accountability Office analysis of Afghan National Police units indicated that none of 433 units were fully capable of operating independently.[78] However, when managed carefully, PSC-delivered contracts such as the US Africa Contingency Operations Training and Assistance program, which has trained 369 contingents of peacekeepers since 2005, provide substantial benefit.[79]

The fourth design principle is the requirement to frame and communicate an unambiguous narrative that supports DE activity. If planned and conducted effectively, strategic communication should reduce the risk of generating or exacerbating a security dilemma that may arise through misunderstanding or misperception of UK actions and intentions. The narrative must be nested within the context of the wider full-spectrum approach and must be communicated clearly across the region where the United Kingdom plans to act and to allies and competitors. Increased media transparency and visits by international observer teams to forces conducting DE can also help mitigate the risk of misperception.[80]

The fifth design principle is the necessity to pursue DE as a long-term endeavor if it is to offer genuine value to a strategy of building resilience. It must not be viewed as "a transitory ad hoc reaction. . . . It is a medium and long-term proactive strategy intended to identify and create the enabling conditions for a stable and more predictable international security environment."[81] Any sense of short-termism or veering and hauling of priorities for DE will be harmful not only for military-to-military relationships but also to the wider cross-departmental approach. The long-term, persistent relationship between US Special Operations Forces and the Iraqi Counter Terrorist Service (CTS) offers an excellent illustration of this issue. In the face of the Islamic state onslaught in 2014, a third of Iraqi Army and Police brigades melted away, leaving the US-trained CTS to stem the tide of the attack and then spearhead the counterattack. Not only did a long-term approach engender trust and confidence on both sides, but collocation and daily contact between US advisors and the CTS enabled the inculcation of professional ethics within the CTS.[82] Important wider benefits of partnering in this manner are that the "control" issue can be addressed, in part, by achieving a degree of oversight of the partner force's conduct and providing feedback from combat to measure the effectiveness of capacity-building.

The final design principle is to consider expanding the United Kingdom's forward-basing profile in regions of greatest national interest. This fundamental step would mark a strategic tipping point in the value of the United Kingdom's engagement, by converting episodic activity to permanent presence. The result would be a significant improvement in understanding and a quantum leap forward in reassurance of partners, as allies perceive forward-stationed forces as a sign of a stronger, more enduring commitment.[83] It would also be highly likely that a forward-deployed posture would alter adversaries' risk calculus of competing openly with UK interests. The greatest value of forward deployment is the depth it offers to resilience by affording a level of understanding and agility that would not otherwise be possible. The speed with which France responded to the Mali crisis in 2013 highlights this point—set against UK MOD's expectation of six weeks' lead time before delivering effect on the ground, France responded in seventy-two hours.[84]

The heavy UK forward presence in the Gulf reflects the strategic significance of this region and the importance of our relationships with the Gulf Cooperation Council (GCC) members.[85] It follows that a similar approach should be applied to other priority regions. Certainly the threat of instability spawning migration and growth of violent extremist organizations in sub-Saharan Africa indicates scope for additional investment. The case for this approach is strengthened further by the level of competition in this region, albeit principally economic, with China. Aside from permanent basing of deployable forces, the United Kingdom might seek to replicate the GPOI model by developing UK-led training hubs for peacekeeping. Low-cost options for doing so might include exploiting capacity at the army's training center in Kenya. In a similar manner, the United Kingdom may wish to confront Russian subthreshold competitive behavior in the Balkans[86] by adopting a permanent presence in the region. An equally strong case could be made for expanding the United Kingdom's presence in Asia-Pacific beyond the garrison in Brunei as a means of meeting the regional competitive challenge of China.

Unforeseen events that are the likely result of competition and conflict appear the only certainty in our complex modern world. Consequently, the pursuit of a strategy of conflict prevention on a "Global Britain" scale and scope is not viable—the means are insufficient to achieve the ends; and DE, independently, as a way will certainly not succeed. However, a nuanced approach that employs the Fusion doctrine to combine the efforts of all government departments to generate resilience to those unforeseen events by addressing instability and conflict drivers will be far more effective. The role of the military in this endeavor will remain significant but supporting, with DE being employed actively as a tactical tool to support broader strategic-stability outcomes.

The United Kingdom's focus must now be on optimizing the contribution of DE to make it fit for purpose in the era of constant competition. Rooted on a platform of comprehensive understanding, the United Kingdom must look to apply DE with precision, to forward base where it is logical to do so, and to leverage burden-sharing opportunities appropriately so as to amplify the positive effect of UK military-to-military relationships where they will make the most significant contribution. If strategy is "the art of creating power,"[87] then it seems DE will remain an immensely valuable tool for the United Kingdom in generating power through developing and maturing relationships with partner forces around the globe that will counter instability and malign competitive influences. However, the greatest barrier to any implementation of a coherent or effective DE program is a problem of the United Kingdom's own making: Brexit.

Brexit and the Implications for Future Defense Engagement

In the 2015 National Security Strategy/Strategic Defence and Security Review (NSS/SDSR),[88] Prime Minister Cameron set out his vision for a secure and prosperous United Kingdom with global reach and influence. Moreover, the NSS/SDSR posited that the United Kingdom enjoyed a "position as the world's leading soft power which gives us international influence."[89] There are many well-founded reasons why the United Kingdom should consider itself in such a position. As the SDSR reminds us, we sit at the heart of a rules-based international order, and we are the only nation to be a permanent member of the UN Security Council and in NATO, the EU, the Commonwealth, the G7 and G20, the Organization for Security and Cooperation in Europe, the Organization for Economic Cooperation and Development, the World Trade Organization, the International Monetary Fund, and the World Bank. A key element of achieving the prime minister's vision was to direct that DE become a core, funded MOD task. Though the concept of DE was not new in itself, this was the first time that it became a core task, although in truth it attracted no additional funding; rather, the MOD was directed to prioritize DE alongside other core tasks. However, at a time when elements of the armed forces are heavily committed to operations, alongside significant financial challenges, winning wars will likely take priority over DE tasks. The result is that by necessity DE takes second place to operational activity.

DE does not operate in a vacuum. A sound DE plan will be coherent with all relevant government objectives and synchronized with other levers of power. However, the 2015 NSS/SDSR was written prior to the United Kingdom's decision to leave the EU. This decision has had a profound effect on UK international relations, and this is likely to increase the demand for DE activities. The first part of this section will examine only the international-relations aspects of the Brexit decision insofar as they can be deduced at this stage. No apology is made for avoiding, where possible, the political dimensions, and no opinion will be offered as to the benefits or otherwise to the United Kingdom of leaving the EU.

Having examined how Brexit affects the United Kingdom's position in the world, the second part of this section will focus on how DE might be used to mitigate such effects. Subtle shifts in strategic policy are already detectable, with the United Kingdom government promising to strengthen defense and security ties across Europe in the wake of Brexit. Although there will clearly be a tension between resourcing and capacity, it is likely that there are more effective ways to conduct such activity; however, in so doing, the United Kingdom may well need to limit its ambition in order to focus more on where the best value or highest-impact activity might take place.

THE UNITED KINGDOM'S POSITION FOLLOWING THE BREXIT DECISION

While much has been written and discussed on Brexit, it is almost always biased by whether the commentator is a "Remainer" or a "Brexiteer." Accepting that it will be impossible, therefore, to find an unbiased view, perhaps the most illuminating picture on how the United Kingdom's position in the world has been impacted can be drawn from how the United Kingdom is seen through the UN lens. Oral evidence taken by the House of Commons Foreign Affairs Committee presents a stark picture of the decline in the United Kingdom's world standing following the Brexit decision. Sir John Sawers, a seasoned diplomat who, by the time he became the United Kingdom's permanent representative at the UN in 2007, had some thirty years of diplomatic and foreign policy experience, described how the United Kingdom was viewed during his tenure at the UN: "We were an admired country, and that gave us weight at the United Nations."[90] However, in the same committee session, in responding to questions on how the United Kingdom recently lost its influential position on the International Court of Justice (ICJ) for the first time in the ICJ's seventy-one-year history, Lord Hannay[91] offered that "it was a complex issue and a lot of other matters were in play. It was seen, I am sure, by many in the General Assembly as a way of chipping away at permanent member privileges. . . . The fact that they chose us to pick on is perhaps a worrying tendency."[92]

When asked which factors affect the United Kingdom's influence in the world, Sawers offered that

there are three factors that affect our influence in the world and at the United Nations. First, the performance of our economy—the more effectively our economy is growing, the stronger the UK; that plays very well, very effectively, into our foreign policy influence. Secondly, the leadership shown by our Prime Minister and Foreign Secretary of the day is really effective if it is done very well indeed. They have authority and can play a leadership role. Thirdly, there is the investment we make in the tools of having an impact on the world—our diplomatic service, our aid budget, our armed forces, our intelligence service. In the last few years aid and intelligence have both been funded quite well and effectively—I certainly can't criticise on that score—but in diplomacy and the armed forces it is a different picture, and that is undoubtedly making it more difficult to carry weight in the world, when those budgets are being held steady or cut back.[93]

A simple examination of the performance of the United Kingdom economy since the referendum shows that immediately after Brexit the United Kingdom suffered a 15 percent devaluation of its currency (which has since recovered to 10 percent). Moreover, prior to the vote the United Kingdom sat at the top of the G7 table of GDP growth performance; just eighteen months later, the United Kingdom is at the bottom in economic terms. In April 2017, Mark Carney, the governor of the Bank of England, indicated that "households looked through Brexit-related uncertainties initially. But more recently, as the consequences of sterling's fall have shown up in the shops and squeezed their real incomes, they have cut back on spending, slowing the economy."[94] Carney also suggested that "businesses have been somewhere in between. Since the referendum, they have invested much less aggressively than usual in response to an otherwise very favourable environment. The balance of these effects has led overall UK growth to slow in the first half of 2017, even as growth in the rest of the G7 was picking up, and UK growth looks set to remain weaker than the G7 average until mid-2018."[95] Using Sawers's assertion that economic strength is one factor that affects a nation's influence in the world and at the UN, the United Kingdom would appear to have lost a degree of its foreign-policy influence.

In considering the leadership role played by the prime minister and foreign secretary, both are, by necessity, focused on daily issues surrounding Brexit. Hardly a day goes by when tabloid front pages are not reporting serious fractures within the Conservative Party over issues relating to negotiating strategy, customs arrangements, and border control. Although such details, important though they may be, are outside the scope of this chapter, such reporting cannot be helping to positively promote the United Kingdom's image of a strong and stable world-leading power in the eyes of our European partners.

While defense spending looks positive, with the United Kingdom committing to the 2 percent of GDP required by NATO, it is well documented that there is a significant resource challenge for defense in the years to come. Meanwhile, the Foreign Office budget has seen a 40 percent reduction over the past five years. In Sawers's words, "We are undoubtedly going through a bit of a dive. . . . At the end of this process we will need to work out how to rebuild our economy and rebuild our standing in the world."[96]

In adding to Sawers's comments, Lord Hannay suggested that there are

two other factors that count a lot, particularly on the Security Council, [which] are our relationship with the United States and degree of influence in Washington, and our relationship and position as one of the two European permanent members of the Security Council. That is about the degree to which we can, with France, help to shape European Union policy at the Security Council—there is always at least one more and sometimes even two more European Union members on the Council. It just goes without saying, I'm afraid, that since June of last year those two pillars of our influence at the UN have been shaken.[97]

More recently, Sir Simon Fraser[98] gave oral evidence at the House of Commons Foreign Affairs Committee on the subject of Global Britain. He offered that "I think many other countries around the world are looking at us at the moment in a state of some concern. . . . To be frank with you, a lot of countries think, for the time being, that we have slightly lost the plot in terms of where we intend to go."[99]

The polarizing nature of Brexit means that it is challenging to find unbiased views on what such a decision means for the United Kingdom's world standing. However, informal discussions with UK-based foreign defense attachés reveals a degree of surprise and a feeling of immense self-inflicted injury by the Brexit decision. Foreign Office colleagues invariably indicate a sense of European disappointment with the United Kingdom's decision—for a country that appeared so diplomatically skilled and admired for its ability to extract the very best deals within the construct of the EU, there does appear to be a sense of dismay. All of this is couched in diplomatic niceties, but one cannot escape the deep-rooted feelings apparent among our European partners. As one senior Whitehall figure put it, "We've done enormous self-harm. I've attended meetings with Foreign Ministers where we've been derided and belittled—it's well disguised, but it's there."[100] When viewed through this particular lens, the rationale and language used in Prime Minister May's Lancaster House Speech on January 17, 2017, was clearly aimed at reassuring our European partners that "we are leaving the European Union, but we are not leaving Europe."[101]

In concluding the first part of this section, irrespective of whether one believes that Brexit is a positive or negative for the United Kingdom, there is a clear underlying belief, from many in key positions with insight, that the United Kingdom has lost some of its respect and influence, at least for the time being. The laudable aspirations of a Global Britain, in which as Prime Minister May puts it, the United Kingdom aims to be "a country that goes out into the world to build relationships with old friends and new allies alike,"[102] can only be built on trust and respect that, at this stage, seems in short supply. Moreover, the Global Britain agenda does not quite sit alongside the significant cuts to the Foreign Office budget. A recent announcement suggested that the Foreign and Commonwealth Office (FCO) plans to hire fifty extra staff for embassies within the EU, funded by making cuts in embassies across Asia-Pacific, south Asia and Afghanistan, and the Americas and Africa.[103] This hardly appears to be a consistent message alongside a coherent approach.

DE AS A MITIGATION

In considering how DE can be used to mitigate the effects of Brexit in terms of international relations, one must first define the term. It is worth repeating here that the International Defence Engagement Strategy defines DE as "the use of our people and assets to prevent conflict, build stability and gain influence."[104] This definition does, however, somewhat overstate the idea, and an alternative proposal is taken from the Royal Air Force (RAF) DE policy, which states that "if done successfully, across the full spectrum of military intervention and activity, it has the potential to alter the momentum of campaigns and conflicts and enable the timely provision of life saving support in times of crisis and enhance operational output by improving the efficiency of our force elements and those of our partner air forces and fellow coalition members."[105] In any event, it would seem natural that, sitting within the context outlined above, Defence will be asked to do more, specifically within Europe, but not at the expense of engagement farther afield, which appears to remain a high-level aspiration.

The current UK experience would suggest that Defence is indeed attempting to be everything everywhere. While it is true that cross-Whitehall systems exist to coordinate DE activity, the reality is that existing plans are made years in advance, meaning such plans are presented as a fait accompli—the very best stakeholders can expect is to seek opportunities within existing DE plans. This is all understandable given that DE has been a core task only since 2015, and the lead time for planning activity on a global scale is significant. Moreover, stark differences exist between individual services' approach to DE, highlighted by the British Army's Regionally Aligned Brigades—no such arrangement exists within either the RAF or the Royal Navy. Without a more centrally directed approach, Defence is inefficient in the way that it conducts DE activity. A more focused and nuanced approach is required if Defence is to fulfil its commitment to increase its engagement activity in the wake of Brexit.

So, what would such an approach look like? In the first instance, Defence needs to seek a degree of clarity on where the government's priorities lie. Are we attempting to remain a global nation with global influence, or should we seek to focus more on Europe? Of course, there are no easy answers to this, and one could not reasonably expect such clarity at the national level. This lack of clarity is precisely where the tension lies between the ambitions es-poused in the Global Britain agenda and the resources available to Defence in order to support such aspirations. Notwithstanding the current lack of clarity, one can safely assume that the UK-US relationship retains primacy; however, the scale and complexity of the US-UK relationship is such that DE activity, as defined above, forms but a small part. This relationship is deeply ingrained; that is not to say that the United Kingdom can afford to take it for granted, but it is not characterized by DE—close military co-operation is more a by-product than a key enabling function. With this in mind, as the United Kingdom prepares to leave the EU, it would not be unreasonable to focus Defence's attention on Europe as a primary DE aim.

US FIRST, EUROPE ALWAYS—THE PRIMARY DE FOCUS

The 2015 NSS/SDSR placed the United States as the United Kingdom's "pre-eminent partner for security, defense, foreign policy and prosperity,"[106] and despite perturbations in this relationship in recent months, there is no reason the United Kingdom should change its long-term approach toward the United States. In considering the United Kingdom's future relationship with Europe, Britain has a broad range of existing defense arrangements with European na-tions. NATO remains the bedrock of our national defense.[107] Additionally, the United Kingdom features heavily in the Northern Group,[108] the Joint Ex-peditionary Force,[109] and the Combined Joint Expeditionary Force (CJEF). Furthermore, in outlining the United Kingdom's future defense relationship with Europe post-Brexit, in September 2017 the government stated that "the United Kingdom wants to build a new, deep and special partnership with the European Union. . . . The UK is unconditionally committed to maintaining European security."[110] It seems, therefore, that while UK-US relations will take primacy, the message to Europe is clear: Britain wishes to remain engaged. In DE terms, this would most effectively be achieved through a centrally MOD-managed increase in our engagement with NATO through perhaps a concerted effort to place our very best people within NATO structures and by acting as a driving force behind the development of an ambitious NATO exer-cise plan. The United Kingdom should be at the forefront of discussions about the future of NATO.[111] This would appear to be an easy win through which the United Kingdom can influence twenty-eight partner nations.

The NSS/SDSR explicitly lists both France and Germany as the next most important partners after the United States. In considering France, the on-going development of CJEF, alongside other commitments made as part of the Lancaster House agreements and more latterly the Sandhurst talks, underline the United Kingdom's commitment. DE links with Germany rarely feature so prominently, but they exist all the same. Given the current strategic considerations it is unsurprising that, in his speech at the Royal United Services Institute on January 22, 2018, General Sir Nick Carter, chief of the General Staff (CGS), stressed the need for a forward mounting base and offered that "we are actively examining the retention of our infrastructure in Germany where we store our vehicles in Ayrshire Barracks in Rheindahlen; and our training facilities in Sennelager."[112] These views actually relate to CGS's concerns relating to a resurgent Russia; although, with the very clear commitment that the United Kingdom government has made toward Europe, one might question whether it is time to revisit the withdrawal of the British Army from Germany.

THE NEAR-ABROAD — MATRIX MANAGED?

In accepting the importance of Europe to the United Kingdom, and a focus on NATO, JEF, and the Northern Group, CJEF could hardly be described as living up to the rhetoric of a Global Britain. Noting the "everything everywhere" maxim, in such a resource-constrained environment a secondary focus on the near-abroad would seem appropriate.[113] In proposing a more nuanced approach, one must examine the strengths of each of the services to determine where they might be best employed. For example, as a secondary DE aim, the army might be more suited, in influence terms, to engaging in areas where both the United Kingdom has national interests and the host nation land forces enjoy primacy. This, when combined with the British Army's extensive presence in Kenya through British Army Training Unit Kenya (BATUK), suggests that Africa might offer a natural DE target for the army. Moreover, when one considers the significance of the air sector to UK defense sales throughout the Middle East,[114] the RAF might best be focused in that region. In addition, with the prospect of trade deals driven farther afield by Brexit, alongside the introduction into service of the Queen Elizabeth class carriers, the senior service could be directed to turn their attention to building relationships in the western Indian Ocean region. Given the critical dependence that India has on sea lines of communication, an India looking West for allies with similar security concerns can meet a United Kingdom looking East for open markets and economic prosperity.[115] Critically, there is no suggestion of a permanent presence by any of the services within their respective area of responsibility; rather, this should be viewed as each service's taking on responsibility for coordination of effect within each of the above-named regions, thus allowing for individual service chiefs to be held to account for the development of such relationships. While the default setting would be for the nominated service to "own" the relationship, it would also act in a coordination role to request assistance from either of the other services when required (in effect a matrix-managed approach), thus ensuring efficiency, consistency of messaging, and a coordinated approach based on strategic and operational domain awareness and expertise.

THE POLITICAL REALITY

While focusing on the near-abroad might seem an attractive proposition for Defence, the political reality is that the government is committed to a Global Britain approach. Moreover, Defence is already committed in certain instances to operating farther afield — the Five Powers Defence Arrangement is but one example. That said, Defence has proven that it can deliver global effect; the recent exercise Eastern Venture, undertaken in late 2016, saw the simultaneous deployment of the Royal Air Force Aerobatic Team (RAFAT) to over nineteen destinations, culminating in a four-day presence in China, while a Typhoon Squadron exercised with Malaysia, Japan, and South Korea. This particular RAFAT deployment, and indeed a 2017 deployment throughout Europe and the Middle East, was carried out under the banner of the Great Campaign and reinforces the contribution that defense assets can make to the United Kingdom's prosperity agenda.[116] However, such endeavors are not resource-neutral and in a fiscally constrained environment must be balanced against what are more pressing priorities, as the strategic landscape shifts under the weight of Brexit. This will likely require hard choices to be made to limit the scale of Defence's contribution to the United Kingdom's international ambition. What is clear, however, is that any DE activity has the greatest effect when it is coordinated with a whole-of-government approach—forming relationships at the tactical level carries significant advantage but has little impact at the strategic level. Using DE as a tool to expand the United Kingdom's influence through a whole-of-government approach has the potential to deliver significant effect.

In concluding, irrespective of whether one sees Brexit as a golden opportunity or a looming threat, the decision taken by the United Kingdom public on June 24, 2016, appears to have taken some toll on the United Kingdom's international standing, albeit potentially temporarily. In mitigation, the UK government is promising to keep Europe at the heart of its thinking on defense and security while touting a Global Britain, making new friends, and renewing old acquaintances. While the Global Britain agenda is laudable, it is not yet matched by demonstrable actions—the Foreign Office reductions throughout Africa and the Asia-Pacific regions to offset the Brexit manpower bill underline the tensions evident in such an ambitious agenda. DE can, in part, mitigate some of the effects of the United Kingdom's impending departure from the EU. Assuming the enduring UK-US relationship remains, a clearer focus on European engagement through existing institutions such as NATO offers the advantage of reaching twenty-eight nations through a single aperture. However, to do so, Defence will need to apply additional horsepower to NATO to become a leading advocate for reform and the development of a challenging and demanding exercise program. Our closest European allies, France and Germany, will continue to require a particular focus. Second in priority should be the near-abroad, but managed in a way that enhances efficiency and plays to the strengths of each of the services—the suggestions contained herein are based on a personal perspective, and there is likely to be sensible refinements to ensure that every engagement adds maximum value. Moreover, DE influence is maximized when combined with a well-constructed whole-of-government approach—aims must be clearly articulated and combined with a large dose of DE-level artistry. If the same rigor is not applied to DE as one would apply to operations, then the chances are that opportunities will be missed. Finally, although national-level clarity on government engagement priorities might be sought, such clarity does not exist. What is clear is that "everything everywhere" will not deliver the outcomes sought, so perhaps it is time for a rethink as to the scale of Defence's contribution to the United Kingdom's internationally focused ambition. This might be true at least in the short term, as the United Kingdom focuses on its departure from the EU.

Clearly the place and character of defense engagement in the United Kingdom national-security-strategy environment will be ongoing and contested topics of debate. When placed against the historical evidence presented throughout this volume, indications would appear to be that the concept will not live up to the political expectations attributed to the defense-engagement policy. Limited resources in terms of manpower and time, and lack of clear political direction, lack of coordination between the various domains (air, land, and sea), as well as a lack of agreed definitions and objectives for any defense-engagement policy, mark it as a trend that will soon revert to the more traditional ad hoc uses of UK military power in the pursuit of leverage, influence, and assurance.

NOTES

1 MOD UK, *UK International Defence Engagement Strategy* (IDES), 1st ed. (London: Ministry of Defence UK, 2017), 2.
2 Cabinet Office, *The Strategic Defence and Security Review* (Norwich, UK: Stationery Office, 2010), 18.
3 *Strategic Defence and Security Review*, 1.
4 *Strategic Defence and Security Review*, 6.
5 IDES, 11.
6 Stockholm International Peace Research Institute (SIPRI), *SIPRI Yearbook 2017: Armaments, Disarmaments and International Security* (Oxford, UK: Oxford University Press, 2017), 26.
7 UNHCR, "Figures at a glance," accessed January 26, 2018, http://www.unhcr.org/uk/figures-at-a-glance.html.
8 *SIPRI Yearbook 2017*, 23.
9 For example, Robert Cooper, "Hard Power, Soft Power, and the Goals of Diplomacy" in *American Power in the 21st Century*, ed. David Held and Mathias Koenig-Archibugi (Cambridge, UK: Polity, 2004), 167–180.
10 Joseph Nye, *Soft Power: The Means to Success in World Politics* (New York: Public Affairs, 2004), 5.
11 Nye, *Soft Power*, 5.
12 Nye, *Soft Power*, 8.
13 Kira Peterson, "Four Types of Power in International Relations," paper for IPSA, 22nd World Congress of Political Science (Madrid, July 2012), 12.
14 See Nik Gowing and Chris Langdon, *Thinking the Unthinkable: A New Im-*

perative for Leadership in the Digital Age (London: Chartered Institute of Management Accountants [CIMA], 2016), http://thinkunthinkable.org/downloads /Thinking-The-Unthinkable-Report.pdfhttp://thinkunthinkable.org/down loads/Think ing-The-Unthinkable-Report.pdf.

15 See, for example, Lawrence Freedman, *Strategy: A History* (Oxford, UK: Oxford University Press, 2015), chap. 35.

16 IDES, 2.

17 Rob Johnson, *The Case for Persistent Engagement*, presentation to UK 1st Division Defence Engagement Study Day, November 2017.

18 The Independent-on-line, *The Winograd Report*, accessed February 6, 2018, http://www.independent.co.uk/news/world/middle-east/lebanon-the-wino grad-report-in-full-776000.html.

19 Committee of Privy Counsellors, *The Report of the Iraq Inquiry: Executive Summary* (London: Williams-Lea Group, 2016), 134.

20 Malcolm Chalmers, *Strategic Think Tank Analysis: The Role of Defence in Conflict Prevention* (London: Royal United Services Institute [RUSI], 2014), 16.

21 In contrast, Defence defines conflict prevention as action to modify the causes of potential conflict and prevent its onset: DCDC *Joint Doctrine Publication 0-01.1* (Shrivenham, UK: Development, Concepts and Doctrine Centre [DCDC], 2011).

22 United Nations Security Council Resolutions (UNSCR) Report 2017, *Can the Security Council Prevent Conflict?* (New York; UNSCR, 2017). http:// www.securitycouncilreport.org/atf/cf/%7B65BFCF9B-6D27-4E9C-8CD3 -CF6E4FF96FF9%7D/research_report_conflict_prevention_2017.pdf.

23 Chalmers, *Strategic Think Tank Analysis*, 9.

24 "Defence Secretary strengthens ties between UK and Oman," www.gov.UK, accessed January 26, 2018, https://www.gov.uk/government/news/defence -secretary-strengthens-ties-between-uk-and-oman.

25 Mike Butler, *UK Defence Diplomacy: A Realist Analysis* (Oxford, UK: University of Oxford Foreign Service Programme, 2017), 21.

26 Zachary Selden, *Alignment, Alliance, and American Grand Strategy* (Ann Arbor: University of Michigan Press, 2016), 118.

27 Point raised by an official in conversation with HCSC, 18.

28 Robert Johnson, "Upstream Engagement and Downstream Entanglements," *Small Wars & Insurgencies* 25, no. 3 (May 2014): 647–668.

29 Stabilisation Unit, "A Few Thoughts on the Military Contribution to Stabilisation 2017," accessed January 23, 2018, http://sclr.stabilisationunit.gov.uk/top -ten-reads/uwm-1/1236-a-few-thoughts-on-the-military-contribution-to -stabilisation/file.

30 Saul Kelly and Gareth Stansfield, "Britain, the United Arab Emirates and the Defence of the Gulf Revisited," *International Affairs* 89, no. 5 (2013): 1203–1219 at 1205.

31 Kelly and Stansfield, 1218.

32 Babcock International, "Case Studies," accessed February 17, 2018, https:// www.babcockinternational.com/Case-Studies/What-We-Do/Marine/Facili ties-and-Infrastructure/DUQM-Naval-Dockyard.

33 Kelly and Stansfield, "Britain, the United Arab Emirates," 1205.

34 Kenyan Embassy, "Kenyan Cut Flower Industry," accessed February 17, 2018, http://www.kenyarep-jp.com/business/industry/f_market_e.html.

35 Center for Historical Analysis and Conflict Research (CHACR), "Contribut- ing to Strategic Influence and Prosperity," *Ares and Athena: CHACR Occa- sional Paper* (Summer 2015), accessed February 17, 2018, http://chacr.org.uk /docs/Ares-Athena1.pdf.

36 Department for International Development (DfID), *Statistics on International Development 2017: Final 2016 UK ODA Spend Statistics*, https://www.gov.uk /government/uploads/system/uploads/attachment_data/file/660062/SID -2017b.pdf.

37 DfID brief to HCSC, January 31, 2018.

38 DfID brief, January 31, 2018.

39 AAG, "Malthusian Theory of Population," http://cgge.aag.org/Populationand NaturalResources1e/CF_PopNatRes_Jan10/CF_PopNatRes_Jan108.html.

40 DCDC, *Global Strategic Trends Out to 2045*, 5th ed. (Shrivenham, UK: DCDC, 2017), https://espas.secure.europarl.europa.eu/orbis/sites/default/files/generated /document/en/MinofDef_Global%20Strategic%20Trends%20-% 202045.pdf, 6.

41 Chalmers, *Strategic Think Tank Analysis*, 7.

42 Hannes Mueller, "The Economic Cost of Conflict," International Growth Centre Working Paper (April 2013), https://www.theigc.org/wp-content/up loads/2014/09/Mueller-2013-Working-Paper2.pdf.

43 Elliot Cohen, *The Big Stick: The Limits of Soft Power and the Necessity of Mili- tary Force* (New York: Basic, 2016), 195.

44 Clay Dillow, Jeffrey Lin, and P. W. Singer, "China's Race to Space Domina- tion," *Popular Science*, September 20, 2016, https://www.popsci.com/chinas -race-to-space-domination#page-3.

45 Chalmers, *Strategic Think Tank Analysis*, 9.

46 Camilla Schippa, "Conflict Costs Us $13.6 trillion a Year: And We Spend Next to Nothing on Peace," World Economic Forum, January 5, 2017, https://www.we forum.org/agenda/2017/01/how-much-does-violence-really-cost-our-global -economy.

47 UK MOD & FCO, *UK's International Defence Engagement Strategy* (2017), 1.

48 Chalmers, *Strategic Think Tank Analysis*, 15.

49 Ewan Lawson, "The UK National Security Capability Review and the Fusion Doctrine," rusi.org, commentary, April 4, 2018, https://rusi.org/commentary /uk-national-security-capability-review-and-fusion-doctrine.

50 Theresa May Speech at Conservative Party Conference, October 2, 2016, in *UK's International Defence Engagement Strategy*, 2.

51 Chalmers, *Strategic Think Tank Analysis*, 41.

52 US Department of Defense, *Summary of the 2018 National Defense Strategy of the USA* (2018), 5.

53 Cabinet Office, *National Security Strategy and Strategic Defence and Security Review* (2015), chapter 5.

54 J. J. Messner, "Fragile States Index 2017," Fund for Peace, May 10, 2017, https://reliefweb.int/report/world/fragile-states-index-2017.

55 Patrick Porter, "Why Britain Doesn't Do Grand Strategy," *RUSI Journal* 155, no. 4 (2010): 9.

56 Senior Whitehall Official Remark to HCSC, January 29, 2018.

57 Andrew Cottey and Anthony Forster, *Reshaping Defence Diplomacy: New Roles for Military Cooperation and Assistance* (London: Oxford University Press, 2004), 27.

58 Senior DfID Official Remark to HCSC, January 31, 2018.

59 James Chandler, *UK International Defence Engagement Strategy Lessons from Bassingbourn* (London: Chatham House, 2016), 13.

60 The Fragile State Index 2017 (see note 54) lists six states at very high alert and a further nine states at high alert.

61 Antonio Giustozzi, *Decoding the New Taliban: Insights from the Afghan Field* (New York: Columbia University Press, 2009), 1.

62 David Schnabel and Albrecht Carment, eds., *Conflict Prevention from Rhetoric to Reality*, vol. 1 (Oxford: Lexington, 2004), 11.

63 John Mearsheimer, "Why Ukraine Crisis Is the West's Fault: The Liberal Delusions That Provoked Putin," *Foreign Affairs* (September-October 2014): 5.

64 Cottey and Forster, *Reshaping Defence Diplomacy*, 18.

65 Joseph Nye, *The Future of Power* (Philadelphia: Perseus, 2011), 86.

66 Multinational Capability Development Campaign (MCDC), *Understand to Prevent: The Military Contribution to the Prevention of Violent Conflict* (November 2014), https://assets.publishing.service.gov.uk/government/uploads/system/uploads/attachment_data/file/518617/20150430-U2P_Main_Web_B5.pdf, 102.

67 Johnson, "Upstream Engagement and Downstream Entanglements," 650.

68 Johnson, "Upstream Engagement," 663.

69 Chandler, *UK International Defence Engagement Strategy Lessons*, 13.

70 David Ralph, Preventing Conflict: A Paper for Discussion, General Dynamics United Kingdom Limited, July 2010, https://www.generaldynamics.uk.com/wp-content/uploads/2016/06/WW_Preventing_Conflict_20100726.pdf, 5.

71 Boutros Boutros-Ghali, quoted in *Conflict Prevention from Rhetoric to Reality*, vol. 1, ed. Albrecht Schnabel and David Carment (Lanham, MD: Lexington, 2004), 4.

72 Ralph, *Preventing Conflict*, 7.

73 The Iraq Inquiry (Chilcot) Report (2016) highlighted groupthink as a fundamental weakness in government decision-making.

74 MCDC, *Understand to Prevent*, 70.

75 GPOI was launched in 2005 as the US response to a G8 action plan for expanding global capability for peace support operations.

76 Tony Chafer, "The UK and France in West Africa: Toward Convergence," *African Security* 6 (2013): 249.

77 The Conflict, Stability and Security Fund (CSSF) uses both Official Development Assistance (ODA) spend and non-ODA spend to deliver and support security, defense, peacekeeping, peace-building, and stability activity. Further details are available at https://www.gov.uk/government/publications/conflict -stability-and-security-fund-cssf/conflict-stability-and-security-fund-an -overview, accessed February 20, 2018.

78 Denis James, *Strengthening the Private Sector's Role in UK Defence Engagement*, Chatham House, August 2017, https://www.chathamhouse.org/sites/de fault/files/publications/2017-08-25-defenceengagement1.pdf, 12.

79 James, *Strengthening the Private Sector's Role*, 9.

80 John Deni, *Military Engagement and Forward Presence: Down but Not Out as Tools to Shape and Win* (Carlisle, PA: Strategic Studies Institute, 2016), 12.

81 David Carment and Albrecht Schnabel, *Conflict Prevention: Path to Peace or Grand Illusion?* (New York: UN University Press, 2003), 20.

82 Michael Knights and Alex Mello, "The Best Thing America Built in Iraq: Iraq's Counter-Terrorism Service and the Long War against Militancy," War on the Rocks, July 2017, https://warontherocks.com/2017/07/the-best-thing-america -built-in-iraq-iraqs-counter-terrorism-service-and-the-long-war-against-mili tancy/.

83 John Deni, *Rotational Deployments vs. Forward Stationing: How Can the Army Achieve Assurance and Deterrence Efficiently and Effectively?* (Carlisle, PA: Strategic Studies Institute, 2017), 38.

84 Chalmers, *Strategic Think Tank Analysis*, 16.

85 In addition to an extensive network of attachés and advisers, the region also enjoys permanent bases for the Royal Navy, British Army, and Royal Air Force.

86 It is widely accepted that Russian operatives were responsible for the attempted coup in Montenegro in October 2016.

87 Lawrence Freedman, *Strategy: A History* (New York: Oxford University Press, 2013), xii.

88 United Kingdom Prime Minister's Office, *National Security Strategy and Strategic Defence and Security Review* (London: 2015).

89 Prime Minister's Office, *National Security Strategy*, 13.

90 House of Commons, Oral Evidence on the United Kingdom's Influence in the

UN, HC 675, December 19, 2017, before the Foreign Affairs Committee, evidence of Sir John Sawers.

91 A seasoned diplomat with over forty years FCO experience and who served as permanent representative to the UN (1985–1990) and permanent representative to the UN (1990–1995).

92 House of Commons, Oral Evidence on the United Kingdom's Influence in the UN, HC 675, December 19, 2017, before the Foreign Affairs Committee, evidence of Lord Hannay of Chiswick.

93 House of Commons, Oral Evidence, evidence of Sawers.

94 Mark Carney, "What a Difference a Decade Makes," speech given at the Institute of International Finance's Washington Policy Summit, Washington DC, April 20, 2017).

95 Carney, "What a Difference a Decade Makes."

96 House of Commons, Oral Evidence, evidence of Sawers.

97 House of Commons, Oral Evidence, evidence of Hannay.

98 Sir Simon Fraser served as a British diplomat from 1979 to 2015 and was the permanent undersecretary of the Foreign and Commonwealth Office from August 2010 to July 2015.

99 House of Commons, Oral Evidence on Global Britain, HC 780, February 6, 2018, before the Foreign Affairs Committee, evidence of Sir Simon Fraser.

100 Conversation with author, April 2018.

101 Theresa May, "The Government's Negotiating Objectives for Exiting the EU: PM speech," *Lancaster House, London, January 17, 2017.*

102 May, "Government's Negotiating Objectives."

103 Lizzy Buchan, "Boris Johnson's 'Global Britain' Claims Mocked as UK Cuts Back Embassies around World to Fund More EU diplomats," *Independent*, December 30, 2017, https://www.independent.co.uk/news/uk/politics/boris-johnson-eu-brexit-diplomats-foreign-office-global-britain-a8134506.html.

104 Joint Ministry of Defence and Foreign and Commonwealth Office, *UK's International Defence Engagement Strategy*, https://assets.publishing.service.gov.uk/government/uploads/system/uploads/attachment_data/file/596968/06032017_Def_Engag_Strat_2017DaSCREEN.pdf, 1.

105 United Kingdom, Ministry of Defence, *RAF Defence Engagement Policy*, London, March 10, 2017, 1.

106 United Kingdom, Prime Minister's Office, *National Security Strategy and Strategic Defence and Security Strategy*, London, 51, para. 5.29.

107 *National Security Strategy*, 51, para. 5.29.

108 Britain, Poland, Germany, the Netherlands, Denmark, Finland, Iceland, Norway, Sweden, Estonia, Latvia, and Lithuania.

109 Britain, Sweden, Denmark, Finland, Estonia, Latvia, Lithuania, the Netherlands, and Norway.

110 United Kingdom, HM Government, "Foreign Policy, Defence and Development, a Future Partnership paper," London, September 12, 2017, 1.

111 John Bew and Gabriel Elefteriu, "The UK and the Western Alliance: NATO in the New Era of Realpolitik," *Policy Exchange* (March 2017), 11.

112 Nick Carter, "Dynamic Security Threats and the British Army," speech delivered at Royal United Services Institute, London, January 22, 2018, https://rusi .org/event/dynamic-security-threats-and-british-army.

113 The near-abroad is defined as Europe, the Mediterranean, African countries within which the United Kingdom has national interests, and the Middle East, and given the economic interests, extending into the Western Indian Ocean.

114 UK Defence and Security Organisation, *UK Defence and Security Export Statistics for 2016*, Department for International Trade, July 25, 2017, https://www .gov.uk/government/publications/defence-and-security-exports-for-2017/uk -defence-and-security-export-statistics-for-2017.

115 Steve Moorhouse, "From a UK Perspective, To What extent Can 'the' Special Relationship with the United States Be Bolstered by 'a' Special Relationship with India?," HCSC 18 Futures Paper, Joint Services Command and Staff College, 7.

116 While it is impossible to attribute inward investment directly to this DE activity, the Great Campaign has indicated that the 2016 RAFAT tour of the Far East aided contracts worth some £140 million in Thailand and £1.34 billion in Singapore.

NOTES ON CONTRIBUTORS

Tyler Bamford is the Leventhal Research Fellow at the National World War II Museum in New Orleans. He received his PhD from Temple University and his BA from Lafayette College. He was a 2011 Beinecke Scholar and his research has been supported by the Army Heritage Center Foundation, the Center for the Study of Force and Diplomacy, and the Society for Military History.

Olly Brown is a career infantryman who has served with the British Army for twenty-two years. He has extensive experience with counterinsurgency, security force assistance, and capacity-building from multiple deployments to Northern Ireland, Afghanistan, Iraq, and Northeast Nigeria. Currently, he commands a brigade focused on capacity-building with partner forces in North Africa.

Poppy Cullen is a teaching associate at the University of Cambridge. She earned her PhD from Durham University in 2015. She is the author of *Kenya and Britain after Independence: Beyond Neo-Colonialism* (2017).

Douglas E. Delaney holds the Canada Research Chair in War Studies at the Royal Military College of Canada. He is the author of *The Soldiers' General: Bert Hoffmeister at War* (2005), which won the 2007 C. P. Stacey Prize for Canadian Military History, *Corps Commanders: Five British and Canadian Generals at War, 1939–45* (2011), and *The Imperial Army Project: Britain and the Land Forces of the Dominions and India, 1902–1945* (2017).

Tim Hadley is a former US foreign service officer and is currently an adjunct professor at the Diplomatic Academy of Vienna, Austria. His book, *Military Diplomacy in the Dual Alliance: German Military Attaché Reporting from Vienna, 1879–1914*, was published in 2016.

Geraint Hughes is a senior lecturer at the Defence Studies Department, teaching at the Joint Services Command and Staff College. He is the author of two books: *Harold Wilson's Cold War: The Labour Government and East-West Politics, 1964–1970* (2009) and *My Enemy's Enemy: Proxy Warfare in International Politics* (2012). His next project is to write a book on the Dhofar War in Oman (1963–1976).

C. J. Jenner is associate research fellow, King's College London, research fellow, University of Oxford, and senior research fellow, Institute for China-America Studies. He holds master of studies and doctor of philosophy degrees in modern history from the University of Oxford and has held various fellowships and teaching posts in Asia and the United States. Focusing on twentieth-century strategic policy engagements in the Indo-Pacific, his interdisciplinary publications range across history and international relations. In addition to his academic work, he undertakes governmental analytical assignments and contributes to internationally televised documentary series.

Greg Kennedy is a professor of strategic foreign policy at King's College, London, and joined the Defence Studies Department in June 2000. He has taught at the Royal Military College of Canada in Kingston, Ontario, in both the History and War Studies Departments. He is an adjunct professor of that university. His PhD is from the University of Alberta, with an MA in war studies from the Royal Military College of Canada, and a BA (honors) in history from the University of Saskatchewan. He has published internationally on strategic foreign policy issues, maritime defense, disarmament, diplomacy, and intelligence.

Chaz Kennett is a group captain in the RAF. He is currently the director of the United Kingdom's Qatar Typhoon Programme. From July to December 2018, he was group captain international engagement in the Ministry of Defence. Prior to that, October 2017 to July 2018, he was part of the Combat Air Strategy team, developing and writing the United Kingdom's Combat Air Strategy. From 2014 to 2016, he was the RAF's station commander at RAF Akrotiri.

Ken Kotani is a professor in the College of Risk Management, Nihon University. He obtained his MA from King's College, London, and a PhD from Kyoto University. He was a senior research fellow of the National Institute for Defense Studies, Ministry of Defense, Japan, and a visiting research fellow of the Royal United Services Institute, UK. He is the author of *Japanese Intelligence in World War II* (2009).

Athol Yates teaches at the Institute for International and Civil Security, Khalifa University, Abu Dhabi, United Arab Emirates. The institute offers a master's degree for emirati security professionals. He teaches civil security, which covers professional security practice, internal security, and disaster management. His current research focuses on the contribution that expatriates have made to the UAE military since the 1950s.